D0489226

Contents

Notes on contributors

Waqar Ihsan-Ullah Ahmad is a Senior Research Fellow at the Social Policy Research Unit, University of York. Previously he was a lecturer in health studies at the Department of Social and Economic Studies, University of Bradford. He is the editor of *The Politics of 'Race' and Health* (Bradford: Race Relations Research Unit, University of Bradford/BICC, 1992).

Elizabeth N. Anionwu was born in England and is of Nigerian/Irish parentage. She has community nursing experience and obtained a PhD in health education. From 1979 until 1990 she was head of the Brent Sickle and Thalassaemia Counselling Centre. She is presently a lecturer at the Institute of Child Health, University of London.

Raj Bhopal is Professor of Epidemiology and Public Health Medicine at the University of Newcastle upon Tyne. He is a major contributor on ethnic minority health issues.

Errol Francis has contributed to debates in 'race' and mental health for a number of years. He was, until recently, Director of the Afro-Caribbean Mental Health Association.

Jenette Golding is at the Royal College of Nursing and was, for some time, its adviser on minority health care.

Mark R.D. Johnson is Senior Research Officer at the Centre for Research on Ethnic Relations at the University of Warwick. He has researched on 'race' and health for more than a decade and writes the six-monthly update on 'race', health and welfare in the journal *New Community*.

Alison Macfarlane is statistician at the National Perinatal Epidemiology Unit, Oxford. She researches and writes on perinatal epidemiology and health policy. Her publications include *Birth Counts* (two volumes, 1984), with M. Mugford (London: HMSO).

Luise Parsons is a consultant epidemiologist working in Tower Hamlets in London. Her research interests include issues concerning maternity care and birth, on which she has published several articles.

Naina Patel currently heads the 'race' programme for the Central Council for Education and Training in Social Work (CCETSW). Among other national developments, Naina has designed and managed a major curriculum development project in anti-racist social work resulting in seven publications (available from CCETSW) and involving some 400 people during the project's three phases. Naina is also the author of *A 'Race' Against Time? Social Services Provision to Black Elders* (London: Runnymede Trust, 1990).

Sashi P. Sashidharan is a senior lecturer in psychiatry at University of Birmingham and consultant psychiatrist at All Saints Hospital, Birmingham. He has written widely on the racialization of mental health and racism within psychiatry.

Paul Stubbs is a sociologist and formerly lecturer in social work at Bradford University. He is now a freelance writer and researcher. His most recent publication is *Anti-racist Social Work Education: Improving Practice with Children and Families*, co-written with four others (CCETSW 1992).

Laurence Ward has studied and taught philosophy and mathematics at British universities. He was, until recently, principal planning officer at Brent Council.

Martin White is senior lecturer in public health medicine at the School of Medicine, University of Newcastle upon Tyne. He has researched and written on aspects of public health, including health promotion.

Acknowledgements

Though all of the chapters in this book were specifically commissioned, most were first presented at the Bradford conference 'Race' and Health in Contemporary Britain (9–11 September 1991). My thanks to the Department of Health and Bradford Health Authority who partly funded the conference. Many people have offered advice and suggestions. Among them I am particularly grateful to Charles Husband, who is generous with both his time and ideas. Elizabeth Anionwu, Trevor Sheldon, Russell Murray, Marie Macey, Jenny Douglas, Paul Stubbs, Reg Walker, Alyson McGregor and Charles Husband commented on various chapters. Brian Howlett provided much appreciated technical help. Jacinta Evans, Carolyn Medd and Janet Howatson at Open University Press, who were patient and helpful. To all of them my grateful thanks. I am especially grateful to Win Healey who prepared the manuscript.

At a family level, Nayyar, Saffi, Samee and Maryam are a constant source of support and strength. My family in Pakistan have given freely their love while expecting little in return from me. This effort is dedicated to Abba Ji, Ammi Ji, and Masi Ji, for they always faced adversity with courage and believed in the value of struggle.

1

Introduction

W.I.U. AHMAD

This book aims to provide a critical introduction to the study of health, illness and health care provision in the lives of Britain's black population. Part 1 of the book problematizes research enterprise on 'race' and health. Part 2 reviews some of the major areas of concern in differential health and health care provision. Part 3 evaluates trends in health policy directed, arguably, at decreasing inequalities in health care provision and in the employment of black staff in the National Health Service. The concluding chapter focuses on recent reforms in the National Health Service, locating these within the context of both a shrinking welfare state and the assault on local democracy, and assesses the options for black people's struggles for equity in health status and in access to health care resources.

The World Health Organization's strategy for 'Health for All 2000' acknowledges the centrality of social, economic and environmental factors, broadly defined, to our experience of health and illness and access to health care provision. Any cursory study of the position of the black population in relation to housing, income, employment, education and other indices of quality of social existence will show abundant evidence of racial inequalities (see Bhat *et al.* 1988; Skellington and Morris 1992). The situation is rife for generating inequalities in both health and health care, as shown by contributions to this volume and other research (Donovan 1986; Ahmad *et al.* 1989).

The role of ideological considerations has been largely ignored in health and health service research on black populations. There are two main trends in research and writings on black people's health. One is a vehemently 'culturalist' approach, where realities are constructed and explained in terms of 'cultural differences' – difference usually equating with deviance and pathology (see Pearson 1986). In this perspective, racialized inequalities in both health and access to health care are explained as resulting from cultural differences and deficits. Integration on the part of the minority communities, and cultural understanding and ethnic sensitivity on the part of the health professional, then become the obvious solution; personal and institutional racism and racial discrimination have no part in this equation. There is no shortage of proponents of this perspective, including black writers (for discussion, see Lawrence 1982a; 1982b; Pearson 1986; for an example of the approach, see Qureshi 1989). The following example, from a report on the work of Dr Qureshi in the *Guardian* newspaper (29 September 1992, p. 5) shows the prominence of this perspective, attractive for its lack of political insight and comforting to health professionals and policy-makers because of the potential of its accommodation within existing institutional structures:

> He [Dr Qureshi] cited the case of a 40-year-old Pakistani labourer who went to see his GP in Norfolk complaining about abdominal pains and fever. He was asked if he had blood in his stool and replied No because 'I don't know' is seen as weakness in Asian cultures. He did not know because examining one's stool 'is taboo for Hindis [*sic*] and Sikhs', said Dr Qureshi.
>
> The GP sent him to hospital for an appendix examination but the patient refused a rectum examination – another cultural taboo – and returned to his GP. He was given iron tablets.
>
> A blood sample was sent for testing and the patient told to return in a week. He failed to keep the appointment. Later, the doctor received a hospital notification of his death from cancer of the colon.

The second approach is of supposedly benign epidemiology, the notion of an unconcerned, value-free scientific observer making objective pronouncements on the basis of carefully collected evidence which uses rigorous scientific methodology. This is a prized tradition in clinical medicine and the scientific researcher who dismisses such political 'irrelevancies' as 'race' and class is much applauded for upholding the traditions of good science (for example, see Carney 1989).

In Chapters 2 and 3 Ahmad and Stubbs take issue with these approaches. Waqar Ahmad (Chapter 2) reviews the relationship between medicine and the ideologies of 'race', and discusses the long history of medical legitimation of racialized oppressions. He evaluates the current health and 'race' research, and argues that medicine and medical research are political issues. The racialization of black health issues – understanding and explaining black people's health needs and racial health inequalities in terms of individual 'cultural'/'biological' differences when they are in fact located in iniquitous social relationships – is the logical consequence of the institutionalized and personal racism within and outwith the health services. The 'intellectual apartheid' of excluding black people from defining their own realities, as researchers and as the 'subjects' of research, and the internalization of racist stereotypes and dominant (white) research paradigms by black researchers are considered by Ahmad to be major problems to confront. Ahmad argues that the challenge needs to be taken up by black communities and black professionals, as well as progressive white people.

Paul Stubbs (Chapter 3) extends this discussion of the politics of 'race' and health, emphasizing that the frameworks and models utilized by researchers and policy-makers alike, to construct black people's 'problems' or 'needs', do matter. He discusses the relative merits and problems of two broad models, 'ethnic sensitivity' or multi-culturalism and 'anti-racism', employed in both research and policy, not just in health but also in other fields such as education and social services. Stubbs argues that we need to go beyond crude anti-racism to an anti-racist approach that acknowledges and values differences within the black populations and is committed to building links with other oppressions. After concerted attacks from the right, and pronouncements on the 'end of anti-racism' from the left (cf. Gilroy 1990), 'anti-racism' may be badly bruised. However, its potential has never been fully realized and there is a strong need to revitalize anti-racism. It is required in the field of 'race' and health in particular, as other models do not acknowledge the need to transform the racialized inequities in social relationships between black and white people which are at the base of racial health inequalities. Equally, these racial inequalities structure black people's interaction with state health services.

Part 2 of the book concentrates on a selection of pertinent health issues. The areas chosen have been of concern to both the black populations and the health service providers. However, it is not claimed that these should take precedence over other issues which are not included in the volume. In particular, the book says little on the 'forgotten minorities' such as the Bangladeshis, Chinese, Vietnamese and people from the Middle Eastern countries. The issues concerning these communities may be similar to those discussed in this volume but they merit a specific volume for detailed consideration. (See Williams 1992 and Li 1992, respectively, for discussion of issues concerning the Irish and the Chinese communities.) Part 2 provides a critical overview of four areas of research and policy: maternity care and birth-outcome; haemoglobinopathies; mental health; and black elders.

One broad area which has attracted particular attention from researchers and policy-makers alike is pregnancy, birth and maternity care. In Chapter

4, Luise Parsons, Alison Macfarlane and Jenette Golding review the relevant research findings and policy debates. They emphasize the need to set the problems encountered by black women in the wider context of poor and impersonal maternity services in general. The research on pregnancy and birth is based on 'ethnic' data of dubious quality, and therefore needs to be interpreted with care. They show that the assumptions made about the maternity care needs of ethnic minority women are based largely on stereotypes rather than careful analysis of valid information. The picture they carefully present is one of heterogeneity of experience and outcome – in terms of fertility, pregnancy, birthweight and perinatal and infant mortality – between different ethnic minority groups. Parsons, Macfarlane and Golding conclude that:

> It is important to recognize that the 'problems' of how to provide appropriate care will not disappear once the majority of women using the services can speak English. In fact, the need to provide for cultural diversity and raised expectations may well become more pressing . . .

An issue which has attracted particularly vigorous attention from sections of the black community and an apathetic response from policy-makers concerns the prevention of and the provision of care for haemoglobinopathies, particularly sickle cell and thalassaemia. These inherited disorders of red blood cells, which mainly – but not exclusively – affect black and minority ethnic groups, have received proportionally considerably less attention and resources than the inherited disorders such as phenylketonuria and haemophilia which affect predominantly the white population. As Anionwu argues in Chapter 5, the history of winning recognition of need in this area is the history of struggle against institutional and individual racism within the health service. As the first director of Brent Sickle Cell Centre and a leading writer and campaigner on services for haemoglobinopathies, Anionwu is particularly well placed to consider the history of this struggle, and to assess the contemporary situation. She also provides insights into the anger and the agony of the sufferers and their carers through the use of case studies based on research conducted in Bradford and in London. She cites evidence of progress, albeit painfully slow and still inadequate, in many parts of Britain. The overall picture is, however, one of unequal recognition of black people's needs; the case for concerted community action for this recognition is strong.

Perhaps the strongest site of black people's struggles in health and health care has been in the area of mental health, particularly the 'schizophrenization' of young Afro-Caribbean males. In psychiatry, the research debates have focused on notions of biological and/or cultural pathology, consequences of 'culture shock' after migration and 'culture conflict' on the one hand, and, on the other, possible misdiagnosis because of white psychiatrists' unfamiliarity with minority cultural traditions. In relation to Asians, Rack (1980) and others have popularized the notion of 'somatization', that Asians do not acknowledge psychological distress as culturally legitimate and express this through ill-defined aches and pains which have no organic basis. Black activists, including some black psychiatrists, have resisted the racialization of black mental health; Sashi Sashidharan and Errol Francis have been at the forefront of this resistance. In Chapter 6 they provide a powerful critique of the epidemiology of schizophrenia. After outlining the main debates in 'race' and mental health they engage in a vigorous review of some of the major comparative studies of racial differences in schizophrenia. They argue that 'studies to date are seriously flawed in that they try to understand excess hospital admission rates for schizophrenia found in Afro-Caribbeans as indicative of individual pathology . . . [T]he process of hospitalization itself is rarely considered as meriting serious study.' They conclude that 'the alignment of mental illness and ethnicity or race is indicative of underlying political ideologies rather than the product of empirical findings'.

In contrast to mental health, the area of health and social care provision to black elderly has only recently gained recognition. Authorities and professionals have legitimated their continued neglect of black elders by using traditional stereotypes – of extended caring families or the notion that the elderly will retire to their countries of origin – and by forwarding arguments about relatively small numbers of black elders. Naina Patel, in Chapter 7, sets out the case for putting black elders' health and social needs on the agenda. She locates their needs in the historical and social factors of dislocated families and their disadvantaged situation in the job market, arguing that 'Black elders' health and health needs cannot be understood without reference to their experience of employment, housing and income'. She discusses *racisms* in service delivery, operating at different levels and in different guises – institutional practices, mono-culturalism and rigid application of rules to disadvantage black people; ideas and policies in relation to 'cultural accommodation' and 'cultural pluralism'; and direct or individual racism. This discussion is equally applicable to other areas of health service delivery. Patel concludes with a consideration of the NHS and Community Care Act for black elders and exhorts health professionals to meet their responsibilities towards black elders: 'Health professionals cannot remain on the sidelines: to do nothing would be to accept racism, the marginalization of communities and the consequent ill health of black elders.' This is an area which will become increasingly important in years to come, and Patel stresses the urgent need for action in terms of assessing the black elders' needs and the formulation of appropriate policies. However, as Patel argues: 'At the same time, work must focus on raising black elders' expectations of health and social services rather than accepting their tolerance of problems "as normal".'

Part 3 of the book concentrates on selected but broad issues in health policy. Chapter 8, by Raj Bhopal and Martin White, focuses on health promotion. The need for health promotion focused on minority ethnic communities was acknowledged in official policy initiatives such as the Stop Rickets Campaign and the Asian Mother and Baby Campaign as well as other smaller-scale and local initiatives. Overall, health promotion with ethnic minorities has lacked clear focus and coherence and, as critics have highlighted (Pearson 1986; Rocheron 1988, among others), has tended to locate health inequalities in presumed individual and/or cultural shortcomings. Bhopal and White provide an overview of health promotion activities directed at minority ethnic communities in Britain and make suggestions for improvement. Their focus is particularly on health professionals, especially those involved in health education and promotion, though they acknowledge that other agencies and individuals can, and indeed do, play a part in promoting health.

The inadequate response from the NHS to black people's health issues has gone hand in hand with the marginalization of black health services staff. Bhopal and White note this in relation to health promotion and health education. Laurence Ward, in Chapter 9, provides a wider overview of the experiences of black staff in the National Health Service. He reviews major policy initiatives and practical innovations in the health service over the past two decades. His focus is on the employment patterns and experiences of doctors and nurses; the situation of other black employees such as auxiliary nurses or domestic staff is not considered in this overview and remains to be charted. Ward marshals considerable evidence of black doctors being channelled towards unattractive, low status specialities, having their promotion blocked, and suffering racism at both a personal and an institutional level. Black nurses likewise are marginalized, and Ward sees little hope for progressive change in the Project 2000 initiative. Equally, using the examples of psychiatry and geriatrics, he argues that the existence of a high proportion of black staff in a speciality does not of itself guarantee racial equity in service provision. Indeed psychiatry, with a high proportion of black doctors and nurses, is one of the most problematic areas of health care (as also discussed by Sashidharan and Francis in Chapter 6). There is, therefore, also the need to politicize the black workforce, an area in which black health workers can learn from black social workers (Central Council for Education and Training in Social Work (CCETSW) 1991a; 1991b).

In Chapter 10, Mark R.D. Johnson discusses continuities and changes in the delivery of health services to minority ethnic communities since the 1950s. He notes the continued emphasis on 'cultural difference' as the basis of understanding racial health inequalities, and as the dominant criterion for adequate service provision. Equally the belief that the minority ethnic communities abuse health services continues (instances of this are cited by Patel in Chapter 7). Johnson notes that the response of health services to the needs and concerns of the black population remains uncoordinated and patchy. Even recent exhortations to do better, such as the National Association of Health Authorities (1988) report *Action Not Words*, have failed to make significant improvements. However, he does acknowledge limited positive outcomes of some policy initiatives. For example, whereas the ideological basis of the Asian Mother and Baby Campaign has been severely criticized (Rocheron 1988; Ahmad 1989), Johnson notes that many of the participating health authorities have, as a consequence, maintained a commitment to the provision of 'link-workers' or 'liaison officers' and thus eased communication difficulties. However, the liaison officers are themselves marginalized and the policy will achieve little in the absence of wider recognition of black communities' needs and the political commitment to meet these equitably. As Johnson shows, in terms of the health services' commitment and ability to affect positive change, history is against the optimists.

In the concluding chapter Waqar Ahmad considers some wider issues in promoting equitable health and health care. Rejecting health as the outcome of interventions by medical 'technicians', he locates racial health differentials in the wider racial inequities in contemporary Britain. He provides a critical overview of changes in the health service, including the government's strategy for health promotion, and argues that at a general level they offer little hope to the black communities. He develops the argument that the fight for equitable health and health care is fundamentally located in the black communities' wider struggles for substantive citizenship rights. In an era when repeated and concerted assaults by the central government have badly weakened local democracy, made public services less rather than more accountable at the local level, and shrunk the democratic base drastically, there is a strong need for political action, and not just by the black population. Equally, links between racial oppression and other forms of oppression are highlighted by Ahmad. He concludes that:

> Racial inequalities in health are a part, and a consequence, of racial inequalities in substantive rights of citizenship. Equally, although the scope for reducing racial inequalities in health lies largely outside the NHS, equity of health care provision is also of paramount importance. These struggles for equitable health and health care are essentially located in the wider struggles for equity and dignity which have been a part of black people's history.

This book is a humble contribution to these struggles.

Part I

POLITICS OF RESEARCH

2

Making black people sick: 'race', ideology and health research

W.I.U. AHMAD

Introduction

'Race' and health research is a major industry. However, its benefits to ethnic minorities in terms of understanding illness or improving health care are minimal (Bhopal 1992; Sheldon and Parker 1992). The literature is heavily skewed, reflecting the interests of health professionals and at odds with the priorities of minority ethnic communities (Webb 1982). It espouses a naive empiricism and cultural reductionism that would not be tolerated in other branches of medical or social research (Ahmad *et al.* 1989; Sheldon and Parker 1992; Sashidharan and Francis, this volume). This chapter analyses how this research enterprise constructs black peoples' health issues: how it 'makes them sick'.

Although the focus of this chapter is on 'race' and health research it is set within a broad context. Health, illness and health care are structured within social relationships, shaped by historical developments and contemporary socio-economic realities, and mediated through professional ideologies (Friedson 1970; Stainton-Rogers 1991; Cockerham 1992). Racism in medical research cannot be analysed in isolation from a wider discussion of racial oppression and its historical context (Husband 1982; Bhat *et al.* 1988). Equally, racial oppression has links with other forms of socially reproduced oppressions (Bryan *et al.* 1985); therefore, links have been made between racism and other oppressions, sexism and heterosexism.

I start with a brief look at the status of and interplay between the two constructs 'race' and 'biomedicine', and their potential for social control. This leads to a discussion of the racialization of health research and the politics of research on black peoples' health. Unlike some of the contributors, I use the political category 'black' when referring to 'non-white' minority populations. This does not deny that the category 'black' is contoured by differences of ethnicities, histories, and possibly, experience of racism, in the same way as individuals and groups may be differentially located in terms of class, gender and sexuality. However, the commonality of experience of racism and need for political unity are of greater significance than 'ethnic' differences within the 'black' populations. Hence, my choice of the collective label 'black'.

I do not review the field of health and 'race' research; the reader will find this in other contributions to this volume as well as elsewhere (for example, Donovan 1984; 1986; Pearson 1986; Ahmad 1989; Ahmad *et al.* 1989, Sheldon and Parker 1992). I aim simply to provide a critical analysis of health and 'race' *research* within its structural and ideological context. Neither is it my intention to 'deskill' potential or established researchers, medical or social, white or black. But both medical and social researchers, whether white or black, need to become aware of the racial politics of health research – a point few researchers have grasped.

'Race', medicine and ideologies of oppression

The construct 'race' has been used to support colonization of a socially constructed 'Other', a supposedly inferior people or nation, while the construct 'biomedicine' has been employed to support the increasing colonization of human life. 'Race' has legitimated exploitation on the basis of the 'scientific' and 'natural' superiority of some over others, natural selection taking over from divine hierarchies; differential worth attached to the cultures of the conqueror and the conquered; and an undermining of the values, history, frameworks of knowledge, laws and customs of the colonized.

Biomedicine, too, can be seen as an instrument of oppression, controlling deviance and maintaining conformity – here there is agreement among a range of critiques of biomedicine, from the culturalist (Zola, 1972; Illich 1977), the Marxist (Navarro 1976; Doyal 1979), the feminist (Scully and Bart 1978; Oakley 1980) and the social constructionist (Friedson 1970) perspectives. Biomedicine depoliticizes and individualizes ill health, treats the afflicted in isolation from their social, economic, and citizenship context and thus legitimates structural inequalities and supports the status quo. It diverts attention away from the production of ill health to its distribution among individuals and, by relating it to their lifestyles, perpetuates the ideology of victim blaming (Crawford 1977).

Like 'race,' it legitimates the colonization of new territories, so convincingly argued by Zola (1977). In discussing the increasing medicalization of life, he identifies four concrete ways in which medicine extends its claims of expertise:

1 Through the expansion of what in life is deemed relevant to the good practice of medicine.
2 Through the retention of absolute control over certain technical procedures.
3 Through the retention of near absolute access to certain 'taboo' areas.
4 Through the expansion of what in medicine is deemed relevant to the good practice of life.

He goes on to show how treatment of 'psychosocial' states has become a major preoccupation of medicine, where drugs are now available:

> To help us sleep or keep us awake. To stimulate our appetite or decrease it. To tone down our energy level or to increase it. To relieve our depression or activate our interests. To enhance our memory, our intelligence and our vision – spiritually or otherwise.

Elsewhere, Zola (1972) claims that biomedicine has taken over from religion and law as the new repository of the truth, becoming the articulator and the guardian of a new, secular morality. On the emergence of biomedicine, he writes: 'Instead of a fixity of the universe, of hierarchical relations promulgated by God, we now had a universe fixed by laws . . . Medical science became the ultimate articulator and conveyor of the message of Darwin and Spencer.' Social Darwinism also formed the basis of scientific racism (Husband 1982).

Common to both is to some extent the complicity of the colonized. The legitimacy of colonial rule was rarely effectively challenged by the colonized; any rebellion was harshly crushed. Likewise, patients rarely challenge the hegemony of medicine or the expert status of the doctor; medicine monopolizes the definition of 'truths' about health and ill health, their causes and cures. Notions of appropriate and inappropriate behaviour in illness are dictated by medicine and relate directly to labels of 'good' and 'bad' patients. The functionalist model of the sick person stipulates conformity to the medical diagnosis and treatment as a precondition for the legitimacy of status as a 'sick person' (Parsons 1951). The function of the 'sick role' is seen by Parsons as maintaining social order and cohesion where society accepts, and sympathizes with, sick people's predicament and assists in bringing them back to 'normality' as long as they behave within the confines of the 'sick role'; normality here is a return to the sick person's role in society, that is, as parent, teacher, or whatever.

'Alternative' therapies are also marginalized, judged by the yardsticks of biomedicine (whether or not these yardsticks are appropriate); and their users and practitioners demonized (Ahmad 1992b). Both 'race' and medicine have a fascination with technical solutions. Medicine provides technical/ scientific 'fixes' for impaired biology or diseased organisms through surgical, electrical, chemical, rhetorical (see Posner 1991), or public health interventions. The concept of 'race' led to various fixes, from 'civilizing' the savages through a long period of 'pupillage' under the rule of the civilized colonial powers before 'graduation' to self-rule (Said 1978), to the current fascination with equal opportunities policies as a technical activity.

Neither the structures built on the 'race' theory nor on biomedicine tolerate challenges. The freedom movements in British ex-colonies were explained in terms of 'return to savagery' and the 'end of civilization and democracy', thus legitimating their brutal suppression on the pretence of caring for the masses (Fanon 1970; Said 1978). Medicine's suppression of alternative therapies, and the patients who may use these, has a long history (Ahmad 1992b), including the ideologically motivated removal of lay midwives from maternity care during the medicalization of childbirth. The British Medical Association's (1986) 'Report of the Board of Science Working Party on Alternative Therapy' confirmed the medical orthodoxy's paranoia regarding alternative therapies. Recently, attempts to 'scientify' the failure of non-orthodox cancer therapy (Bagenal *et al.* 1990) led to heated debates (*Lancet* 1990:1185-8; Stacey 1990) and eventually acceptance of methodological flaws by the authors (cited in Stacey 1990).

When alternative therapies are granted credibility it is through the ritual of 'scientific' evaluation, or embracing the religion of science and therefore proving a commonality with scientific medicine (Swayne 1989; Kleijnen *et al.* 1991). Such conversions help maintain the dominance of scientific medical ideology while suggesting objectivity and openness, and are similar to bringing 'approved' black people into the folds of white institutions, to create an illusion of change while maintaining the status quo (see King 1992).

Racist ideology permeates British and other Western societies and their institutions although racism may be articulated and experienced in different forms. Similarly, the permeation of the discourse of medicine into the collective psyche is apparent from the use of health jargon as metaphor; for example, one hears of racism being the 'cancer' of our society that needs to be 'incised' to return society to 'full health'. Health services are granted or witheld on consultants' or general practitioners' moral judgements. A prime example here is the variation in the availability of abortions between consultants and district health authorities. The common fears about black women 'over-breeding', and about poor quality of parenting in black homes have been reflected in the relatively generous availability of abortion and birth control services to black women, whereas this has been a prime site of white feminists' struggles for such services against medical orthodoxy (Bryan *et al.* 1985).

Neither the construct of 'race' nor the institution of medicine has survived on the basis of some intrinsic merit or truthfulness; both are socio-political constructs supported by and supporting dominant orthodoxies and ideologies, often reinforcing and legitimating each other. Gordon (1983) illustrates this with reference to the role of medicine in racist immigration control. An analysis of medicine's claims to be scientific and of science being neutral, objective, value-free, ahistorical and universal is beyond the scope of this chapter (but see Anderson 1976; Rose and Rose 1976; Anees 1988 and for a critique of 'left approaches to medicine', see Figlio 1980). However, scientific medicine needs to be acknowledged as political, often oppressively so. Medicine played a frontline role in colonialism as an essential and integral tool of colonial foreign policy – the need to institute the London and Liverpool Schools of Hygiene and Tropical Medicine signifies this (Fanon 1978; Paul 1978; Doyal 1979). It kept the colonizers healthy and its benevolent face softened up the 'natives'. It undermined and often destroyed indigenous systems of health care with the knock-on effect of destroying morale and self worth, and created long-term dependency – a dependency all too apparent in the contemporary health care systems of many underdeveloped ex-colonies (Doyal 1979; Zaidi 1988). Fanon (1978) states that the colonized people equated accepting foreign medicine with accepting foreign rule.

Earlier still, medicine 'naturalized' slavery by coining diagnostic labels such as *drapetomania* (the 'irrational' and pathological desire of slaves to run away from their masters) and *dysaethesia Aethiopica* (or rascality) (Bryan *et al.* 1985; Littlewood and Lipsedge 1989). Freedom from slavery was not seen as an answer; Littlewood and Lipsedge (1989: 37–8) quote fears about emancipation:

> Enlarged freedom, too often ending in licence, excessive use of stimulants, excitement of emotions, already unduly developed [could lead to insanity. The black people] are removed from much of the mental excitement to which the free population . . . is necessarily exposed in the daily routine of life, not to mention the liability of the latter to the influence of the agitating novelties of religion, the intensity of political discussion . . . They have not the anxious cares and anxieties relative to property. They were taught from infancy obedience and self-control . . . The cause of insanity and other diseases with them now, from which they were exempted in slavery, is the removal of all healthful restraints that formerly surrounded them.

Even in the recent past (1950s) it was suggested that mental illness among black people in America was due to political activity, for which presumably their brains were not sufficiently developed. New 'scientific' theories purported to demonstrate that while the whites possessed determination, power, self-control and rationality the black people lacked all of these. The theories were often contradictory – for example, showing black people as more sensitive and at other times as less sensitive – but they always confirmed the superiority of white people over black people (see Littlewood and Lipsedge 1989: 38).

The testing of drugs on men, women and children in the underdeveloped world before marketing in the West as well as using drugs banned in the West in the underdeveloped countries has become commonplace (Doyal 1979). Doyal cites numerous examples of this taking place in Latin America, Africa and Asia, and quotes Silverman's study of drug promotion (Doyal 1979: 268):

> in nearly all of the products investigated in this study, the differences in the promotional or labelling material were striking. In the United States the listed indications for each product were usually few in number, while the contraindications, warnings, and potential adverse reactions were often in extensive detail. In Latin America, the listed indications were far more numerous, while the hazards were minimized, glossed over, or totally ignored. In some cases, only trivial side effects were described, but potentially lethal hazards were not mentioned.

At the time of writing there is a renewed campaign against the policy of the multinational conglomerate, Nestlé, of aggressive marketing of baby milk in underdeveloped countries, a policy which has a disastrous history in Africa (Doyal 1979).

There are parallels with other areas of medical influence. The medicalization of sexuality, where non-heterosexuality once equalled clinical mental disorder, scientifically legitimated the oppression of gays and lesbians. This continues to the present day with the recent attempts to find genetic explanations for homosexual behaviour and more generally, gender roles (*Newsweek* 1992). The respectable current affairs weekly, *Newsweek*, devoted eight pages to the subject in one issue and advertised it on its front cover with the heading superimposed on the picture of a child: 'Is This Child Gay? Born or Bred: The Origin of Homosexuality.' A further example of medicine expropriating the moral guardianship of society is the past treatment of unmarried mothers, including their confinement to mental institutions for 'moral imbecility', medicalizing and 'naturalizing' patriarchal gender roles (Ehrenreich 1978; Doyal 1979).

Scully and Bart (1978) provide an excellent account of this process in gynaecology textbooks, which both reflected contemporary societal views of women's role and sexuality and structured the medicalization of womanhood. Contemporary treatment of women as patients, and gender divisions in health service employment, also provide evidence of this. The changing fashions in obstetric medicine constantly redefine the boundaries of acceptable maternity behaviour; examples include hospital versus home births, delivery positions, care regimens during pregnancy and after birth, 'active management of birth' leading to increases in induced births, and Caesarean sections.

To see the development and practice of scientific medicine as mediated through socio-political and ideological processes is not scientific nihilism (Rose and Rose 1976). I am not arguing that scientific medicine can simply be reduced to ideology or social relations, as, for example, Young (1977) argued about science. That scientific medicine is value-laden is not in doubt; that it is valueless or that its ideological biases can dissolve the phenomenon itself must be contested (see, for example, Rose and Rose 1976; Ford 1988). Nevertheless, the institution of scientific medicine and its construction of health and illness have a strong ideological basis (Strong 1979; Turner 1987; Billig *et al.* 1988: chs 5–6), and oppressive relations – be they related to 'race', gender, social class or sexuality – are effortlessly reproduced through professional ideologies and institutional administrative practices (Stubbs 1985; Husband 1991; Torkington 1991). As Stuart Hall states (quoted in Lawrence 1982a):

> [Ideologies] work most effectively when we are not aware that how we formulate and construct a statement about the world is underpinned by ideological premises; when our formulations seem to be simply descriptive statements about how things are . . . or of what we take for granted.

Just as 'common-sense neutral' views about gender roles and the family legitimate gender oppression, so similarly, common-sense ideas about black people become part of the collective wisdom. This is a cyclical relationship. White racism keeps black people in low status in terms of education, employment, housing, health or position in society; this then confirms racist ideas about black inferiority. An anti-racist analysis of black people's experience of health and illness and the response of the health services requires an understanding of racism in British society and its reproduction in institutions, including in medicine.

Neutrality is not enough, for neutrality is culturally and historically specific. The dominant culture portrays the 'Third World' negatively, giving a reading of imperialism as 'civilization', portrays colonialists as 'pioneers' and 'explorers' who, for example, 'discovered' America and Australia (the fact that the Aboriginal and American Indian people, respectively, had inhabited these parts for hundreds of years is thus of no consequence). Here Christianity is seen to have saved their souls, and European science and education to have given them enlightenment, progress and democracy. Such views are reinforced through news coverage of world events, suggesting a continuation of the 'white man's burden' of having to control the 'natives' for their own good, upholding international law, order and democracy, and shouldering the responsibility of policing the 'Third World'. With this background of racism within and without medicine, to be 'neutral' is to be oppressive. Racism does not require formal tuition to be reproduced; it passes on through socialization, through literary and audio-visual media, literature and the arts, education, humour, and most importantly through 'common sense' – by being a full member of a racist society. Ideologies impose limits on thought and action: within a racist society the dominant and professional ideologies are inherently racist and oppressive. It is therefore not surprising to see particular constructions of black people's health problems, their explanations and solutions.

Racialization of black people's health

The concept of 'racialization', according to Miles (1989) was first used by Fanon and has been defined as 'the way in which scientific theories of racial typology were used to categorize populations' (Banton 1977). According to Cashmore (1988: 246), it:

> refers to a political and ideological process by which particular populations are identified by direct or indirect reference to their real or imagined phenotypical characteristics in such a way as to suggest that the population can only be understood as supposedly biological entity.

This process has a long history and can be witnessed in areas other than health. Such processes are apparent in the definitions and explanations of, among other areas, black people's reproductive capacity, sexuality, intelligence, ability to control the universe, 'rascality', mental breakdown, desire to run away from their slave-masters, lack of political achievements, and so on. Racialization legitimated ('scientifically') the oppression of black people in the past, as it does now (Centre for Contemporary Cultural Studies (CCCS) 1982; (Husband 1982). Miles (1982: 127) illustrates this with reference to employment: 'Since the 1950's, the British labour market has been racialised in this way. Employers have signified certain physical and cultural characteristics . . . and this signification has structured recruitment processes.'

Racialization assumes that 'race' is the primary, natural and neutral means of categorization, and that the groups are distinct also in behavioural characteristics, which result from their 'race'. With reference to Fanon, Miles (1989) states that by defining the 'Other' (usually as an inferior) one implicitly defines oneself against that definition (as normal and superior).

Europe has historically defined itself in opposition to the notion of an 'exotic east', a process well summarized by Said's (1978) powerful study of 'orientalism'. Peteirse (1991) argues that this process is being re-enacted in an attempt to unify the European states into 'fortress Europe'. 'The vision of

Europe, informed by the myopic conceits of "Western civilization" and tied to a "Plato to Nato" historical lineage, is narrow and wrong', he argues. (The editing out of black history from the history of the world, as if black people have no history, is the subject of Bernal's (1987) *Black Athena*).

A major issue in the racialization of health research is that it is assumed that the populations can only be meaningfully divided into 'ethnic' or 'racial' groups, taking these as primary categories and using these categories for explanatory purposes. Stratification by class, income and so on, is then seen as unimportant; issues of institutional and individual racism as determinants of health status or health care become peripheral at best, but are usually seen as irrelevant, unscientific, 'political' and polluting (Sheldon and Parker 1992). As a leading writer on transcultural medicine (Qureshi 1992) writes:

> Transcultural Medicine means the science and art of dealing with patients from different cultures . . . This approach may be useful in cross-cultural contact during a medical consultation as short as 12 minutes or a detailed medical examination lasting an hour. I recognise four realities – patriotism, neocolonialism, racism, and fundamentalism – as political issues of our times, but leave them to other experts who specialise in these fields.

Racialization takes place in terms of notions of cultures being static and homogeneous and having a biological basis. This is then extended to notions of cultures having direct relationship to attitudes, expectations and behaviour. 'Cultures' here take on a rigid and constraining shape, rather than being nurturing and sustaining forces. These culturalist assumptions ignore issues of power, deprivation and racism. They result in culturalist explanations and feed into culturalist health policy options, as I will illustrate.

Chirimuuta and Chirimuuta (1989) provide an excellent account of Western scientific attempts to racialize AIDS through linking it first with Haiti and then Africa. This may seem odd considering that at the time AIDS was largely confined to America, and to white populations. The Chirimuutas show how Haiti became the focus of concern for American researchers and 'thus the "gay plague" changed overnight to the "Haitian disease"' (1989: 128). They state that although the Haitian hypothesis collapsed, 'the idea of black people as the source of AIDS was too attractive to abandon. Attention shifted to the African continent itself. Racism, not science, motivated the search for the origins of AIDS' (1989: 128).

In Britain, the right-wing weekly, *Spectator* (1986), sought to focus on West Indians along with the New Right's other favourite demons, homosexuals:

> But there is another endangered group. To alert or protect them will require still more unfashionable candour than to address the homosexuals.

That group is the West Indians. Their men sire their children, and often move on to another partner . . . To talk to West Indians about Aids will require more plain-speaking – and risk more cries of 'racism' - than has been dreamt of in Lord Whitelaw's philosophy.

This fascination continues with a recent report in the *Lancet* 'showing' that women of African origin were more likely to be HIV positive than British-origin women (Chrystie *et al.* 1992). Blood samples given for anonymous testing by pregnant women were analysed to provide the link with Africa. This was achieved through testing the blood samples for malarial antibodies, and on the basis of this adducing ethnicities of the pregnant women.

In the late 1950s and 1960s medical researchers expressed fears about the incidence of tuberculosis in the recent (largely black) immigrants to Britain (Emerson 1961; *British Medical Journal* 1962; Springett 1964), particularly in as far as this posed a threat for the white population. This was tempered with relief that the immigrants had shown little tendency to integrate and therefore not spread the disease to the local population. In this scenario, tuberculosis became a 'disease of immigrants', an imported disease, and among the many 'exotic' diseases to be associated with black immigrants. The researchers did not acknowledge the extremely high mortality (over 400 deaths per 100,000 in the nineteenth century) from tuberculosis, and of its reduction largely through improvements in standards of living, including nutrition, housing, and public health facilities (McKeown 1976).

An editorial in the *Lancet* pleaded for X-ray examinations of immigrants on ports of entry as no other explanation than the importation of tuberculosis by black immigrants was acceptable. The editorial writer was astonished that 'the search for tuberculosis in immigrants is still not compulsory. It should be'. And continued: 'This is not racial discrimination; it is simply humane' (*Lancet* 1974). As stated earlier, health checks at ports of entry and health concerns about 'immigrants' generally have become essential weapons for supporting and legitimating racist immigration policies.

A number of other areas can be mentioned in this respect. The Stop Rickets Campaign, the Asian Mother and Baby Campaign (Rocheron 1988), and less high-profile campaigns against surma (an eye cosmetic also used for medicinal purposes) and sikur (a form of clay that some women are believed to eat, especially during pregnancy) were all attempts at defining, in this case, Asian peoples' health problems in terms of their 'pathological' culture. If the cause lies in their culture then so must the solution. The aetiology of rickets, once a common disease among white children, was thus racialized. Rickets was acknowledged as a disease of poverty which was controlled through fortifying margarine with vitamin D, improvements in standards of living, improved nutrition and universal availability of free milk to school children.

With the knowledge of its higher prevalence among Asian children in the 1970s it now emerged as an 'Asian' disease signified by a new name, 'Asian rickets'. It was explained in terms of un-British eating and living habits, and perhaps a genetic deficiency in absorbing vitamin D into the bloodstream or in synthesizing vitamin D from sunlight. Vitamin D deficiency in Asian women was said to be due to the oppression of women in Asian cultures, where men insist on modest dress and impose restrictions on women sunbathing (Ahmad 1989). Thus Goel *et al.* (1981) predicted that 'the long term answer to Asian rickets probably lies in health education and a change towards the Western diet and lifestyle'. This was reflected in the official response of the DHSS working party and in the resultant Stop Rickets Campaign.

Higher rates of consanguinity among Asians, particularly Pakistanis, in Britain has become the ultimate 'explanatory hypothesis' within medicine. This includes serious researchers who wish to disentangle the complex interplay between socio-economic, lifestyle, environmental and health service factors in influencing, for example, birth outcome – perinatal mortality and congenital malformations. A larger group, however, is happy to hang anything from poor birth 'outcome' to blood disorders, cancers, diseases of the eye, and much more onto this new found explanatory peg. This concern is already being expressed in scientific literature (Bundey *et al.* 1989; *Lancet* 1991) and research on consanguinity is likely to become a major sub-industry soon. Among obstetricians and midwives it is 'common knowledge' that higher perinatal deaths and congenital malformations among Asians are due to consanguinity.

Recently, in one day I met three consultants – a paediatrician, a haemotologist and an opthalmologist – who linked consanguinity to significant aspects of their work with Asian patients. Since then I have met a consultant clinical oncologist who believes consanguinity to be the cause of 'unusual tumours' in Asians. It has been argued that the medical scientific community has failed to maintain high standards in research on black people and has favoured interpretations which locate problems of health care in black people's cultures and genetics (Peach 1984a; 1984b; Bhopal 1992; Sashidharan and Francis, this volume).

Consanguinity is fast becoming the 'cause' of all the health problems of the Pakistani and Muslim minorities – that the research literature on consanguinity remains inconclusive (Rao and Inbaraj 1977; Macluer 1980; Saedi-Wong and Al-Frayh 1989) can be conveniently sidestepped. That in studies of effects of consanguinity it is nearly impossible to control for numerous confounding variables – including social class, education and quality of health care – is easily ignored. It provides an excellent way of blaming the victim and absolving health services and wider racial inequalities from responsibility; better still, by not doing anything you claim to be an anti-racist, as the only action you could, in this scenario, recommend would be for communities to abandon this alien and deleterious habit.

My point is not that culture and genetics – keeping in mind that humans share approximately 85 per cent of their genes (Jones, S. 1991) – are of no significance in health; it is simply that these are among a host of possible determinants and explanations. Through racialization problems become redefined and a different range of explanations are applied to black than to white people. For black people this focus is almost exclusively on cultures and ethnicities, genetics and metabolisms, being different and therefore inferior.

Politics of health research

Research problems do not emerge in a vacuum; they are shaped within particular social, economic, professional, theoretical, ideological and historical contexts. The identification of research issues is similar to the construction of social problems. Space precludes detailed discussion of the literature on the construction of social problems, or more widely on the construction of reality, but suffice to say that at any given time a range of issues have the potential for being identified as a social problem, needing attention. What is put on to the agenda is less the result of the intrinsic characteristics of the issue and more a consequence of the complex interplay between professional interests; community and pressure group politics; interests and influence of 'champions' of various 'causes' such as the media, politicians, clergy and pressure groups; and the potential perceived threat to the moral, economic and social structures of the society, or the threat to the 'national character' and other such concerns (Berger and Luckman 1979; Manning 1987; Hulley and Clarke 1991).

Social problems also have a historic and cultural specificity: illegitimacy is less of a 'problem' in contemporary Britain than historically (historic specificity), and more of a 'problem' in Saudi Arabia than in Britain (cultural specificity). The construction of research problems is akin to the construction of social problems, with perhaps the professional ideologies playing a more significant part in the former's identification. So the areas which are selected for attention reflect the concerns of certain individuals and groups with the power to define the agenda, and along with the presentation and interpretation of findings construct a particular, highly selective vision of reality. This construction also carries with it explicit or implicit theories of appropriate causes (thus allowing construction of hypotheses), interventions and outcomes.

Professional ideologies are particularly effective tools for reproducing oppressive relations, including racism.

I will look at some of the issues involved in research on the health of black populations, under two broad headings: 'clinical bias of race and health research'; and what I have called 'intellectual apartheid'. The structuring of material under the two headings is little more than arbitrary, and is justified only in terms of ease of presentation.

Clinical bias of 'race' and health research

I have noted elsewhere that health research on black people is concentrated in a small number of areas, largely of clinical interest (Ahmad 1989; Ahmad *et al.* 1989). Within this it has often concentrated on exotica. One can begin to make sense of this concentration by looking at the processes involved in the construction of this research. One reason may be the continued fear of and fascination with what in the West have been defined as exotic people, exotic customs and exotic diseases, and the tendency to reduce complex phenomena to cultural or genetic factors alone. So interesting cultural quirks (Bhopal 1992) or peculiar diseases are more often the subject of research than racism within medicine and the racial production of ill health.

Secondly, whereas traditionally medical researchers have provided the majority of research on clinical and epidemiological aspects of populations' health, sociologists of health have researched a range of issues concerning social aspects of health and health care. This has included research on concepts of health and illness, analysis of medical institutions, the relationship between service users and providers, perceptions of health status and health concerns, factors associated with help-seeking behaviour, and issues around gender, social class, health and health care. The range and depth of this material can be witnessed in any textbook on the sociology of health or in journals (such as *Sociology of Health and Illness* and *Social Science and Medicine*).

As far as 'race' and health are concerned medical sociology has pretended to be an ostrich.[1] It has not kept in touch with the social realities of 'multi-racial' Britain. It keeps its head buried in the sand of white health concerns, is made up of almost exclusively white researchers, works from white perspectives, and publishes in white journals with white editorial boards. The main medical sociology journals in Britain are good examples of this editing out of black people, as a focus of research and as researchers. They offer virtually no coverage of 'race' issues and are controlled by and serve the white medical sociologists.

If British sociology – so severely criticized by Bourne and Sivanandan

(1981), Ben-Tovim and Gabriel (1982), Carby (1982), Lawrence (1982a; 1982b), and others – is white in its personnel, concerns and perspectives then its sub-discipline, sociology of health, is considerably whiter. At a recent conference on health and society there were about half a dozen black people among around 400 delegates.

A white sociologist, with impeccable radical and feminist credentials, at this conference went through the so familiar and patronizing 'some of my best friends are black people' and 'bending over backwards to please black colleagues' routine and complained about black colleagues being impossible to please. Another white colleague gave a paper on the health service reforms, talking about the consumer as if the consumer only had a class position but was neutral in terms of 'race'. When challenged by a black delegate that the 'reforms' will have a differential impact on black and white people and that this needed to be acknowledged, he replied that he could only do so much in the time given.

The major *Health and Lifestyle Survey* (Blaxter 1990), which included academic knights and leading sociologists, used the 'eyeballing' definition of ethnicity (that is to say, defined ethnicity on the basis of interviewer observation) in 1984. By then medical sociology's parent discipline had built huge edifices and illustrious individual careers on studies of 'ethnic' inequalities in all walks of life, and on 'ethnic' categorization, albeit as 'cheerleaders and ombudsmen' (Bourne and Sivanandan 1981).

Widely used medical sociology texts have edited out 'race' and racism in health and medicine as legitimate areas of scholarship or at best provide patronizing cultural reductionist, stereotyped accounts of Asian and Afro-Caribbean patients (see Tuckett 1976; Hart 1985; Morgan *et al.* 1985; Cunningham-Burley and McKegany 1990; Lock and Gordon 1990; Gabe *et al.* 1991, among a range of textbooks). The racism within medical sociology perpetuates the racism in medicine as medical under- and postgraduates, practitioners, other health professionals and policy-makers are denied material and instruction in racial structuring of British society and the inequalities in health and health care.

The health inequalities debate, including the famous *Black Report* (Townsend and Davidson 1982) and the *Health Divide* (Whitehead 1987), generally either ignores 'race' or marginalizes it to a few paragraphs. A spate of papers and special issues of journals on the tenth anniversary of the *Black Report* failed to notice that Britain is no longer all white, and that the black populations have a greater share of these inequalities, be they in terms of health status or the quality of health care (Davey-Smith *et al.* 1990; Morris 1990; special issue of *Social Science and Medicine* on health inequalities in Europe published in 1990).

Within sociology, white feminists have provided valuable and challenging research literature on gender in relation to, among other areas, caring for the sick, masculinization of medicine, feminization of nursing, the journey from being a women to becoming a mother, the sexist nature of medical ideology and institutional structures, and positivist methodologies. They, however, are equally guilty of excluding black women. Black women are nowhere to be found in the work of leading British feminist writers such as Ann Oakley (1980) or the early work of Hilary Graham (1984).

The white feminists' concerns with the availability of birth control or abortion were never shared by black women – the dominant ideology, shared by the medical profession, of an over-fertile black population and fear of black people outbreeding whites meant that fertility control, including Depo-Provera, and sterilizations were aggressively thrust upon black women (Bryan et al. 1985). The concentration on the domestic division of labour neglected the fact that black women did not just labour in their own homes but also in the homes of white women. Their (often exclusive) emphasis on patriarchy neglected the dimension of 'race' and that for many black women black men were essential allies against white racism.

This is not to deny sexism in black cultures, but simply to reiterate some of the powerful criticisms by black feminists who have felt excluded and found the feminist movement often irrelevant and at times oppressive (Davis 1981; Carby 1982; Parmar 1982; Bourne 1983; Bryan et al. 1985; Bhavnani and Coulson 1986). This exclusion is now acknowledged as problematic by some white feminist writers (Graham 1991). So whereas the feminist sociologists and writers may have been the champions of white women's rights – and much of this writing has concentrated on medicine – they have singularly failed black women.

The often heated debates on the relationship between 'race', class and gender which have characterized the development and formed the basis of the editorial policy of the social policy journal Critical Social Policy, are yet to take place in medical sociology. This broader neglect of 'race' by sociologists of health is itself significant in shaping the type of research that we find on black populations: 'clinical' and 'scientific', devoid of sociological analysis or at times even social awareness, divorced from any attempt to set the findings against the backdrop of oppression, discrimination and internal colonialism.

The majority of research in this area has been funded by the Department of Health; largely through its Locally Organized Research Schemes (LORS). The research funds are administered by the 14 regional health authorities (and the special health authorities) to researchers in their respective district health authorities and trusts, and family health service authorities on the basis of regional research competitions. The Scottish and Welsh Offices run equivalent schemes. The research funded by the Department of Health amounted to about 59 per cent of all health research, according to the register of medical sociology, *Medical Sociology in Britain* (Field and Woodman 1990) – the total proportion, including clinical research, is likely to be considerably higher.

The membership of most LORS research committees is white and male, and almost exclusively from the clinical sciences. For example, at the time of writing, one regional health authority's research committee, consisting of eighteen members, has one black, no women and two members whose specialties are described as 'health services research' and 'health economics' (others being medical specialists). Thus, the mechanism for the distribution of this research is such that research focusing on issues such as clinical aspects of (say) vitamin D deficiency, effects of maternal characteristics on birth outcome, biochemical and physiological correlates of diabetes, the genetic basis of schizophrenia and so on is much more likely to be both proposed and funded than (say) studies of black women's experiences of pregnancy and maternity care, doctors' attitudes towards patients from minorities, or racist practices within the health care structures. The scheme excludes, by and large, studies based on 'non-scientific' qualitative methodologies.

A second factor is related to the discipline of the researcher. The applicants for research grants are mainly doctors, and evidence of 'hard' clinical research ability and productivity is important for many in terms of prestige, recognition and promotion. Equally, white physicians who focus on racism as opposed to cultural peculiarities or the genetic basis of disease are likely to be considered both as not 'real scientists' and as dangerous. It would therefore make sense for them to concentrate on clinical rather than service and structural issues. Related to this, even when field researchers are social scientists they still play by the rules of their medically qualified supervisors, again reinforcing the clinical bias in research.

Lastly here, my arguments earlier about medical practitioners wanting to keep research 'pure', 'scientific' and 'professional' also apply. Carney (1989), commenting in an editorial for the *British Medical Journal* on two papers by senior medical researchers (Balarajan *et al.* 1989; Gillam *et al.* 1989) looking at consultation rates in general practice by patients of different 'ethnic origins', emphasized the need for scientific purity as studies of this kind need to be 'objective so as not to be construed as having political or racial overtones'. As stated earlier, professional ideologies generally are an effective vehicle for the legitimation and reproduction of oppressive relations; the efficiency of medical ideology in reproducing racism is hard to match.

Medicine has based its legitimacy on its status as a science; like the natural sciences it searches for underlying realities and fundamental truths: the 'black' genes in schizophrenia, the black culture in rickets and birth experience, and now a 'godsend' in the guise of consanguinity as the 'cause' of all that is alien and pathological among Asians. It does not acknowledge that 'facts' are socially created, it wants to discover new ones without being polluted with politics. My argument does not imply that all researchers on black peoples' health, medical or sociological, are socially and politically naive. There are some rare exceptions, but I am more concerned with the overall picture, which remains depressing.

Intellectual apartheid

One of Illich's (1977) criticisms of medicine is that it has expropriated health and illness – its definition, treatment and cure – from the individual. I do not want to elaborate on this but wish to discuss another type of expropriation – white medicine has colonized black people's health issues. This is not unique to health, but rather is an extension of other forms of expropriation, historical and contemporary, where the dominant whites have defined black peoples' realities. (Said (1978) shows how this was considered as the 'white man's burden').

Sivanandan (1990) and other black writers have recently emphasized the need for black people to reappropriate their lives, to reinterpret these from their own experiences, through black perspectives. Such debates inevitably run to the issues around what can be seen as the efforts of the state to resist this through 'ethnicization'. A massive infrastructure to promote the integration of black people is built on such fragmentation of a potential black political unity. Task Forces, Section 11, Urban Programmes and so on give state handouts to distinct 'ethnic minorities', depoliticize black oppression, fragment both internal black alliances as well as alliances with other oppressed groups and bureaucratize what were grassroots anti-racist struggles (Sivanandan 1990). The political exclusion of black communities from defining their own realities, including in terms of health research, as community representatives, grant holders for research, researchers and publishers constitutes such an expropriation.

This can be seen to have an effect on the agenda for research, a white middle-class, largely male professional agenda which maintains the status quo, focusing on the minorities themselves rather than challenging racism. Within this white professional agenda institutional practices remain intact but black communities become pathologized. Any challenges to the professional status become 'political', disruptive and polluting – clearly an affront to the value free, scientific, rational and objective nature of medicine, its practitioners and researchers.

There is also the implicit assumption that black people cannot be rational, particularly about their own communities. This was exemplified in a research application by a team consisting of white medical sociologists focusing on food choices of a particular Asian community in the South of England. The researchers proposed to employ two assistants from the relevant community to facilitate trust and communication. They were not worried about their own 'objectivity' as obvious outsiders parachuting into this community for largely personal gain. However, they expressed concern about the Asian research assistants' ability to be objective in this context. To take it to its illogical conclusion, this line of thinking would suggest that medical sociologists should perhaps have employed exclusively black researchers to work with white communities – as they would supposedly be more 'objective' researchers. However, it seems that it is only black researchers that we need to worry about.

Let me move on to a related issue in this debate on 'intellectual apartheid'. Part of what happens under colonization is that values, educational paradigms, cultures, histories and languages of the colonized are devalued, not necessarily through putting up billboards pronouncing their inferiority but more insidiously through instituting new, officially sanctioned, supposedly superior systems. The institutions of the colonized are subtly, sometimes forcibly, subverted through institutions based on the values of the colonizer – education, law, medical systems are examples. The imposition of Western medicine in India through discrediting and undermining, both 'scientifically' and administratively, of the popular and more accessible Unani and Auyrvedic systems of health care is an example of this (Hume 1977).

Fanon (1967; 1970) has written about the difficulties which the African decolonized intellectuals faced in trying to construct a cultural future in their countries after liberation. The liberation, to be meaningful, needs to extend to frameworks of knowledge, perspectives and values. The history of being steeped in Western frameworks of knowledge, uncritically, without challenge, without the freedom to develop new frameworks – or at least to evaluate Western models – makes a sudden rejection of the dominant white perspectives difficult.

In the contemporary world, this cultural hegemony is still extended to the under-developed countries (UDCs) through international aid; through Western models of education both inside UDCs and in the West marketed to 'overseas' students; through the one-way (North to South) flow of news; and through satellite television.

Here black health professionals are in a difficult situation. They are themselves marginalized and suffer racial discrimination (Anwar and Ali 1987; McKeigue *et al.* 1990; see also Ward, this volume). There is ample evidence to show that Asian doctors and West Indian nurses find themselves channelled into unattractive specialties, have promotion blocked, and suffer racial abuse. This extends to British-qualified black health professionals.

However, many black health professionals appear to have internalized the white stereotypes of black people. Writings by some black authors on health issues facing sections of the black populations, in this case Asians, have been as damaging and problematic as those criticized earlier (Qureshi 1989; Healey and Aslam 1990; see also the critique by Ahmad 1992b). Such writers, through their 'scientific' and 'cultural' pronouncements, legitimate white racism. Consider the following quotes, some from these writers:

> one cannot change peoples' attitudes or the way they think by legislation: indeed, one must be grateful for that. A change in such views, indeed what is little short of a revolution in thought of this island race, will result only by long term education. The emphasis must by strictly on education, not implied 'brain-washing'. A better understanding of each other's views and aspirations must be achieved. People must want to accept each other. *Equally, nor should the 'blame' be considered entirely one-sided. If the Asian community really wants to integrate it has to grasp the view, at least in part, that 'when in Rome, do as the Romans'. Any group cannot come into a community into which it expects to be accepted without being prepared to contribute, at least in part, by an attempt to adapt to the mores of the society [it is] adopting.* (Healey and Aslam, 1990: 76; emphasis added)

> To suppose that the habits of the mass of immigrants, living in their own communities, speaking their own languages and maintaining their native customs, will change appreciably in the next two or three decades is a supposition so grotesque that only those could make it who are determined not to admit what they know to be . . . (Powell 1969: 307)

> Unfortunately, the real problem arises with the section of the community which is least able to look after itself – those people whose lifestyle is more akin to the rural village farmer than to a Britain heading rapidly to the prospects of scientific revolution held by the 21st century. Regrettably, this is actually the majority of that community. (Healey and Aslam 1990: 77)

They carry the same sentiments of black people not integrating, of problems created by the existence of an alien wedge among British culture, of the onus for change being on the 'immigrants' and so on. Drs Aslam and Healey, on the back cover of their book, are described as 'acknowledged leading experts in traditional Asian medicines and practices'. Dr Aslam's scientific work is also in the same mode of pathologizing Asian patients and demonizing practitioners of *hikmat* (for a critique, see Ahmad 1992b), and is heavily, and uncritically, cited by white researchers, including sociologists of health (Scrivens and Hillier 1982).

Dr Qureshi is a general practitioner who is a prolific writer on Asian people's health problems. He is popular with the white dominated medical scientific journals and highly regarded by the white scientific community as a scientist and cultural expert. Over the last few years he has served on the editorial boards of *Health Trends, the Journal of Royal Society of Medicine* and the *Journal of Royal Society of Health*. His ability to provide stereotypes and gross generalizations of 'multi-ethnic' patients is unsurpassed:

> English patients are shy of revealing their age and reluctant to discuss their religion or political persuasion because they consider this a part of their personal privacy. An ethnic minority doctor should be very tactful when asking about their ages or religion. However, the reverse is the case among ethnic minorities. *An English doctor should be bold in asking the age or religion when taking the history from an Asian, African, Chinese, or other such patients because they feel proud to give this information. In general, they live by the religion.* (Qureshi 1992; emphasis added)

There are problems particularly in psychiatry and general practice; ironically, both these specialities have sizeable proportions of black doctors. Black general practitioners seem to be even more likely to hold negative attitudes towards black patients than white GPs (Ahmad *et al.* 1991; MORI, unpublished data, personal communication). A more radicalized black workforce in health services is required to mount an effective challenge to the system from within.

With this background, will a greater number of black researchers, researching on the health issues and concerns of their own communities, make a qualitative difference considering that the structures of internal colonialism will persist, and that these researchers will be colonized into white professional and educational frameworks? The evidence from black health professionals is discouraging. However, there is reason for optimism in that a small nucleus of black health professionals is emerging who are beginning to challenge racist research and practice in psychiatry (Burke 1989; Fernando 1991; Sashidharan and Francis, this volume). Within the voluntary and academic sectors, too, there is some hope – Kobena Mercer (1986), and Errol Francis (1991a, 1991b) and Torkington (1991), among others, deserve mention.

The NHS, both in its research and practice, is not an island. It is time it learned from experiences in social services and education. There are lessons here for the black health professionals also. Black social workers have had a radical impact on their discipline and forced it to examine its curricula, training and practice (Central Council for Education and Training in Social Work (CCETSW) 1991a; 1991b; Husband 1992; Rhodes 1992). Black professionals provided the political impetus as well as the intellectual labour for this change, though they have benefited from moral and intellectual help from white colleagues. In this example, there is hope for black health professionals making a significant impact on the research agenda for black populations' health and health care through political commitment and action.

This is not an argument for excluding white researchers: some of the most powerful analyses of racism in health research and delivery of care have come from white colleagues such as Donovan (1986), Pearson (1986), Rocheron (1988) and Sheldon and Parker (1992). Progressive white researchers must continue their efforts. Nor am I arguing for expropriating power from black non-professionals, the majority of the population. Rather, this is a plea to empower ourselves as black people and to reappropriate the responsibility for defining our own realities, to resist labelling and pathologization.

Concluding comments

We need a radicalized and politicized field of 'race' and health. I do not see this to be at odds with the historical tradition of sections of medical practitioners and researchers, particularly the psychiatrist and the public health physician or the sociologist of health. Nor do I see it as problematic in that 'good' science is not supposed to be political or radical, but neutral: my argument is that all science is political but that 'good' scientists are aware of the political nature of their enterprise.

There is a tradition of radical materialist epidemiology (McKeown 1976) and sociology of health in Britain, and this needs to be extended to the study of 'race' and health. But there is a danger that a radical field of 'race'/health research will encourage material reductionism where all phenomena are reduced to material disadvantage or class oppression. 'Race' has important historical and contemporary overlaps with class, but is not reducible to class. The reformed researcher, to be credible and useful, needs to be conversant with the history and politics of 'race' and with the minority communities as having a 'political' existence quite apart from having distinct cultures. But, significantly, neither are the minority cultures of no significance – to argue this is to deny them their rightful identities and ignore the sustaining, nurturing qualities of cultures, especially in a hostile environment.

I do not deny the need for clinical research. But too often it is based on problematic assumptions and has been conducted at the expense of challenging racism in defining health needs and service delivery. There needs to be a 'social research agenda' concentrating on black people's perceptions and perspectives on health and health care delivery; not concerned with fundamental biological/aetiological truths but with making the system fit the needs of the population. Critical analysis of the institution of medicine and professional practices should be central to this agenda. This will necessitate a rejection of culture reductionist models of 'race'/health research, so prevalent in this area (Sheldon and Parker 1992). Equally, it will be absurd to continue the 'intellectual apartheid' in 'race'/health research: black researchers need to play an important part in helping their communities gain a voice on health and health care.

I have argued that black women's health issues have been excluded from wider feminist critiques. The literature on their health and health care has tended to be victim-blaming and based largely on studies of clinical aspects of pregnancy and 'birth outcome'. A new focus on black women's health is required that empowers them to define their own priorities. Black women have voices, as is apparent from powerful recent critiques of health and welfare (Bryan et al. 1985; Douglas 1991) – their voices will need to become louder and stronger.

Knowledge can be both oppressive and emancipatory. Too often in history it has been used to oppress sections of the population – defined with reference to 'race', gender or sexuality – for sectional gains. A new radicalized field of 'race' and health research is needed more now than ever before, to challenge the pathological constructions of black people's health and health needs and to focus attention on structures. White colleagues can play an important role in this, but like their black colleagues in social work, black activists, researchers and health care providers need to take the lead.

Note

1 A version of this discussion was published in *Medical Sociology News*, the newsletter of the British Sociological Association's Medical Sociology Group, in April 1992 (see Ahmad 1992c). The editors gave Mildred Blaxter, the editor of the Medical Sociology Group's journal, *Sociology of Health and Illness*, the right to reply in the same issue, reproduced here in full.

During the three years to March 1992, five papers were submitted to *Sociology of Health and Illness*, which dealt in any way with 'race'. Of these, three were published (11, 4, 253; 13, 3, 293; 14, 1, 23), one was rejected, and the fate of one remains to be decided. Maybe this proves Ahmad's point – few medical sociologists are writing about these issues – but it is in fact a higher than average acceptance rate. It is certainly not true (though I am sure the suggestion was not made literally) that SHI *ever* 'ignores, erases or edits out Black people'. Papers on 'race' and health are positively welcomed.

May I add a note about the *Health and Lifestyle Survey* (since this was specifically castigated) and similar population surveys? Interrogation about ethnic origin is notoriously difficult (v. the Census) and the use of crude proxies, in the interests of avoiding offence, is perhaps defensible. It is anticipated that 'race' might well not be a usable variable anyway, and indeed it was not used in published analyses. Only slightly fewer people of 'non-white race' were identified than the 'proper' number, given the sample size and sampling areas, but this is still only a few hundred. This number could not possibly represent both genders, all ages, many different ethnic groups, and all areas of the country. Surveys of 'race' and health – and there would be a general agreement that they are needed – have to be specifically targeted.

There is, however, an important point which Ahmad does not raise. SHI often publishes analyses of national statistics (as distinct from sample surveys) in which 'race' might be a very relevant dimension. It is always absent, and the reason is simple: it is not available. Those who record population and health statistics – of death, disability, disease prevalence, hospitalization, medical consultations, and so on – will say that distinguishing 'race' is unacceptable and is resisted. Thus Black people do become invisible. Is there an answer to this dilemma?

Rather than defend British medical sociologists, I believe Blaxter proves my point. Further, the editors of *Medical Sociology News* invited replies and comments on my paper. By the time of the next issue (three months later), they had received one reply, and that from a medical anthropologist.

Acknowledgements

This chapter has been some time in the making. I have presented sections of it at various seminars and have benefited from participants' comments. My particular thanks to Charles Husband, Russell Murray and Paul Stubbs for their comments on the complete version.

3

'Ethnically sensitive' or 'anti-racist'? Models for health research and service delivery

PAUL STUBBS

Introduction

This chapter argues that the models or frameworks which are explicitly or implicitly utilized by researchers and policy-makers in the field of 'race' and health actually matter. It goes further, indeed, to suggest that the dominant or orthodox frameworks represent, at best, a skewing of priorities and, at worst, a dangerous, if not racist, tendency to 'blame the victim'. The chapter goes on to suggest that more radical challenges to these orthodox frameworks, while being necessary, can also face certain problems of partiality and narrowness of focus.

The attempt to provide an overview of these issues derives, in part, from my own research, writing and practice concerned with challenging racism in social work and social services. Like education, this is a field, or an arena of struggle, which has seen considerable changes in models of research and service delivery in response, often unacknowledged, to black people's challenges to and criticisms of dominant theories and practices. Debates about the relevance of 'culture' as against 'racism', of 'multi-cultural' as against 'anti-racist' policies and practices, and recently a debate about 'black perspectives' are beginning to surface in the health arena. There may be a great deal to learn from the field of social work and social work education (cf. Central Council of Education and Training in Social Work (CCETSW) 1991a; 1991b) where, as a result of black people's pressure, significant changes have occurred and are still occurring.

A major question must be, given that black people have campaigned against the unfavourable health care they receive, why it is that there has been massive resistance to change from health care professionals and policy makers. In a changing relationship between health professionalism and the state, in the context of an increasing emphasis on market mechanisms and consumer choice, it is important to examine the failure of health services to address the concerns of black health workers and consumers.

Models of research

It is in the light of these issues that different models of health care research must be addressed. Most importantly, there needs to be a debate about whether, in fact, a separate, separable, field of research called 'race and health' is itself problematic, both in terms of research and service delivery issues. Three themes immediately suggest themselves. .

First, how far does the specialism 'race and health' mean that much sociological or social scientific research, and policy on health, actually has an 'under-racialized' view of the world, ignoring the existence of black and ethnic minority populations? If these populations are seen to form a 'special group' to be studied only by specialist researchers, there might be a failure to examine, much less account for, black people's specific positioning within health inequalities and the differential impact of health service provision on black groups. The tokenistic acknowledgement of 'race' and racism in supposedly radical analyses, which focus overwhelmingly on socio-economic or class-based inequalities, is also a serious problem (cf, for example, Townsend and Davidson 1982; Whitehead 1987; Widgery 1988).

Second, as Sheldon and Parker (1992) have persuasively argued, concepts of 'race' and 'ethnicity' have been operationalized in highly problematic ways in a great deal of (primarily epidemiological and clinical), health research. Here, a distorted view of the world emerges in which 'race' becomes seen as a variable which is not contextualized in any sense, but rather becomes an objective 'fact'. The separation of 'race and health' encourages the ignoring of a sociological truth that 'race' is not a biological essence but a socially constructed category (cf. Husband 1982). Sheldon and Parker suggest that health research, where it has been 'racialized', has become so in ways which utilize contradictory, contested, and sometimes irrelevant categorizations. These are given the status of real entities able to be correlated with other real entities in a supposedly meaningful scientific way. The dominance of clinical and epidemiological studies is problematic since there is a tendency to reduce complex sets of social relations to particularly crude kinds of variable.

A third problem is the dominant research focus, which is 'problem-taking' rather than 'problem-making' (Young 1971). Rather than posing fundamental problems of their own making, researchers in 'race and health' tend to operate within a particularly narrow framework of 'policy relevance'. Many studies lack any historical, theoretical and political depth. Instead, studies tend to operate within a technical framework in which particular projects are studied relating 'objectives', in a linear way, to 'outcomes'. As Sonja Hunt (1987: 166) has pointed out, '"outcome" is an artificial freezing of a dynamic process'. Even when the 'outcomes' for particular racial groups are addressed, the importance of the processes of delivering services, and the racial biases underpinning them, tends to be downplayed. These processes are of little concern to the funders of research or to policy-makers. Orthodox research, then, tends to neglect or downplay the vexed questions of power relations, including racism, which must be central to any critical research (cf. Harvey 1990).

The politics of 'race and health research'

If research is not neutral or value-free, but is itself situated in a political context, then we must address the complex politics of 'race and health research'. The process begun by Maggie Pearson (1983) must be reassessed and added to. In a series of interventions, Pearson raised fundamental problems about the construction of a research orthodoxy of 'ethnic minority health studies'. She did this through a reading of black people's critiques of 'race relations sociology' in the United Kingdom led by writers from the Birmingham Centre for Contemporary Cultural Studies (cf. Lawrence 1981; CCCS 1982).

Pearson examined a number of interlinked issues, many of which remain relevant today. First, she suggested that most research had an uncritical acceptance of medical models and a mechanistic understanding of disease. One consequence of this was that the historical links between Western medicalization and the development of 'scientific racism' remained unexplored. More generally, research tended to operate within frameworks provided by the powerful definitions of doctors. This led to a skewing of research priorities in a number of ways (cf. also Bhopal 1992; Ahmad, Chapter 2, this volume).

Second, she argued that research tended to be divorced from what she called 'committed action'. In consequence, black people became the objects of more and more essentially white research which made little difference to their lives. At its simplest, this argument raises questions about the role of white researchers studying 'ethnic minority health' both in terms of ethics and research validity. More complexly, a model of white research could be said to continue to operate in a number of studies conducted by black researchers since the concept refers as much to the assumptions made as to the 'racial origins' of the researchers.

Third, and clearly connected to this, she suggested that there existed a dominant research focus on 'culture' at the expense of a concern with power relations and structures including, of course, racism. This echoes the arguments of Errol Lawrence, who noted 'scholars' propensity to discover and tackle any "problem", except the burning problem of racism' (Lawrence 1982a: 19).

Fourth, she suggested, again closely following Lawrence's argument, that the effect of all of this was the tendency to see black people's cultures as inferior, deviant, or pathological so that health issues tended to be explained in terms which 'blamed the victim'. The following quote from her paper to the Medical Geography Conference (Pearson 1983: 16) captures much of her argument:

> the focus on cultural distinctiveness or racial difference as an explanatory factor *per se* has led to some misleading and simplistic conclusions and definitions of 'problems'. Over generalisations abound, and the influence of social factors such as occupational class, unemployment and housing conditions are often denied in simplistic analyses which reduce such complex social phenomena to grossly over generalised stereotyped racial and ethnic categories. Such interpretations neglect the subtle and crucial effects of racism and racial discrimination.

Since this was written, there have been two types of study which have been, and continue to be, of immense importance in challenging this dominant research model. The first type of study has attempted to describe and account for the operation of institutional racism within health care, in terms of both service delivery and employment. Rather than seeing black and ethnic minority health problems as deriving from 'culture' or a series of unfortunate 'accidents' resolvable by 'better communication', this work has seen health and health care as structured systematically in terms of a pervasive racial inequality, discrimination and disadvantage. Black people are seen as receiving fewer health services and more of the social control aspects, their employment is skewed, and health problems are either not addressed or addressed in racist ways. Protassia Torkington's work (see Torkington 1983; 1991) is a good example of this tradition, examining the politics of health in Liverpool. She makes the connections between a number of issues which are usually treated separately, and is thus able to make racial inequality a central focus. There is clearly a need for more research and published material examining institutional racism in health care provision.

The second type of study questions the dominance and relevance of Western models of health and disease ('the medical model', as white research would have it) and looks at the existence of diverse and different models of health and disease and the continued importance of non-Western traditions of health and medicine. This is a body of work which, potentially, has a great deal of policy relevance not least in terms of challenging the ethnocentrism or Eurocentrism of much of existing research and practice (for a recent piece on the role of 'hakims', see Ahmad 1992a). In addition, the influence of Western models of health and illness throughout the world is a subject which needs addressing given the international context of the politics of 'race' and health (cf. Navarro 1976). Both of these issues, the study of institutional racism and the challenge to Western models, need to be conceptualized within a coherent framework which, I would suggest, necessitates a shift from 'ethnic sensitivity' to 'anti-racism'.

From 'ethnic sensitivity' to 'anti-racism'?

It is significant to note that the debate about 'ethnic sensitivity' and 'anti-racism' has a long history in the literatures on social work and education in both the United States and the United Kingdom. However, there has been virtually no reference to this debate in the health service literature, despite its applicability. Stated simply, the debate is between two conceptual frameworks which have attempted to replace crude 'colour-blind' or 'assimilationist' models through which black and ethnic minority populations were either ignored or seen as 'integrating' into the supposed norms of the 'host society'.

The 'ethnic sensitivity' approach

'Ethnic sensitivity' seeks to focus on the distinct ethnicities of ethnic minority groups, seeing ethnicity as a key determinant of life chances generally and, in particular, in structuring access to services, at both an interpersonal and an organizational level. In a key construction reiterated in a report from the United Kingdom Association of Directors of Social Services (ADSS/CRE 1978), ethnic minorities were seen to have special needs as a result of three factors: being immigrants of fairly recent settlement; facing community hostility, resentment and discrimination, and through the existence of different cultural patterns.

In the institutionalization of 'ethnic sensitivity' within welfare services, it is the last of these three, the existence of different cultural patterns, which has been emphasized, underpinned by an ideology of 'multi-culturalism'. In terms of service delivery, the argument is that there needs to be a better understanding of such things as the customs, traditions and religious activities of ethnic minority groups.

Even a cursory examination of health care services reveals the dominance of this model of 'ethnic sensitivity'. In her important study of the Asian Mother and Baby Campaign, Yvette Rocheron (1988) notes two key elements of this, namely, teaching health service professionals about 'ethnic minority cultures', and health education programmes aimed at ethnic minority communities. From her own example, it is possible to add a third, namely, the development of 'specialist' services including the employment of ethnic minority workers in particular positions.

Within each of these strands, particular points can be made about the skewing of priorities. First, in terms of ethnic minority cultures, there has been much more attention to 'Asian' cultures (cf. Henley 1980) than to other black groups, particularly Afro-Caribbeans, and other so-called 'ethnic minorities'. This may relate to colonialist and racist constructions of the 'strangeness' of the cultural patterns of 'Asian' groups; in contrast, Afro-Caribbean cultures are often viewed as impoverished versions of 'indigenous white British' culture – whatever that may be!

Second, health education programmes, again tending to focus on Asian communities, have been directed primarily to the issues of 'diet, ante-natal care, and birth control' (Rocheron 1988: 16). Colonialist constructions are also in play here, relating to a Western model of 'the problems of the Third World' which concentrates on over-population and the failure of (particularly) women to learn and inculcate 'civilized' patterns of life.

Third, in terms of service delivery, there has been much greater attention to link-workers and interpreters, usually low-paid, casualized, and exploited, rather than to issues concerning the role of black workers at senior levels of the medical and health professions. Skills such as community languages (a euphemism for undervalued, non-European languages) and 'cultural awareness' are not seen as prerequisites for the recruitment of medical students, GPs, consultants, or administrators.

One partial exception to this is the development of 'transcultural psychiatry' where there have been discussions of the role of 'Asian' and Afro-Caribbean psychiatrists (cf Littlewood and Lipsedge 1989) – for a useful critique, see Mercer (1986) and Francis (1991a). Transcultural psychiatry is, however, in many ways, a prime example of the 'ethnically sensitive' approach and does, in fact, have very close links with the relevant literature relating to social work. Farrar and Sircar (1986: 202), in their discussion of the development of a Unit working with 'Asian' patients, saw the key issues as 'language difficulties, differing expectations about what the service should provide, and different concepts about what constitutes mental illness'. This emphasis on language and difference, almost in a vacuum, is at the centre of ethnic sensitivity and, in my view, of its partial and inadequate understanding of health care provision. There is no discussion, for example, of the possibility of mental health services being perceived as an apparatus of social control; in this sense 'ethnic sensitivity' might be little more than a smokescreen for the excesses of state power.

'Ethnicity', like 'culture', is a very vague, static, and narrow concept which can serve, then, to deflect attention away from broad structural processes, including racism. Rocheron (1988: 18) sums this up when she states that 'the cultural approach in no way entails any fundamental change in the structural position of ethnic minorities vis-a-vis the NHS'. It is thus based on a benevolent model of health service provision in which the solutions to problems are essentially technical and professional rather than political. There is an assumption that with greater knowledge of different cultures, with improved skills in cross-cultural communication, and through the creation of particular ethnic specialisms, services will be improved.

Even more worryingly, the 'ethnic sensitivity' approach tends to focus on the supposed 'problems' of ethnic minority groups. Hence, health models see many of these problems as internally generated through inappropriate cultural, familial and community traditions. The approach seems to be based on the construction of 'a pathology of Black family life, identity crisis, cultural conflict and generational conflict' (Parmar 1981: 29). This is clear in the psychiatric literature where, for example, Aggrey Burke, who is one of the more progressive writers, can still argue that 'there is no doubt that family stress is the major aetiological factor in the disorders of West Indian patients' (Burke 1986: 187). There is a tendency to downplay issues of racism; where racism is mentioned, as in the article by Farrar and Sircar (1986), the authors ask merely that it be 'noted'.

Anti-racist perspectives

Despite considerable controversy about what is meant by 'anti-racism' and, indeed, recent pronouncements concerning 'the end of anti-racism' (Gilroy 1990), it is still possible to outline an anti-racist perspective which offers a coherent critique of 'ethnic sensitivity'. In her influential book *Anti-racist Social Work*, Lena Dominelli (1988: 3) suggests that 'anti-racist perspectives focus on transforming the unequal social relations shaping interaction between black and white people into egalitarian ones'. In this definition, anti-racist analyses and practices take us into a radical political arena which is precisely that which is ignored by the 'ethnic sensitivity' approach.

Anti-racist perspectives, then, have as their starting point not 'culture' but 'racism'. It is important not to see racism as a fixed essence but, rather, to see it as changing and dynamic. Indeed, it may be preferable to refer to 'racisms' rather than 'racism' in recognition of the different, interconnecting levels at which racism operates and, also, the ways in which racisms change over time (see also Patel, this volume). An understanding of the production and reproduction of relations of dominance and subordination based on different 'racial' categorizations can refer to three interlinked levels: the interpersonal, the organizational/institutional and the structural/societal. Hence, racism is seen as more than just the sum total of individual prejudices and institutional practices and, rather, is seen as a pervasive reality structuring all social interactions.

There are a number of elements which I see as necessary for the development of an anti-racist perspective on health care. Inevitably, this must go beyond the study of racism in one institution – the NHS – to examine the importance of structural inequalities and the existence of a pervasive racism within the welfare state in a society in which black people have been defined ideologically as a 'problem' or a 'threat'. My analysis in this regard is informed, particularly, by Fiona Williams's book, *Social Policy: a critical introduction* (1989), which provides a framework which aids understanding of racism and health care.

The first point to make is that general inequalities within a society have a racialized dimension and that this is of central importance in understanding black people's health needs. Stated crudely, it surely matters that structural racism tends to consign disproportionate numbers of black people to structurally subordinate, oppressed, and ill health-producing positions in terms of material poverty, housing, employment and unemployment, and so on. The existence of the 'inverse care law' (Tudor Hart 1971), which suggests that those whose health needs are the greatest tend to receive the least, is clearly relevant to black people, making the neglect of racialized inequalities in many studies of this issue all the more problematic.

Williams (1989: ch. 6) argues that the historical cast of welfare reforms, including the creation of the NHS in 1948, cannot be understood outside of an awareness of its underpinnings in nationalism, imperialism and racism. The NHS, as a part of the welfare state, was based on the attempt to create a 'fit race and people' after the ravages of war. This concern was not extended to the 'new' black settler populations of the 1950s onwards. Indeed, of far greater concern was a fear of the abuse of services by 'immigrants' and 'foreigners' and the burden which 'immigrants' would place on health services. It is no accident that Enoch Powell's interventions in the 1960s spoke of the plight of white mothers unable to obtain hospital beds for 'our' sick children (cf. Barker 1981). Doubts about black people's entitlement to services continued to the present day, of course, with accounts of black people being made to show their passports at hospitals. In addition, as others have suggested (Ahmad in Chapter 2 and Anionwu in Chapter 5, this volume), numerous reports and health reforms have failed to address specifically the needs of black people.

Second, there is the linked issue of social reproduction and the importance, within the welfare state, of a particular construction of 'fit motherhood'. A whole series of policies and practices, deriving from eugenicist ideas in which 'fitness' is equated with 'whiteness', have been incorporated into health services. As Bhavnani and Coulson (1986) have suggested, we must recognise that 'different women are treated differently' within the welfare state. Policies and practices concerning reproduction can be seen as offering 'birth control for white women and fertility control for black women' (cf. Bryan *et al.* 1985). Black women's different relation to reproductive rights can be seen in debates about abortion, sterilization, and the use of the contraceptive Depo-Provera. All of these issues have an international dimension which returns us to the question of global relations of dominance and subordination.

Third, there is the question of the NHS as an employer. This is a complex issue but it is certainly the case that, historically, the NHS has relied on black workers, originally those trained overseas, to offset rising costs. Black workers remain an exploited group within many different sectors of health care, be it as ancillary staff (cf. Doyal *et al.* 1981), nurses, or GPs. The concentration of mainly 'Asian' doctors in the less prestigious areas of psychiatry, geriatrics, and general practice, is an important manifestation of racism. In addition, we must ask questions about the internalized racism manifested by some black doctors (cf. Ahmad, Chapter 2, this volume), and the lack of any serious attempt within the NHS to develop coherent equal opportunities policies, much less to challenge documented instances of discrimination in recruitment and promotion (cf. Johnson, and Ward, this volume).

The fourth issue concerns the role of health services in a web of social control which oppresses black people. The most obvious example, already referred to, is that of mental health and the issues of misdiagnosis, compulsory hospital admissions, police involvement, referral to secure hospitals, and treatment with large doses of psychotropic drugs. Much of the literature has concentrated on the Afro-Caribbean population (cf. Francis 1991a; 1991b), especially men, although there are also issues about the treatment of 'Asian' women in terms of the label 'depressed' (cf. Westwood *et al.* 1989; Sayal 1990). (See also Sashidharan and Francis, this volume.)

Anti-racist perspectives, then, address the ways in which state and professional ideologies and practices tend to reproduce racism at a number of levels. Instead of seeing black communities as 'underserved', the dominant racist construction is of those communities as 'undeserving', with cultural explanations overused at the expense of a concern with structural inequalities, the racist assumptions of powerful medical definers, and so on (cf. Clarke and Clayton 1983; Ahmad *et al.* 1991, for a discussion of some of these processes).

All of these issues warrant further investigation. What is important is the development of theoretical and research approaches which are able to examine the complex interrelationships between different factors. In addition, a central aspect of anti-racist analysis must be a rejection of determinism and an attempt to aid the process of challenging and changing racist practices and outcomes. Research is not valuable for its own sake, but for its role in this process.

Even more importantly, anti-racist perspectives have to acknowledge the existence of resistance to orthodox models and frameworks led by black communities. For example, no anti-racist perspective on health can ignore the importance of black-led self-help initiatives and campaigns which have, in many cases, led to real change. The campaign to get sickle cell disease taken seriously is a case in point (cf. Anionwu, this volume), as is the challenge to racism in mental health led by the Black Health Workers and Patients Group (1983) and now by the Afro-Caribbean Mental Health Association (Francis 1991a, 1991b). There is a need for more accounts of these struggles in the context of NHS reforms and, in particular, privatization which, yet again, appears unwilling to address the needs of black people.

The problems of racism and anti-racism

At this point, it is important to note some of the problems with anti-racism which are being addressed in some recent writings. I wish to argue that there remains a partiality in some radical research and analytical frameworks which seek to make racism central. Four themes seem to me to be the most important.

First, there is a danger that 'racism' will be invoked as a catch-all category with no real analytical value at the expense of a clear demonstration of the processes through which racism operates. Indeed, it could simply become another variable like culture to be measured empirically. In my own work (see Stubbs 1987), I have suggested that it may be through ideologies of 'professionalism' that racism is reproduced within social work. Given the importance of doctors' claims to professional status, it is useful to explore this issue with regard to health care. It may be precisely through notions of 'medical autonomy' that a racist professional common sense is constructed, very close to a Powellite common sense in the political domain (see Ahmad, Chapter 2, this volume).

Second, while it is absolutely right to suggest that much less emphasis should be placed on studying black and ethnic minority groups, and much more emphasis should be placed on studying the realities of white racism, there is a danger that this will produce a one-dimensional picture of black people as passive victims of racism. By (often but not exclusively white) researchers following this line, there is a relative neglect of challenges and resistance to racism. I am not suggesting that this is anything other than a dilemma, as Karenga (1982) recognized:

How does one prove strength in oppression without overstating the case, diluting criticism of the system and absolving the oppressor in the process? How does one criticise the system and state of things without contributing to the victimology school which thrives on litanies of lost battles and casualty lists, while omitting victories and strengths and the possibilities for change inherent in both black people and society?

The role of white researchers must be questioned much more than it has been up to this point in health research. This is not to deny the insights which white researchers can bring nor to produce an essentialist argument that research validity is inextricably a product of racial identity. It is, however, to acknowledge the importance of power relations, at all levels, within research and a suggestion that radical, black-led, research agendas would, at the very least, be different and certainly challenging of existing orthodoxies. 'What is this research for?' is a valid question to ask any health researcher, who may be no more immune from the problems of professionalism than the medical personnel which she or he is purporting to study. Accounts by recipients (or non-recipients) of services are vital in analysing racist processes provided the research relationship itself is understood as political and open to abuse.

Third, while I acknowledge the importance of the category 'black' as a term denoting a shared experience of, and opposition to, racism, it is possible to address the ways in which black groups experience racism differently in a manner which does not return us to a culturalist 'list' of ethnic minority groups. The studies of the so-called 'forgotten minorities' (cf. Li 1992; Williams 1992) are one part of this process.

In the broader context, a debate is raging currently about the political usefulness of the category 'black'. The work of Tariq Modood (1988) has suggested that the use of the term 'black' within anti-racist discourse has not only minimized the differences between different 'black' groups but has, effectively, acted to promote the interests of Afro-Caribbean groups over, in particular, 'Asian' groups and, for Modood, over Muslim groups. This is a complex debate which may be important in allowing for an increasing sophistication and recognition of difference and diversity in the development of anti-racist perspectives on health and illness. There is a real danger, however, that this critique will lead to a dismissal of any political anti-racism, and its replacement with a 'new ethnicism', in which the claims of different groups will be played off against each other in the health care marketplace. In many cases, black groups will be competing for the crumbs.

A recent attempt, certainly within social work education at least, to suggest that anti-racist perspectives need to be supplemented, if not replaced, by 'black perspectives', is more valuable (cf. Ahmad 1990). There is a concern that anti-racism is a limited, white-dominated project which fails to understand, or respond to, demands for black autonomy. Again, there are dangers of essentialism here but the debate focuses attention, once again, on the Eurocentrism of much existing research and practice and the importance of 'black-led agendas'. Within this, it seems to me, there is scope to widen the range of approaches which seek to understand racism in health care and the possibility of challenging that racism while avoiding simplistic and crude categorizations about 'who is black'.

Fourth, just as there are problems in the separation of 'race and health' studies, I would suggest that there are problems in the separation of racism from other forms of oppression based on gender, class, sexuality, age and disability. Too often, black people are discussed in research as if they do not also occupy classed and gendered positions. Radical analyses must make connections in terms of the explanation of health inequalities rather than treat racism as if it were an autonomous social process. If we reject a concern, solely, with 'race and health' it becomes possible to discuss the 'Anglocentrism' of health provision and the connections between health and other welfare services, in terms of their construction of a 'mythical norm' of a white, two parent, middle class nuclear family, and the centrality of models of black family pathology in different spheres of the welfare state.

An illustration

To try to illustrate some of these important issues I want to look briefly at the area of Irish people and mental health. There is some evidence to suggest that Irish people face particularly high rates of being diagnosed as mentally ill and, indeed, of being compulsorily admitted to hospital under the Mental Health Act in Britain (cf. Williams 1992). If this is the case, consider the effect of simply including Irish people in a catch-all category, 'white', which would actually serve to reduce the difference between rates for white as against black people. In addition, if the two main groups which give rise for concern are single men and married women, it is surely remarkable, at least in the research and analysis which I have read, that the issue of gender is given very little prominence.

There is clearly a need for more research into the issues. However, there are dangers in a crude explanation of the research which sees migration, colonialism and racism as sufficient explanatory frameworks. For example, Dr Marie O'Shea (n.d.), writing for the Brent Irish Mental Health Group, is surely right to suggest that 'centuries of imperialist oppression culminating in a racist society' and 'conflicts arising in the country of origin' must be components of 'an acceptable model of mental illness of the Irish in Britain'. But to suggest, as she does, that 'in an impoverished closed rural society, cut off by colonialism from socially progressive ideas, young Irish people have suffered parental restriction, emotional stunting and sexual repression' so that 'the stresses of emigration and anti-Irish racism produce feelings of failure and rejection, and guilt feelings about deserting their country', is to run the risk of perpetuating crude racial stereotypes. In the midst of crude generalizations about Ireland, and a monolithic construction of 'the Irish' regardless of origin, religion, gender, class and so on, the politics of being labelled as mentally ill are downplayed, as are challenge and resistance.

Researchers Harrington and Finnegan (1989) fare little better, invoking, in opposition to O'Shea, an idyllic picture of the strong countervailing tendencies which exist in Ireland and going on to explain the high risk of 'social dislocation, alcoholism and mental ill health' as an automatic consequence of the isolation of Irish people in Britain in a hostile racist society. Hence, from an attempt to develop a progressive political analysis of racism, there remain dangers that crude racial stereotypes will be reproduced which might, in fact, be taken up by those responsible for service delivery.

Conclusions

In this sense, the politics of race and health research is a complicated business. It is not easy to suggest ways forward beyond a simple statement that researchers need to be clear about what it is they are, and are not, studying. It is not particularly useful, for example, for a sociologist to criticize clinical research simply because it is not sociological. Nevertheless, and I think this is one point which I derive particularly from feminist and black writers, we need to embrace a broader understanding about what is to constitute research which, taking on board criticisms of Eurocentrism, breaks down Western barriers between disciplines and approaches.

Any re-evaluation of research must include the validity of testimony and lived experience. We need more accounts like Yvette Rocheron's (1988) important article in *Critical Social Policy* on the Asian Mother and Baby Campaign which tell a different story from orthodox evaluation and effectiveness studies.

This point is best expressed in a book *Third World Women and the Politics of Feminism*. In the introductory chapter Mohanty (1991) makes the point that supposedly 'objective' indices of health by no means exhaust the meaning of women's day to day lives, stating that in much health research 'the everyday, fluid, fundamentally historical and dynamic nature of the lives of third world women becomes collapsed into a few frozen "indicators" of their well-being'. Research concerns actually tell us more about the interests of the powerful than they do about the realities of women's lives.

If we continue to take seriously Maggie Pearson's point about the divorce between research and committed action, then how research can make a difference to black people's experiences of health and health services becomes a key question. If we develop an understanding of the racial politics of health care in terms of an understanding of the centrality of racism, then this must lead to the development of practical strategies for anti-racism. We must reject a timeless, static, frozen understanding of 'culture' whether this is about 'pathology/weakness' or a seemingly more neutral understanding of difference disconnected from individual experience and from racism and other oppressions. Practical strategies must move beyond a view that it is sufficient to understand black people's 'cultural practices' in order to improve service delivery. As is stated in Brent Community Health Council's (1981) publication, *Black People and the Health Service*: 'focussing attention on black people is not necessarily the same as meeting their needs'. Researchers have to look, urgently, at how to avoid being 'part of the problem' and attempt to become 'part of the solution'.

Part 2

CURRENT HEALTH ISSUES

4

Pregnancy, birth and maternity care

LUISE PARSONS, ALISON MACFARLANE and JENETTE GOLDING

Introduction

The evidence we have reviewed . . . suggests very forcibly that the maternity services, as they are currently organised and provided, fall short of meeting women's needs. All too often maternity services have been shown to be inaccessible and inappropriate for reasons of geography, lack of appropriate information and support for women from minority ethnic groups, lack of facilities for women with disabilities, inadequate support for women on low incomes and insufficient staff training in counselling, in disability and wider awareness of the needs of particular groups. (House of Commons Health Committee 1992)

Over the past twenty years, many women have been critical of the maternity care they have received. The problems encountered by black and ethnic minority women must therefore be set in this wider context, rather than being seen as a minority issue. The assumptions that are made about the maternity care needs of ethnic minority women are often based on stereotypes rather than on reliable information. This chapter looks at statistical information about the population, the babies which are born and the maternity care which is offered. It then discusses initiatives which have been taken to try to provide appropriate maternity care for black and ethnic minority women.

Measuring trends in numbers of births

Attempts to estimate trends in numbers of births usually start from birth registration statistics. In England and Wales, these are collected and collated by the Office of Population Censuses and Surveys (OPCS), which is well aware of the problems of estimating numbers of births to women in minority ethnic groups (OPCS 1982). When a birth is registered, information is collected about the parents' ages, occupations and countries of birth, the previous numbers of births to the mother within marriage, the place of birth, and whether the baby was one of a multiple birth. There is no question about 'ethnic origin'.

Because of this, most analyses of national data sets relate to the mothers' countries of birth, and a few to the fathers' or both parents' countries of birth. In this way only 'immigrants' are identified, thus excluding births to people from minority ethnic groups who were themselves born in the United Kingdom. This seriously underestimates the number of births to minority ethnic groups. Conversely, a few women born overseas, in India for example, will be of white European ethnic origin. Also, because birth registration does not record religion, other groups such as Jews, who identify themselves by religion, can not be separately identified. For reasons which are not surprising, gypsies and other travellers are rarely visible in official statistics.

Another source of information about births is hospital statistics. Up to 1985, the Maternity Hospital Inpatient Enquiry (HIPE) collected data about a 10 per cent sample of inpatient stays in maternity departments of NHS hospitals. As with birth registration, it recorded the mother's country of birth but not her ethnic origin. Its successor, the Maternity Hospital Episode System, started in September 1988, and should contain information about every birth, but at the time of writing is still incomplete. Initially it recorded neither the mother's country of birth nor her ethnic origin. Recording of ethnic origin, using the categories in the Census question, will be phased in from April 1993 onwards with the aim of including it on every record by April 1994. Even if the categories are subdivided, as recommended by OPCS and the NHS Information Management Group, the problems will still persist. In addition, like its predecessor, the system does not contain data about social class.

Until the 1991 Census, detailed data from which are not available at the time of writing, the EC Labour Force Survey was the only routine source of data about the population which recorded ethnic origin, by asking people which of a series .of categories they placed themselves in (Haskey 1989; 1990a; 1990b). It was therefore used to compile Table 4.1, which shows the estimated proportions of women in the childbearing age range who were born outside the United Kingdom (OPCS 1991). It uses a more detailed categorization of ethnic origin than does the Census question. Table 4.1 shows a wide variation in the extent to which women in the younger age groups were born in the United Kingdom, and reflects changing patterns of migration.

In 1990, the latest year for which detailed birth statistics were available at the time of writing, there were 706,140 live births, of which 11.6 per cent were to women born outside the United Kingdom. As can be seen in Table 4.2, which shows trends from 1975 to 1990, births to women from the 'New Commonwealth', which consists of Commonwealth countries apart from Australia, Canada and New Zealand, accounted for 7.0 per cent of live births in 1990. There were 26,547 births to women born in India, Pakistan and Bangladesh in 1990. These represented 3.8 per cent of the total number of births. Other significant groups include women from East Africa, many of whom are of Asian origin, and women from the Irish Republic, Caribbean Commonwealth and the rest of Europe.

As has already been mentioned, these figures do not include births to black and ethnic minority women born in the UK. It has been estimated, using data from the EC Labour Force Survey and other sources, that among births in Britain over the period 1984-6, births to women born in the United Kingdom included approximately 6,000 per year to women of West Indian or African

Table 4.1   Estimated percentages of female population of Great Britain of childbearing age who were born outside the United Kingdom, by ethnic group, 1987–9

	Age					
	15–19	20–24	25–29	30–34	35–39	40–44
West Indian	6	7	36	78	87	95
African	26	50	84	91	93	97
Indian	30	68	90	96	100	94
Pakistani	21	75	98	97	98	96
Bangladeshi	71	95	96	100	90	100
Chinese	55	91	90	97	100	94
Arab	55	98	97	100	90	96
'Mixed'	6	20	28	54	62	67
'Other non-white'	38	53	75	85	94	89
White	3	4	4	5	5	5
Not stated	6	37	21	21	16	64
All groups	4	7	8	10	10	8

Note: Some estimates are based on very small numbers of replies and should therefore be interpreted with caution.
Source: OPCS unpublished data.

Table 4.2   Percentage of live births by mother's country of birth, 1975–90

	1975	1980	1985	1990
United Kingdom*	87.9	86.7	87.7	88.4
Irish Republic	2.1	1.4	1.0	0.9
Rest of Europe	1.6	1.4	1.3	1.3
'New Commonwealth'	6.6	8.5	8.0	7.0
India	2.0	2.1	1.7	1.2
Pakistan	1.2	2.1	2.1	1.8
Bangladesh	0.2	0.4	0.6	0.8
East Africa	0.6	1.0	1.1	1.9
Rest of Africa	0.4	0.5	0.5	0.7
Caribbean	1.3	1.1	0.7	0.5
Far East+	0.3	0.5	0.6	0.6
Mediterranean#	0.5	0.5	0.4	0.3
Rest of 'New Commonwealth'	0.2	0.3	0.2	0.2
Elsewhere	1.3	1.9	2.0	1.9
Total number of live births	603,445	656,234	654,417	706,140

Notes:
* Including Isle of Man and Channel Islands
+ Hong Kong, Malaysia and Singapore
# Cyprus, Gibraltar and Malta.
Source: OPCS (1992a).

origin and 6,000 per year to women from ethnic groups originating from the Indian subcontinent (Shaw 1988a).

Table 4.2 shows an expected decrease since the mid 1970s in births to women born in Ireland, India and the Caribbean Commonwealth countries. This is coupled with increases in the numbers of births to women from Bangladesh, Pakistan and East Africa.

As well as being unevenly distributed regionally, ethnic minority communities tend to be concentrated in inner-city areas, as preliminary analysis of 1991 Census data show (Balarajan and Raleigh 1993). This means that the proportion of births to women born outside the United Kingdom is very high in some districts. For instance, in four London boroughs – Kensington and Chelsea, Tower Hamlets, Westminster, and Brent – just over half the live births in 1990 were to women born outside the United Kingdom (OPCS 1992a). In three London boroughs – Newham, Tower Hamlets, and Brent – more than a third were to women born in the 'New Commonwealth'. Boroughs and county districts with more than a third of their births to women born outside the United Kingdom are shown in Figure 4.1. Two of them – Kensington and Chelsea, and Forest Heath in Suffolk (where there are many US military personnel stationed) – stand out as being different from the rest in having many births to white women born outside the UK. In

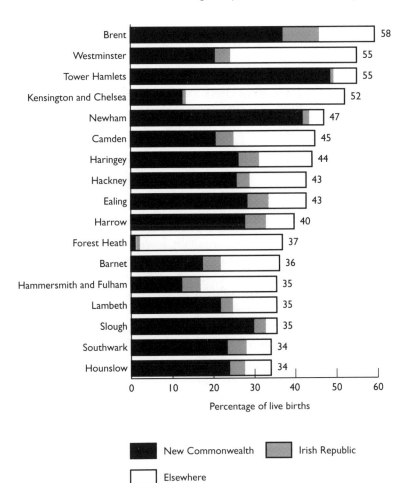

Figure 4.1 Districts with more than a third of births to mothers born outside UK, 1990
Source: OPCS (1992a). Areas are London boroughs or other local authority districts.

contrast many places, such as Birmingham and Bradford, which are well known for their multi-racial character, do not have so many mothers born outside the United Kingdom.

Fertility and contraception

Claims that immigrant and ethnic minority groups have high birth rates continue to play a role in racist propaganda, but the data present a more complex picture. The statistic used to measure fertility is a composite figure called the 'total period fertility rate'. It is derived from the birth rates within each age group for a given year. These are used to estimate the average number of children who would be born per woman if all women were to experience these age specific fertility rates throughout their childbearing lives.

Total period fertility rates for 1981, 1985, 1989 and 1990 are tabulated by country of birth in Table 4.3. OPCS traditionally produces a combined rate for Pakistan and Bangladesh, and estimates are still not made for the two countries separately. The rates for Pakistan and Bangladesh are the highest shown, but fell considerably during the 1980s. Rates for women from India are considerably lower and also fell over the same period. The rate for women from East African Commonwealth countries fell until, in 1990, it was the same as that for women born in the United Kingdom, and the rates for women from the Caribbean and from 'Mediterranean' and 'Far Eastern' Commonwealth countries were marginally lower.

Fertility rates can fluctuate quite rapidly, and usually reflect changes in society. Religion is a factor which can influence fertility in certain groups. For others, the country of birth of their parents may well be less important than factors such as social class and education. The factors affecting the fertility rates in ethnic minority women have not been specifically studied, but the rates may well be lower than those for immigrant women from the

Table 4.3   Total period fertility rates by country of birth of mother, England and Wales, 1981–90

	1981	1985	1989	1990
All birth places	1.80	1.78	1.80	1.86
United Kingdom*	1.7	1.7	1.8	1.8
Total outside United Kingdom	2.5	2.5	2.3	2.3
'New Commonwealth'	2.9	2.9	2.7	2.6
India	3.1	2.9	2.4	2.2
Pakistan and Bangladesh	6.5	5.6	4.7	4.7
East Africa	2.1	2.1	1.9	1.8
Rest of Africa	3.4	3.0	4.2	4.1
Caribbean	2.0	1.8	1.6	1.6
Far East⁺	1.7	2.0	1.7	1.7
Mediterranean#	2.1	2.2	1.9	1.7
Other	2.3	2.3	2.4	2.2
Rest of the world	2.0	2.0	1.9	2.0

Notes:
* Including Isle of Man and Channel Islands
⁺ Hong Kong, Malaysia and Singapore
Cyprus, Gibraltar and Malta
Source: OPCS (1992a).

same group and may well not differ from those of the white population. Furthermore, Ann Phoenix (1990) has pointed to the extent to which younger people are increasingly choosing partners from different ethnic groups. Trends in fertility are believed to be a consequence of the widespread availability of modern contraceptive methods, level of income and attitudes to future prosperity, and an increasing tendency for women of childbearing age to be employed outside their homes (Fuller 1987; Phoenix 1990).

Little information is available nationally about the contraceptive practices and needs of people in ethnic minority groups as most national surveys on contraceptive usage have not recorded respondents' ethnic origin. At the time of writing, only one population based study has been published (McAvoy and Raza 1988), and this was confined to 158 women in one city, Leicester. The population was mainly of Asian origin, but there was considerable heterogeneity within that group.

The survey found that 83 per cent of Asian women approved of contraception, and 70 per cent had used it at some time. As Table 4.4 shows, the most popular methods were the IUCD, the sheath and the oral contraceptives. Hindus favoured the IUCD most and the sheath least, while Muslims and Sikhs preferred the sheath to the IUCD. Contrary to commonly held opinion, religion did not seem to be a bar to contraception.

Knowledge of contraception varied considerably, but 75 per cent were

Table 4.4 Comparison between methods of contraception used by married Asian women in Leicester 1985–6 and women in Great Britain as a whole, 1986

	Percentage using each method				
	Asian women in Leicester, 1985–6				All women married and cohabiting in
Method	Hindus	Muslims	Sikhs	All Asians	Great Britain, 1986
IUCD	41	23	25	33	8
Sheath	23	42	44	31	16
Pill	27	25	31	26	19
Female sterilization	6	10	0	6	15
Withdrawal	2	2	0	2	2
Safe period	1	0	0	1	1
Cap	0	0	0	0	3
Spermicide	0	0	0	0	1
Vasectomy	0	0	0	0	16
Number in sample				158	3,982

Note: Percentages may add up to more than 100 as some women were using more than one method.
Sources: McAvoy and Raza (1988); OPCS (1986).

satisfied with their present method. Among respondents, 73 per cent stated they had been able to get family planning information as easily as they wished. If seeking contraceptive advice, 83 per cent would prefer a female doctor, but only 22 per cent would prefer an Asian doctor. Alternative service provision, such as a domiciliary service and an all-Asian clinic, received limited support, but 82 per cent favoured an all female clinic. Over half suggested improvements in contraceptive services, including provision of interpreters, information at the workplace, and production of more leaflets.

Perhaps the most important message from this and other studies (Beard 1982; Fuller 1987) is that uptake of contraceptive and other services for women is high if they are presented in a sensitive, appropriate and accessible way. This is equally true of sterilization and abortion. While many Muslims and Catholics are opposed to abortion on religious grounds, there may still be variation within these groups and counselling should not be neglected. Acceptance of antenatal screening is growing as is termination on medical grounds if explained adequately, although considerable support may be required for women and their families after a therapeutic abortion. In the population as a whole, male sterilization is becoming slightly more popular as a method of birth control, while the proportion of women who had been sterilized levelled off from 1986 onwards (OPCS 1992a), but there are no data relating specifically to women from minority ethnic groups.

There has been a continuing debate about the availability of genetic tests in pregnancy, such as amniocentesis and chorion villus sampling, and some obstetricians are reluctant to disclose the sex of the foetus. This is because of fears that women from some ethnic groups may wish to abort female foetuses on the grounds of sex alone (Pandya 1988) even though this is not grounds for a termination under the 1967 Abortion Act. Withholding information about sex can discriminate against women who would like to know the sex when it has been determined genetically for other reasons, such as detection of congenital abnormalities. Other ways must be found to prevent abortion on the grounds of gender alone, in particular by improved counselling before screening.

Despite their many gaps and deficiencies, the available data suggest that fertility rates are falling in most, if not all 'immigrant' groups, and it is likely that this applies to minority ethnic groups as a whole. The patchy data suggest that this reflects the acceptability of birth control to women from minority ethnic groups. The next section assesses the data on babies born to ethnic minority women.

Births and infant mortality

Since the late 1970s, reduction of stillbirth and infant mortality rates has been high on the national political agenda (Macfarlane and Mugford 1984).

Despite considerable decreases since that time, the desire for further reduction still featured prominently in the *Health of the Nation* green paper (Department of Health 1991b) and NHS priorities (NHS Management Executive 1991).

There is extensive evidence of the association between mortality and social and economic deprivation (Macfarlane and Mugford 1984; Whitehead 1992a). Analyses of variations in mortality between NHS districts have shown that the districts with the highest mortality rates tend to be those with the highest proportions of fathers in manual occupations and mothers from the 'New Commonwealth' (Botting and Macfarlane 1990).

Despite this, the response has focused predominantly on obstetric and paediatric care. In the face of the pressure to reduce mortality, people from ethnic minorities are often seen as a 'problem' because the belief that their raised mortality rates inflate overall rates for districts. For example, they were highlighted as an example in the second of two 'areas of action' included in the NHS Management Executive's (1991) priorities and planning guidance for 1992–93:

> stillbirths and infant death: regions should agree with their districts and FHSAs targets to reduce stillbirth and infant death and play a full part in the national confidential enquiry. Particular attention should be paid to reducing smoking among pregnant women; issues of access to services for certain groups of women (e.g. those from ethnic minorities); and arrangements for consultant cover of labour wards.

To what extent do the data support these assumptions? Detailed analyses of data for England and Wales have already been published (Balarajan and Botting 1989, Balarajan, Raleigh and Botting 1989; Balarajan and Raleigh 1990) and stillbirth and infant mortality rates for 1990, tabulated by the mother's country of birth are shown in Table 4.5, together with definitions of the rates.

These show that in 1990 the stillbirth and infant mortality rates for babies whose mothers were born in the 'New Commonwealth' were 40 per cent higher than the corresponding rates for babies whose mothers were born in the United Kingdom. There were considerable variations within this group, however. The mortality rates of babies born to women born in Pakistan were about twice as high as that of babies of women born in the United Kingdom. This differential has persisted since the statistics were first analysed this way in the mid-1970s, but for women born in other 'New Commonwealth' countries, the differences have narrowed.

A closer look shows even more diversity, however. Stillbirth rates were relatively high for babies of women born in Ireland and all 'New Commonwealth' countries except the 'Mediterranean' women from Malta, Gibraltar and Cyprus. Stillbirth rates were particularly high for babies

Table 4.5   Stillbirth and infant mortality rates by mother's country of birth, England and Wales, 1990

Mother's country of birth	Stillbirths		Neonatal deaths		Postneonatal deaths	
	Number	Rate[1]	Number	Rate[2]	Number	Rate[2]
All	3,256	4.6	3,171	4.5	2,270	3.2
United Kingdom*	2,762	4.4	2,714	4.3	1,994	3.2
Irish Republic	33	5.1	24	3.7	22	3.4
Rest of Europe	39	3.9	45	4.5	34	3.4
Australia, Canada and New Zealand	7	2.3	16	5.3	6	2.0
'New Commonwealth'	346	6.9	305	6.1	182	3.7
Bangladesh	49	8.6	22	3.9	9	1.6
India	46	5.3	44	5.1	19	2.2
Pakistan	114	9.1	97	7.8	79	6.4
East Africa	46	6.9	37	5.6	13	2.0
Rest of Africa	38	7.6	35	7.1	14	2.8
Caribbean	22	5.7	32	8.4	16	4.2
Mediterranean#	7	3.0	12	5.1	11	4.7
Other	24	4.3	26	4.7	21	3.8
Other countries	61	4.8	67	5.3	31	2.4
Not stated	8	190.5	–	–	1	29.4

Notes:
* Include Isle of Man and Channel Islands
# Cyprus, Gibraltar and Malta
[1] Per 1,000 total births
[2] Per 1,000 live births.
Source: OPCS (1992c).
Definitions:
Stillbirths: late foetal deaths after 28 completed weeks of gestation
Neonatal deaths: deaths at ages before 28 days after live birth
Postneonatal deaths: deaths at ages 28 days and over but under one year after live birth
Infant deaths: deaths at ages under one year after live birth
The definition of stillbirth changed on 1 October 1992, when the lower limit was reduced to 24 weeks.

whose mothers were born in Bangladesh or Pakistan.

Neonatal mortality rates show a different pattern. Mortality among babies whose mothers were born in Ireland or Bangladesh was lower than among those whose mothers were born in the United Kingdom. Rates for babies whose mothers were born in other parts of the 'New Commonwealth' were higher, with particularly high rates for babies with mothers from Pakistan or the Caribbean Commonwealth. In the postneonatal period, mortality rates among babies with mothers from Bangladesh, India and East Africa were well below the rates for babies with mothers born in the United

Kingdom. The only conspicuously high rate was among babies whose mothers were born in Pakistan.

This diverse picture is not new. It was already apparent in two studies done in the 1960s. One, hailing 'immigration' as 'a new social factor in obstetrics' (Barron and Vessey 1966a), found no difference between perinatal mortality rates among babies born during the period 1958-60 in Lambeth Hospital to British, West Indian, Irish and other women. On the other hand, data from Bradford showed that infant mortality rates among babies born to Asian women, most of whom came from Pakistan, were twice as high as those for babies with non-Asian mothers (Aykroyd and Hossain 1967).

Subsequent studies have found similar differences when tabulating mortality by mother's country of birth (Balarajan and Botting 1989; Balarajan, Raleigh and Botting 1989; Balarajan and Raleigh 1990), broad ethnic origin (Griffiths *et al.* 1989, Robinson *et al.* 1982; Gillies *et al.* 1984) or religious group (Terry *et al.* 1980). Relationships have changed over time. For example, in contrast to the earlier data for Lambeth, an analysis of mortality among babies born in St Thomas's Hospital from 1969 to 1976 found raised mortality rates among babies with West Indian mothers (Robinson *et al.* 1982).

Interpreting differences in mortality

Their very diversity makes interpretation of differences in stillbirth and infant mortality rates difficult. For example, a study in Harrow found no difference between mortality among babies born to Indian women born mainly in Gujarat or in East Africa and those born to the local European population, but suggested that as the Indian population of Harrow was relatively affluent, the patterns of mortality may be different elsewhere (Campbell Brown and Willmott 1983). Analyses of data for babies born to Asian women in Bradford suggested that low social class was not a risk factor (Gillies *et al.* 1984), and a study in Leicester found no difference in social class distribution between Asians there and European controls (Clarke *et al.* 1988). On the other hand, analysis of infant mortality rates for England and Wales by mother's country of birth and father's social class revealed pronounced social class differences within each group (Balarajan and Botting 1989, Balarajan and Raleigh 1990). Moreover, social class based on the father's occupation is a relatively crude measure which cannot fully reflect the socio-economic problems that often overwhelm people from ethnic minorities living in the United Kingdom (Bhat *et al.* 1988; Whitehead 1992b; Skellington and Morris 1992), and which should not be ignored.

All too often, however, excessive attention is given to individual factors when trying to explain the high mortality rates among babies born into some minority ethnic groups. For example, high mortality rates among Asian babies are often attributed to the raised mortality rates among babies born to women who have already had several children, despite the evidence that these may well be artefactual (Macfarlane and Mugford 1984). In fact, unpublished data from the Maternity Hospital Inpatient Enquiry (HIPE) show that 24 per cent of women born in Bangladesh and 32 per cent of women born in Pakistan who had singleton births during 1982–5 had four or more previous children, compared with 2.4 per cent for women born in the United Kingdom and Ireland, and well under 10 per cent for all other countries of birth.

Yet, when perinatal mortality rates were tabulated according to the mother's number of previous births within marriage, rates for babies born to women born in Pakistan were higher than the corresponding rates for women born in Bangladesh (Balarajan and Botting 1989). Direct comparison with women born in the United Kingdom is problematic, because births outside marriage are excluded.

As well as the adverse factors experienced by many women from minority ethnic groups, there are others which could be favourable. For example, within the Asian population, few births occur outside marriage or to teenage women, and, until very recently, smoking has been rare among Asian women (Clarke et al. 1988; Lumb et al. 1981).

Views about consanguinity

Lethal congenital malformations make a major contribution to the high stillbirth and infant mortality rates in babies born to Pakistani women. There is considerable controversy over the reasons for this and the extent to which differences between subgroups within Asian populations have been masked in global statistics (Balarajan and McDowall 1985; Little and Nicoll 1988; Balarajan, Raleigh and Botting 1989).

Associations have been found between mortality attributed to congenital malformations and consanguineous marriages, usually between first cousins (Terry et al. 1980; Young and Clarke 1987; Bundey et al. 1991), although other studies have suggested that consanguinity may not be the main factor (Honeyman et al. 1987; Pearson 1991). Environmental and genetic factors and their interactions, together with access to medical care, also need to be considered when discussing possible reasons for differences in mortality (Proctor and Smith 1992). Low uptake of antenatal facilities and lack of screening have been cited as reasons for excess mortality from neural tube defects and chromosomal abnormalities among babies born to women from Pakistan, but may also occur in groups whose mortality is lower.

The main disadvantage of cousin marriage is a raised frequency of autosomal recessive diseases, which include some heart conditions and limb malformations and many metabolic conditions. The rate of serious disease or malformation in the offspring of a first cousin marriage from a family with no previous consanguinity is about 1 in 20, which is twice the rate in the population at large (Fraser and Biddle 1976; *Lancet* 1991). In a family with previous inbreeding, the rate for the offspring of first cousin marriages, will be higher, perhaps about 1 in 11 (Bundey *et al.* 1991). This is lower than the risk of serious disease in the offspring of incestuous unions between first degree relatives, which is about 1 in 2 (*Lancet* 1991). There seems to be disagreement about the long term effects of consanguinity on a population.

Consanguineous marriage has important social functions, compared with which its genetic consequences are relatively minor, and attempts to discourage it systematically on genetic grounds would certainly do more harm than good (*Lancet* 1991). The origins and meaning of the practice of cousin marriage must be sought and the advantages and disadvantages carefully weighed. One reason for consanguinity is a lack of suitable partners outside the family because of geographical, ethnic or cultural isolation. While the frequency of consanguineous marriage is thought to be falling in most populations as a result of social change and increased mobility, there is some evidence that the rate is increasing among British Pakistanis (Darr and Modell 1988).

The causes of this trend have not been investigated, but it is probably linked to constraints imposed by restrictive immigration policies. Indeed, it has been alleged (*Lancet* 1991) that immigration officials seem more ready to consider a planned marriage with an overseas spouse to be genuine if it is between close relatives. Other explanations offered for consanguinity include the preservation of property, particularly land. It has also been suggested that the marriage relationship is more comfortable for the woman if her mother-in-law is also her aunt and she has the reassurance of marrying into a known family background. In countries where consanguineous marriages are common, such as Pakistan and the Middle East, the custom is considered socially supportive (Khlat *et al.* 1986).

Rather than condemning the practice of first cousin marriage, it is essential to confirm the association between consanguinity and socio-economic factors, on the one hand, and the incidence of lethal congenital malformations, on the other, with carefully designed epidemiological studies (Proctor and Smith 1992). There is considerable acceptance of counselling among many ethnic groups (Darr and Modell 1988; Darr 1990; Modell *et al.* 1984), and this is discussed further by Elizabeth Anionwu in Chapter 5 of this volume). More information is needed about the epidemiology of genetic diseases, however, in order to offer appropriate advice. Sensitive education is required for both health professionals and the population at risk and some districts may need additional genetic counselling services. At the same time, more enlightened immigration policies would allow a wider choice of marriage partners for Pakistanis, among others, living in the United Kingdom.

Birthweight

Although low birthweight is not of itself a cause of death, or factor leading to disability, there are strong negative correlations between the percentage of low weight births and the mortality rates for various groups within the population. For this reason, the percentage of low birthweight babies is often used as a proxy measure of ill health among the population to which their parents belong. Published data for England and Wales as a whole show pronounced social class gradients (OPCS 1992c). Cross tabulations by parents' country of birth and their social class are not published routinely, but data tabulated by mother's country of birth suggest that the differences may be more complex.

It has been recognized since the 1960s that 'immigrant' groups differ from each other and from the European population in their birthweight distributions (Barron and Vessey 1966a; 1966b). Subsequent local studies have confirmed this (Grundy *et al.* 1978; Alvear and Brooke 1978; Dawson *et al.* 1982; Campbell Brown and Wilmott 1983; McFadyen *et al.* 1984). It is only since the early 1980s that birthweight data have been available from birth registration on a national basis for England and Wales. Analyses of data for the years 1982-5 combined have been published elsewhere (Balarajan and Botting 1989; Balarajan and Raleigh 1990) and data for 1990 (OPCS 1992b) are shown in Table 4.6. These show considerable variations between the overall percentages of babies weighing under 2,500 g, as well as differences within this group of low-birthweight babies. In particular, the percentage of babies weighing under 1,500 g was very low for those whose mothers were born in Bangladesh, but much higher for those whose mothers were born in the Caribbean or the 'rest of Africa'.

Considerable differences in mean birthweight and in birthweight distributions in babies born to women from different countries were also found in an analysis of Maternity Hospital Inpatient Enquiry data for England for 1982–5 (Macfarlane and Parsons, in preparation). The mean birthweights of babies born to women from Bangladesh, India and East Africa were approximately 300 g lower than those of babies born to women born in the United Kingdom, as Figure 4.2 shows. Babies born to women from the Caribbean and Pakistan were on average 100 g lighter. These differences were greater than would be expected by chance.

Analyses of data for the United States have shown that the associations between birthweight and mortality differ between racial groups (Wilcox and Russell 1983; Behrman 1987). Differences can also be seen in data for

Table 4.6   Percentages of live born babies weighing under 2,500 g at birth by mother's country of birth, England and Wales, 1990

Mother's country of birth	Under 1,500 g	1,500– 1,999 g	2,000– 2,499 g	All under 2,500 g	Number of babies with stated birthweight	Number of live births
	Percentage of live births with stated birthweight				*Number of babies with stated*	*Number of live births*
All	1.0	1.3	4.5	6.8	678,374	706,140
United Kingdom	0.9	1.3	4.4	6.6	600,740	624,160
Irish Republic	1.0	1.3	4.3	6.6	6,011	6,424
Rest of Europe	0.8	1.3	4.1	6.1	9,370	9,988
Australia, Canada and New Zealand	0.6	0.8	3.4	4.9	2,821	2,998
'New Commonwealth'	1.3	1.7	6.7	9.6	47,695	49,790
Bangladesh	0.6	1.2	7.0	8.8	5,401	5,618
India	1.2	1.8	7.9	10.9	8,346	8,570
Pakistan	1.2	1.7	6.6	9.5	12,006	12,359
East Africa	1.2	2.0	9.2	12.4	6,347	6,590
Rest of Africa	2.2	2.0	4.8	9.0	4,522	4,954
Caribbean	2.3	2.0	5.7	10.0	3,589	3,809
Mediterranean	1.3	1.4	3.7	6.4	2,194	2,345
Other	0.9	1.1	4.9	7.0	5,290	5,545
Other countries	1.0	1.1	4.0	6.0	11,706	12,746
Not stated	–	3.2	3.2	6.4	31	34

Source: OPCS (1992c).

England and Wales for 1988–90 combined, analysed by mother's country of birth, in Table 4.7, as well as in earlier analyses of local and national data (Robinson *et al.* 1982; Dawson *et al.* 1982; Campbell Brown and Willmott 1983; Balarajan and Botting 1989). Babies whose mothers were born in Bangladesh and Pakistan had high stillbirth rates in all weight groups, while stillbirth rates were also high for babies born weighing 2,500 g or more to women born in the Caribbean or in Africa other than East Africa. Neonatal mortality was particularly high among babies born weighing 2,500 g or more to women from India, Pakistan and Africa, who had high overall neonatal mortality rates. Babies born to women from the Caribbean had low neonatal mortality rates within each group, but a high percentage of low weight births. Among babies born to women from Bangladesh, mortality was high within each group and overall.

Differences in the gestational age distribution tend, on the whole, to be correlated with the differences in birthweight. Gestational age is not recorded at birth registration but analysis of Maternity Hospital Inpatient Enquiry data found that, on average, women born in Pakistan and India went into spontaneous labour five days earlier than women born in the

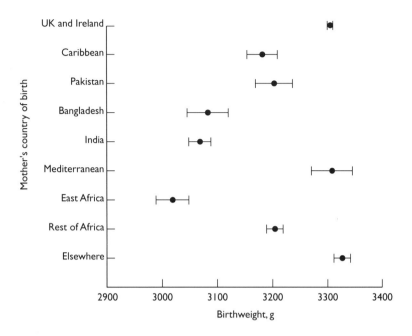

Figure 4.2   Estimated mean birthweight at spontaneous onset of labour together with 95 per cent confidence intervals
Source: unpublished analysis from Hospital Inpatient Enquiry data, in Macfarlane and Parsons (in preparation).

United Kingdom and Ireland (Macfarlane and Parsons, in preparation). Women from the Caribbean, Bangladesh and East Africa also had lower mean gestational ages at the onset of spontaneous labour, as Figure 4.3 shows.

This finding is compatible with an analysis of births in a hospital in North West London (Grundy *et al*. 1978). One explanation that has been suggested is that dates of the woman's last menstrual period are recorded inaccurately. It is hard to imagine, however, that entire populations of women would systematically underestimate their dates, although the extent to which women do so could be affected by cultural attitudes towards menstruation. A more plausible explanation is that Asian women have shorter menstrual cycles or that they ovulate at different points in the cycle. An analysis of births in Hillingdon Hospital suggested that in Punjabi women foetal growth levelled off from 36 to 37 weeks of gestation, in comparison with white European women (Dawson *et al*. 1982). If the differences are real, there may be implications for clinical practice.

The length of human gestation is classically assumed to be 40 weeks. In the nineteenth century, Franz Carl Naegele, director of the Heidelberg Lying-in

Table 4.7 Stillbirth and infant mortality rates by mother's country of birth, England and Wales, 1988–90

Mother's country of birth	Stillbirth rate[1]				Neonatal mortality[2]				Postneonatal mortality[2]			
	Under 1,500 g	1,500–2,499 g	2,500 g or over	All	Under 1,500 g	1,500–2,499 g	2,500 g or over	All	Under 1,500 g	1,500–2,499 g	2,500 g or over	All
All	121.1	25.8	2.0	4.7	233.9	12.8	1.5	4.7	41.4	11.0	2.8	3.6
United Kingdom*	120.0	25.6	1.9	4.5	236.7	12.9	1.4	4.6	39.3	11.3	2.8	3.6
Irish Republic	107.7	29.4	2.7	5.2	178.2	15.2	1.5	4.5	63.2	7.1	3.5	4.4
'New Commonwealth'	133.5	27.5	2.9	7.2	213.1	11.5	2.1	6.1	34.4	8.9	2.7	4.0
Bangladesh	204.7	33.6	3.9	8.2	247.5	12.3	1.4	4.5	29.7	5.4	1.7	2.2
India	139.2	21.3	2.4	6.0	226.5	5.0	2.2	5.8	38.8	6.5	2.1	3.0
Pakistan	201.9	38.5	3.6	9.4	226.7	21.7	2.8	7.7	66.8	16.3	4.2	5.9
East Africa	139.1	16.6	2.1	5.9	161.5	6.4	2.0	5.0	57.7	3.2	1.8	2.7
Rest of Africa	65.1	32.2	3.9	7.2	219.8	11.1	2.2	7.7	47.6	10.0	2.6	4.3
Caribbean Commonwealth	66.9	49.3	3.8	7.3	187.3	7.6	1.5	6.7	71.7	10.8	1.9	5.0
Mediterranean#	102.6	28.6	1.3	3.7	214.3	5.9	2.1	4.5	71.4	14.7	2.9	4.1

Notes:
* Including Channel Isles and Isle of Man
# Cyprus, Gibraltar and Malta
[1] Per 1,000 total births
[2] Per 1,000 live births.
Source: authors' analysis of data in OPCS (1992c).

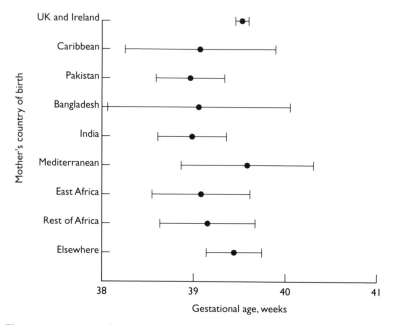

Figure 4.3   Estimated mean gestational age at spontaneous onset of labour together
with 95 per cent confidence intervals
Source: as Figure 4.2.

Hospital, based his famous rule on the common belief that human gestation
was ten menstrual cycles in duration, rather than on empirical data.
Nevertheless, the length of gestation is still taken to be 280 days from the first
day of the last menstrual period or 266 days from ovulation, assuming that
every woman has a cycle 28 days long and ovulates on the fourteenth day of
it. Pregnancies are defined to be post-term if they last more than 42 weeks
and pre-term if they end before 36 weeks. Variations between ethnic groups
in the distribution of lengths of gestational age may therefore have
implications for policies on inducing women for 'post-maturity' (Saunders
and Patterson 1991; Crowley 1993).

Induction of labour and methods of delivery

When labour is induced, it is more likely to be painful than when it starts
spontaneously and more likely to lead to an instrumental or Caesarean
delivery (Crowley 1993). The induction rate for all women delivering in
England and Wales rose to a peak of 39 per cent in 1974 (Macfarlane and
Mugford 1984) before falling to around 18 per cent in the early 1980s
(Department of Health and OPCS 1988).

Induction rates also vary according to the woman's country of birth. These largely reflect the differences in gestational age just described (Macfarlane and Parsons, in preparation). All the same, it is difficult to explain the variations between induction rates for women delivering at 42 or more weeks of gestation. These range from 10 per cent for women born in Bangladesh to 18 per cent for women born in the United Kingdom and Ireland. It could be argued either that the women from Bangladesh had too few inductions, or that those born in the United Kingdom had too many, but this begs the question of whether there is an optimum rate and how it relates to the differences in birthweight and gestational age.

The Caesarean rate in England and Wales rose from 2.8 per cent in 1960 and 4.3 per cent in 1970 to 9.0 per cent in 1980 (Macfarlane and Mugford 1984; Department of Health and Social Security, OPCS and Welsh Office 1986). It then levelled off at 10.1 per cent before rising to 10.6 per cent in 1985 (Hansard 1987a; 1987b). There are considerable variations between NHS regions within England (Department of Health and OPCS 1988).

The combined Caesarean rate for England for the years 1982–5 was 10.1 per cent. Rates varied considerably according to the woman's country of birth, from 8.8 per cent for women born in the Mediterranean, to 16.2 per cent for those born in Africa, excluding East Africa. Women born in Bangladesh also had a relatively high rate of 13.2 per cent.

The Caesarean rates were further analysed to see whether these variations reflected differences in parity, that is, the woman's number of previous live and stillborn children. Among women having their first child, women from Bangladesh had a very high section rate of 20.9 per cent, and women from Africa other than East Africa had a rate of 17.2 per cent, while the rate was 11.1 per cent for women born in the United Kingdom or Ireland. For women with four or more previous births, the rate was 12.4 per cent for women from India, 14.3 per cent for women from Mediterranean Commonwealth countries, 15.0 per cent for women from Bangladesh, 23.6 for women born in Africa excluding East Africa, but only 8.4 per cent for women born in Pakistan and 8.5 per cent for women born in the United Kingdom or Ireland.

Rates of instrumental delivery using forceps or, occasionally, vacuum extractors, were relatively high, at 11.6 per cent for women born in East Africa, 11.3 per cent for those born in United Kingdom and Ireland, and 10.3 per cent for those born in India. Women from Pakistan and Bangladesh had just over half these rates at 6.0 and 6.4 per cent, respectively.

While biological factors such as cephalo-pelvic disproportion could contribute to these differences, the high Caesarean section rates in primiparous women from Bangladesh, a group that contains a high proportion of non-English-speaking women, suggest that communication problems may also play a part by hindering them from discussing decisions with staff.

Risks of childbirth for black and minority ethnic women

Because maternal deaths have become so rare, the possibility that women may die in childbirth tends to be forgotten. In the 1970s, three successive reports on confidential enquiries into maternal deaths drew attention to the relatively high mortality rates for women born in the 'New Commonwealth' (Macfarlane 1986). Attention was drawn to the risks associated with anaesthesia in women with 'dark skins', among whom complications are said to be more easily missed. This warning was repeated in the subsequent report, which also warned of the increased risk of ectopic pregnancies (in which the foetus starts growing in a fallopian tube), but did not include an analysis of mortality data.

A wider study, looking at mortality among 'immigrants', showed that maternal mortality among women from Africa and the Caribbean was higher than that for women from the Indian subcontinent (Marmot *et al.* 1984). Data for 1979-81 and 1982-4 released in response to a Parliamentary question (Hansard 1986), showed that the differences between mortality rates for women born in the 'New Commonwealth' and those born in the United Kingdom were narrowing but had by no means disappeared (Radical Statistics Health Group 1987).

Accessibility and quality of maternity care

The analyses described above pose rather than answer questions about problems with the care provided during pregnancy, labour and delivery. Furthermore, because of the focus on trying to prevent mortality, the question of providing appropriate care for the vast majority of women, from all ethnic groups, who are unlikely to have unsuccessful pregnancies may take second place. Yet paradoxically, the people who most need the health services are often those who are least likely to be able to use them effectively because of institutional and individual racism as well as language and cultural barriers (Phoenix 1990). Despite this, failure to use services is often cited as a reason for raised mortality among babies born to women from ethnic minority groups. Only when it is recognized that there are deficiencies in the services (Clarke and Clayton 1983; Stonham and Sims 1986) or negative attitudes among health professionals (Wright 1983), can the problems be tackled.

Over the past two decades, a succession of reports (Henley 1979; 1980;

Clarke and Clayton 1983; Larby 1985; McNaught 1987; National Association of Health Authorities (NAHA) 1988; Phoenix 1990) have highlighted the continuing concerns about the *ad hoc* approach taken by policy-makers and health professionals to meeting the maternal health needs of women from black and minority ethnic groups. Concern has also been raised about meeting the needs of travellers (Durward 1990; Feder and Hussey 1990). It is evident that in many areas of Britain, policy-makers and health professionals planning maternity services adopt a colour-blind and Eurocentric approach to the needs of black and minority ethnic group users. Consequently, there appears to be little or no attempt to take into account the effect of institutional racism within the NHS (King's Fund 1990b).

The view of many health professionals is that nothing is wrong with the services provided. It is 'those people', with 'special diets', 'strange religious practices', or 'funny maternity habits', who have the problem. Assumptions like these have led many commentators and lobbying organizations (Ahmed and Pearson 1985) to challenge the maternity service providers by asking a number of pertinent questions. These critics have demanded accessible information in appropriate community languages, culturally and religiously appropriate food in hospital settings and respect for minority religious and cultural values and lifestyles.

If all women's cultural values and practices were equally respected then those questions would become redundant. In an article on black women's maternity care, Ann Phoenix (1990) argued that cultural practices should be seen as a result of a complex interrelationship of factors such as class, geographical locality and historical period. It should therefore never be presumed that there are simple one-to-one relationships between a woman's place of origin, colour and religion and the maternity practices in which she wishes to engage.

It is only in those areas where a critical assessment of whom the existing services reach is combined with a fundamental reappraisal of the assumptions on which policies, practices and procedures are based, that there is likely to be an approach to the provision of health care for women and babies that is appropriate, accessible and sensitive to the needs of women from black and minority ethnic groups. The 'spin-off' of this approach to service provision is that it should act to make the services in these localities more appropriate, accessible and sensitive to the needs of all users.

Over the past twenty years a variety of approaches have been taken to improve access to health care for minority ethnic groups, many of whom do not speak English. In the 1970s, teachers of English as a second language were invited to run classes in maternity units. Though not very successful in improving fluency in English, the groups succeeded in raising concerns about the quality of care provided, and the way hospital staff relate to women who did not speak English. Black and ethnic minority groups identify this as the main reason for late booking and poor attendance for antenatal care (Henley 1979; Mitchell and Wilson 1981; Jain 1985).

Organizational procedures and experiences reflect and perpetuate institutional and personal racism. For example, overcrowding at antenatal clinics is said to be caused by Asian women bringing their families. The inability of hospital record systems to deal with Asian names creates confusion and ill-feeling between doctors, midwives and records clerks, all of whom tend to vent their frustration on the women.

Two approaches to support for women who do not speak English

In response to these problems two models of schemes involving bilingual workers evolved. The Asian Mother and Baby Campaign developed the idea of 'link-workers', and continues to be a model used in many places to provide a link between the users of services and the health professionals. The Hackney Multi-ethnic Women's Health Project pioneered a different approach, which used bilingual workers as advocates (Winkler 1986).

The Asian Mother and Baby Campaign was sponsored jointly by the Department of Health and Social Security (DHSS) and the Save the Children Fund and was in operation in 16 NHS districts between 1984 and 1987. It started with health education campaigns, which aimed to make Asian people aware of the services available and the importance of attending for antenatal care. Link-workers were then employed to make links between Asian women whose languages they spoke and people working in the maternity services. Their services were available to women from the time they first booked for maternity care until six weeks after the birth.

The evaluation of the Asian Mother and Baby Campaign suggested that the publicity drive had little immediate impact but that the link-worker schemes were successful and highly valued by Asian women and most professionals (Rocheron 1988; Rocheron and Dickinson 1990; Rocheron, Dickinson and Khan, 1989; Rocherson, Khan and Dickinson 1989). A further evaluation of the Asian Mother and Baby Campaign in Leicestershire (Mason 1990) found that the link-workers provided a much needed interpreter service but were less successful in imparting health education advice to Asian women. The Campaign focused on individual behaviour and promoted a socio-medical model of change. The onus for change was placed primarily on individual women and secondarily on health workers and nursing managers. Furthermore, none of the districts involved in the Campaign developed a sustained anti-racist policy (see also discussion in Chapter 3, this volume).

An advocacy approach has been taken in the Multi-ethnic Women's Health Project, which started in 1980 at the Mothers' Hospital in Hackney and still continues in the district. The project was started jointly by the Community Health Council, Hackney Council for Racial Equality and the City and Hackney Health Authority. The women who work for the project are called 'health advocates' because they do more than just interpret. They mediate between professionals and the women using the services to make sure that they are offered an informed choice of health care. If there are clinical or cultural 'problems' they negotiate, although ultimately they see themselves as advocates for women.

A key feature of the project is the autonomy of the advocates. As the project developed, the advocates frequently described situations where their intervention changed clinical practice. The project steering group commissioned an evaluation (Parsons and Day 1992) to test the hypothesis that health advocacy could improve obstetric outcomes in non-English speaking women. A retrospective study was carried out comparing 1,000 non-English speaking women who delivered at the Mothers' Hospital in 1986 and had been helped by an advocate, with women who delivered at the same hospital in 1979, when there were no advocates.

To attempt to control for changes over time, comparisons were made with another hospital without advocates during the two time periods. The study found significant differences between the groups in their length of antenatal stay, induction rates and method of delivery. In particular, Caesarean rates fell from 10.8 per cent to 8.5 per cent at the Mothers' Hospital, while rising from 11.2 per cent to 17.4 per cent at the other hospital, a difference which was greater than would be expected by chance. It cannot be assumed that these changes are necessarily the direct result of health advocacy, because of the design of the study, but it was considered reasonable to assume that improved communication could have influenced clinical practice. These findings, suggesting that health advocacy may be beneficial, are in line with other research suggesting that social support networks targeted at populations of women at greatest risk may improve the outcomes for their babies (Hodnett 1993). The nature of the support may be critical, however.

The approach used in the Asian Mother and Baby Campaign had much in common with the earlier Stop Rickets Campaign. This was also jointly sponsored by the DHSS and the Save the Children Fund and recommended the use of link-workers. Its other recommendations provoked controversy, which focused on two key questions. These were whether health promotion policies should advocate public health interventions rather than changes in individuals' behaviour; and whose values and norms of behaviour should be fostered by health education programmes (Rocheron 1988), a question which is discussed further in Chapters 8 and 11 of this volume.

In contrast, advocacy schemes had a triple inheritance. They had origins in the 'active birth' movement, which encouraged women to be assertive with health professionals and question routine procedures. They also had links with community health workers in developing countries who worked in a way which aimed to support rather than oppress the community (Werner 1977), and were also influenced by consumerism.

One of the key differences between link-worker and advocacy schemes is that the latter are independent of health professionals. This was illustrated when the Hackney advocacy scheme was taken into mainstream funding in 1988. It became directly managed by the maternity unit, in the same way as the professionals they were trying to challenge. The advocates' role changed to that of link-workers, in all but name. They found this very frustrating, and without support from the Community Health Council, the scheme would have collapsed. When the contract to manage the scheme was given back to the Community Health Council in 1991, the advocates reverted to their earlier role.

Meanwhile, in neighbouring Tower Hamlets, a bilingual service for women using the London Hospital had been provided through the Maternity Services Liaison Scheme, a voluntary organization. When the renamed Royal London became a trust in 1991, the funding was removed and maternity aides were employed instead, and these are not in a position to challenge staff on behalf of women using the services.

Improving maternity services: some conclusions

The available data show that, far from being a homogeneous group having babies with high stillbirth and infant mortality rates, considerable differences exist among minority ethnic groups, in terms of fertility, the birthweight and mortality of their babies and the way their babies are delivered. Initially, failure of communication was the main impetus to develop appropriate services for ethnic minorities. More recently, it has been suggested that the care they received may be improved through receiving support from workers independent of NHS staff. Furthermore, as patterns of immigration change, language may no longer be identified as the predominant barrier, and attention must be directed to providing care which responds to the needs and wishes of all women in our multi-racial society.

It is important to recognize that the 'problems' of how to provide appropriate care will not disappear once the majority of women using the services can speak English. In fact, the need to provide for cultural diversity and raised expectations may well become more pressing, for reasons alluded to in the introduction.

Acknowledgements

Alison Macfarlane is funded by the Department of Health. The authors would like to thank Waqar Ahmad, Janet Sorel and colleagues in the National Perinatal Epidemiology Unit, especially Miranda Mugford and Jo Garcia, for their helpful comments and discussion.

5

Sickle cell and thalassaemia: community experiences and official response

ELIZABETH N. ANIONWU

Introduction

Despite the obvious importance of genetically determined conditions, it is common illnesses and diseases which are the main problems for ethnic minorities, as for other members of society. The specific importance of these two conditions [sickle cell and thalassaemia] is that they provide us with useful bench-marks to assess the willingness and ability of the NHS to respond to specific needs of ethnic minorities. With sickle cell and thalassaemia, the NHS has been continually criticised for its failure to provide adequate services. Apart from an absence of screening facilities in many places, existing services pay little attention to genetic counselling and outreach work with the communities affected. (McNaught 1987: 8)

Sickle cell disorders and thalassaemia (the haemoglobinopathies) are both inherited disorders of the red blood cells which mainly (but not exclusively) affect black and minority ethnic groups. The history of how they were put onto the National Health Service agenda provides useful pointers to: the impact of institutional racism within the NHS; how inequitable services can be challenged by affected families, community groups and committed health workers; and how, in some health authorities, it resulted in the development of more appropriate services for affected families and local populations.

This chapter will illustrate these themes by drawing extensively upon studies that focus on the experiences and views of affected families. Reference will be made to reports produced over the last decade from the voluntary and statutory sector outlining the need for, and the development of, more appropriate services in Britain.

Before reviewing the main features of sickle cell and thalassaemia the common features of inheritance and testing for these conditions will be described.

Inheritance

Sickle cell and thalassaemia are both disorders of haemoglobin, the oxygen-carrying substance found inside red blood cells (Weatherall and Clegg 1981; Modell and Berdoukas 1984; Serjeant 1985; Franklin 1990). Illnesses such as sickle cell anaemia and beta thalassaemia major must be genetically inherited from *both* parents, who will probably both be healthy carriers of a *trait*, for example sickle cell trait, haemoglobin C trait, D and E trait, alpha or beta thalassaemia trait. An individual who has a trait is not ill, cannot develop, and does not have a mild form of the illness. In fact, haemoglobin traits seem to offer some protection against malaria in early childhood (Allison 1957). This accounts for the original geographic distribution of sickle cell and thalassaemia in parts of the world where malaria was or is still endemic such as Africa, Asia, the eastern Mediterranean, and the Middle and Far East. Table 5.1 gives examples of how such haemoglobin traits are commonly found in various populations whose ancestors originated from these parts of the world.

Depending upon which traits a couple have, there is a risk in every pregnancy that their children could be born with either a sickle cell or a thalassaemia disorder. There is also a chance that each of their children could be unaffected because they inherit either a trait or nothing at all (see Figure 5.1).

Testing for sickle cell and thalassaemia

> The haemoglobinopathies are still almost the only group of inherited diseases in which carriers can be detected simply and cheaply, in the absence of a family history. (World Health Organization (WHO) 1988)

Special blood tests, easily arranged through general practitioners, can detect whether a child or an adult has the usual haemoglobin type, is a healthy carrier or has an illness such as sickle cell anaemia or beta thalassaemia major. It is also possible to test the unborn baby as early as nine or ten weeks in pregnancy (Old *et al.* 1982).

Table 5.1   Haemoglobin traits (carriers) in certain ethnic groups: some examples

Haemoglobin type	Ethnic group	Carrier frequency
Sickle cell trait	Afro-Caribbeans	1 in 10
	West Africans	up to 1 in 4
C trait	Afro-Caribbeans	1 in 30
	Ghanaians	up to 1 in 6
D trait	Punjabi Sikhs	1 in 100
Thalassaemia		
Alpha	Chinese	1 in 15 to 30
Beta	Cypriots	1 in 7
	Asians	1 in 10 to 30
	Chinese	1 in 30
	Afro-Caribbean	1 in 50
	White British	1 in 1,000

Note: Certain genes for haemoglobinopathies are also found in ethnic groups not listed above, for example: sickle cell trait, in those originating from Asia, the Mediterranean and the Middle East; D trait, found in various other ethnic groups including white British.
Sources: Weatherall and Clegg (1981), Modell and Berdoukas (1984), Livingstone (1985); WHO (1988); personal communication, Dr Bernadette Modell.

Sickle cell disorders

This is an umbrella term that describes a group of inherited disorders of haemoglobin in the red blood cells and includes sickle cell anaemia (usually the more severe type), haemoglobin SC disease (usually milder) and sickle beta thalassaemia (of which there is both a severe and a mild form). Under circumstances such as a lowered level of oxygen or reduced fluid in the body (dehydration), an increase in the acidity of the blood, infection, sudden changes in temperature and stress, the red cells can change their shape to that resembling a half-moon or farmer's sickle. This can cause a blockage in the smaller blood vessels giving rise to a complex series of problems throughout the body, depending upon which tissue is affected. A child born with the condition does not generally have problems until after the age of four to six months. Problems can then include mild to excruciating pains throughout the body, anaemia, infections, strokes in childhood and damage to various parts of the body including the hips, shoulders, eyes and lungs.

Treatment includes the prevention of certain life-threatening infections by the use of daily penicillin from as early as three months to early adulthood, as well as a vaccine. Patients are encouraged to drink plenty to prevent dehydration, and fluids may be administered into the veins as part of inpatient treatment. Management of the painful 'crisis' depends upon severity, and this can range from mild painkillers such as paracetamol to

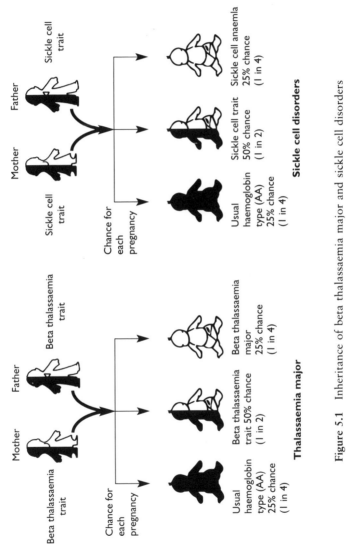

Figure 5.1   Inheritance of beta thalassaemia major and sickle cell disorders

more powerful drugs given during hospital admission such as diamorphine or pethidine. Exchange blood transfusions are occasionally used for certain complications, for example following a stroke. Nearly twenty bone marrow transplants have been undertaken in Belgium to cure sickle cell anaemia (Vermylen *et al.* 1991), but this is still a controversial treatment.

The majority of affected individuals survive into adulthood but there are occasional deaths of young children and adults due to complications such as overwhelming infections and sickling in the lungs. There are no accurate figures for the number of people with sickle cell disorders in Britain. The often quoted estimate of 5,000 cases (based on the Brent register of the mid-1980s and now thought to be too low), is similar to the number of individuals affected by the inherited conditions of haemophilia and cystic fibrosis. Those at greatest risk of inheriting sickle cell disorders (see Table 5.1) are people of African, African/Asian-Caribbean, Eastern Mediterranean, Asian and Middle Eastern origin.

Thalassaemia

This term indicates partial or no production of either the alpha or beta globin chains which make up the structure of haemoglobin in the red blood cells.

Alpha thalassaemia

Alpha globin chains are essential for production of the haemoglobin needed for the unborn baby. Partial absence occurs in those who are 'silent carriers' of alpha thalassaemia trait and who are healthy. There are two main types of alpha thalassaemia, and where both parents are carriers of the more severe type, their unborn baby could inherit a total absence resulting in a stillbirth (known as hydrops fetalis) usually before the expected date of delivery. In addition, there may be some danger to the mother because she is also at risk of developing pre-eclampsia (this can lead to life-threatening high blood pressure and retention of fluid).

The carriers of the most severe form of alpha thalassaemia that can result in hydrops fetalis are generally of Far Eastern origin (see Table 5.1), that is, from Hong Kong, China, Singapore and Vietnam, as well as from Cyprus, Greece and the Middle East. A less severe form of alpha thalassaemia is usually more commonly carried by people originating from Africa, India and Pakistan.

Beta thalassaemia major

A child born with beta thalassaemia major is unable to make a sufficient amount of the beta globin chain necessary for the production of haemoglobin after birth. There is also a generally milder condition called thalassaemia intermedia. A patient with beta thalassaemia major will develop a fatal anaemia in early childhood if not treated with monthly blood transfusions for life. However, this treatment causes too much iron to be stored in the body, so the patient has to be taught from an early age how to use an infusion pump containing a drug (such as Desferal) that helps the body get rid of this excess iron. This requires the insertion of a needle into the abdomen or upper leg, which is then attached to the pump, staying in for twelve hours, five to seven nights a week. Complications of thalassaemia major can include diabetes, delay or failure to enter puberty and other endocrine problems. Through difficulties in compliance with the Desferal pump the patient can experience iron-overload that can result in death from heart failure. Since the advent of early treatment with blood transfusions and the drugs that help get rid of excess iron in the body, more patients are surviving into their twenties and thirties, although early death through non-compliance is not infrequent. In addition, many successful bone marrow transplants have been undertaken for thalassaemia major, particularly in Italy (Lucarelli and Weatherall 1991).

The main groups at risk of inheriting beta thalassaemia (see Table 5.1) are people of Mediterranean and southern European, Asian, Middle Eastern and Far Eastern origin.

Experience of affected families in Britain

Sickle cell disorders

Sickle-cell anaemia is not of great consequence to us in the context of genetic counselling in the United Kingdom. The sickling trait and sickle cell anaemia appear to be confined to peoples of African and Eastern origin. (Stevenson and Davison 1976: 274)

This ethnocentric opinion, published in a genetic counselling textbook in 1976, may account for the fact that so many black families affected by sickle cell disorders complain bitterly about the failure of health professionals to provide them with information both before their child was born and following the diagnosis. The accounts used here are primarily taken from two studies: the first conducted in Brent by the author in 1981 with 22 parents of children with sickle cell disorders (Anionwu 1988); the second, commissioned by the East London Sickle Cell Society (Black and Laws 1986) and undertaken five years later in Newham with 26 affected adults and parents of 16 children.

Only one out of 22 parents of affected children in Brent interviewed in

1981 had ever heard of the condition before their child was diagnosed (Anionwu 1988). This was despite the fact that all the children were born in London, the vast majority in the 1970s. A subsequent check on some of the maternity records revealed that mothers had been identified as having sickle cell trait during their pregnancy but had not been informed or been asked to have their partners tested to see if they also had the trait. Even following the diagnosis, only two were satisfied with the amount of information that they were given. Of the remainder, five were not given any information, one could not remember, and 14 felt that they had received inadequate information. The following responses reflect concerns with inadequate information:

They didn't explain anything, the general practitioner just fobbed me off.

They didn't explain anything except that he wouldn't get over it.

Nine of the 21 children who had symptoms required two or more visits to the general practitioner or hospital before the diagnosis was made. As one of the parents explained:

Month after month he took blood test after blood test. I had to take her back, take her forward, take her back, every month I go they take four different samples of blood, and it took the hospital nearly six years to find out that she had sickle cell.

Following the diagnosis, six out of the 22 families experienced delays of up to one year in being given the result.

My husband was angry and he was very upset because he said 'All this time we knew nothing about it, and the doctor knew'.

Five years later the Newham study identified similar experiences (Black and Laws 1986). The authors state that:

It has been a common theme throughout the respondents' questionnaires that much time was spent going from doctor to doctor and from hospital to hospital trying to confirm the diagnosis. A great proportion of our respondents admitted to not knowing anything about SCD when it was diagnosed and some had never heard of the illness at all.

The Newham study also includes the experiences of two parents accused of battering their children because of the swellings in their hands and joints, a classic early sign of sickle cell anaemia. One of them describes her efforts to identify her son's problem:

'He was crying a lot . . . I didn't know what was wrong with him. So I went back [to the casualty] and he sent me back to my GP. And the casualty officer gave me a letter for the GP, so I opened the letter, and they thought that I battered my son.' The mother went to another hospital where the doctors said it was something wrong with his joints. Then 'After a few months or so they changed their minds. They took a blood test and said he was sickle cell anaemia.'

Another is confronted by the prejudices of a nursing professional:

'The nursing sister said "What have you done? Did he fall? . . . Oh you young mothers, how do you cope? Did you lock him in? . . . What is wrong with him? I bet you're not even married . . . What have you done to him? You can never trust anyone these days." I started crying, I couldn't believe it. I felt the odd one out – the nursing sister was accusing me of battering my child.'

Other issues explored in these studies concerned the impact of the painful crisis. The following quotations (from Anionwu 1988) reflect the parents' feelings:

No one likes to watch a child suffering. I can't stand it when they get the pain.

But when the pain starts it hurts him a lot. I didn't realise how painful it was.

as do these (from Black and Laws 1986):

It's terrible. He doesn't sleep, he doesn't eat. It's just the crying . . . it scares me.

It makes you wish her dead sometimes, the pains are so bad.

Their accounts of hospital experiences centred on delays in treatment, inadequate pain relief and, for the older patients, accusations of being drug addicts.

Prenatal diagnosis
In the Brent study only one out of 22 parents had heard about prenatal diagnosis in 1981, although it had been available since 1974. Five years later several parents in Newham were still unaware of such tests. Both studies found that approximately 50 per cent of parents would be interested in the test. The variability of SCD (compared to thalassaemia major) makes the decision of whether to terminate an affected pregnancy extremely difficult. Key factors (confirmed in a later study in Brent by Anionwu *et al.* 1988), included views about abortion, whether parents already had a seriously affected child and whether or not the test was available early in pregnancy.

Racism

A consultant haematologist in the Midlands commented in 1990: 'Services for sickle cell disease, although improving, are lagging behind the numbers of cases arising in the UK. Major obstacles to progress are the inadequate education of health care professionals, disadvantage within the black community and institutionalised racism' (Franklin 1990). Thirteen years earlier, in reporting on a conference on sickle cell disorders in Brent, Kirby (1977) quoted Neville Clare, an affected individual and founder of the first voluntary group, Organization for Sickle Cell Anaemia Research (OSCAR): 'We have to be extremely cautious . . . You can imagine what the National Front would do with information about this.' In fact the National Front had already made its views known in a grossly inaccurate and virulently racist article by Gilbert (1976) in its newspaper, *Spearhead*:

> Sickle Cell Anaemia now infects 2,500,000 black babies in America and is the cause of 1 out of every 4 negro deaths often before the age of forty . . . another disease introduced into our overcrowded country by our black invaders. Blood transfusions and long periods of rest (on the NHS of course) keep them alive, but now that our physicians are learning more about it they are warning carriers who are considering marriage that they run the risk of infecting their children with the disease.

The perceived effects of racism are incorporated into various accounts of those affected by sickle cell disorders:

> I was hearing that not enough money goes to research on sickle cell. It's not a disease of the white people and they don't know much about it . . .
>
> (Black and Laws 1986)

The following quote is an extract from a tape recorded interview the author conducted in 1980. Debbie was 17 years old and this was her visit to the Brent centre, two years before she died:

> They know that I have got the disease but they don't really know too much about it, and I don't think, this is my personal view, I don't think they're interested because it's not a white man's disease, and I mean, from once it's not a white man's disease, I can't see them really digging into this thing to get any knowledge out of it, because it is black people, and it's black people's problem. (Anionwu 1990)

The way guilt and stigma can arise as a result of the combined effects of racism and lack of information are poignantly summed up in the following quote:

Sometimes I ask myself is what we do to make God give us this? He make them take away us lands. He make them take away us freedom. And now he gave us this. Is what we do? (France-Dawson 1991)

These experiences were not unique to London, as revealed in reports from Liverpool (Torkington 1983) and the Manchester Community Health Group for Ethnic Minorities (MCHGEM 1981). The development of national sickle cell organizations (OSCAR in 1975 and the Sickle Cell Society in 1979) provided a contact point for patients and their families. The Sickle Cell Society built up a dossier of complaints identified at public meetings and through people contacting the organization. In 1981 it made 24 recommendations in a report entitled *Sickle Cell Disease: The Need for Improved Services* (Sickle Cell Society 1981).

Beta thalassaemia major

The two main populations to be affected by beta thalassaemia major in Britain have been the Cypriots and Asians.

The Cypriot experience

Couples requesting testing from their general practitioner at marriage have sometimes been sent away with the comment that 'If all the Cypriots in London were to be tested, there would be no end to it'.
(Modell and Berdoukas 1984: 374)

This account of the British Cypriot experience is mainly drawn from the work of Dr Bernadette Modell, based at University College Hospital, London, and a pioneer in the struggle to improve services (Modell and Berdoukas 1984). One in every six Cypriots is a healthy carrier of beta thalassaemia trait, probably the highest incidence in the world. Modell includes a description by Fawdrey (1946) of the tragic impact of beta thalassaemia major on families in Cyprus after the Second World War, and before the advent of present treatment. Following the eradication of malaria, a major public health initiative concentrated on the management and prevention of beta thalassaemia. Between 1950 and 1967 approximately 10 per cent of the Cypriot population migrated to Britain, mainly to north London, but there was a lapse of about ten years before the high incidence of thalassaemic births began to be appreciated. Here is one typical account from a mother:

In those days we were supposed to bring him down to the hospital for transfusion when he became ill. I took him down every week for a haemoglobin and then when he got bad, for about a week before we took him for transfusion I used to sleep in his bed every night thinking 'Will it be tonight?' (Modell and Berdoukas 1984: 283)

Regular blood transfusions and Desferal pumps to get rid of excess iron dramatically improved survival and the quality of life. However, the treatment still placed a considerable burden on the whole family and it was noted that couples limited the number of children they had rather than risk further affected ones. This also included aborting unplanned pregnancies even though there was a three out of four chance that the child would be unaffected. The introduction of prenatal diagnosis (testing the unborn baby) at 18 weeks of pregnancy in 1974 and then from as early as nine to ten weeks from 1982 was overwhelmingly accepted by Cypriot couples (Modell and Berdoukas 1984).

The UK Thalassaemia Society, established in 1976, was extremely influential in publicizing information about the condition within the Cypriot community, mainly based in London. Social events that raised funds for research – for example, to develop a tablet to get rid of excess iron – also increased awareness about thalassaemia. British Cypriot families also maintained close contact with Cyprus and were aware of the public health initiatives developed in Cyprus to improve both treatment and prevention of the condition.

Alongside a comprehensive range of treatment freely available at specialist centres was a major health education programme involving the media, the schools and the Greek Orthodox Church. Couples planning to marry are required to show evidence that they have been tested, although they are not prevented from getting married if they are both found to have the trait (only 2 per cent of couples decided to call off their marriage in these circumstances). The very high uptake of prenatal diagnosis and termination of affected pregnancies by at-risk couples has resulted in virtually no new births of thalassaemic children (Angastiniotis et al. 1986).

While there is better awareness within the British Cypriot community, the following experience of a 30-year-old member (UK Thalassaemia Society 1991) included in a 1991 UK Thalassaemia Newsletter highlights the serious concerns about the treatment of patients within the NHS:

It's very frustrating when I arrange to have time off for my transfusion only to arrive at the ward and be told that although the blood is ready, there is no bed available. On one occasion my sister and I had to go in on the same day, the nurse phoned me to say that there was only one bed available and only one of us could go. At times like this I feel vulnerable and like an orphan beggar with nowhere to go and having to beg for a bed in order to be treated.

The Society is campaigning for special thalassaemia treatment centres with a trained team of staff.

The Asian experience

From 1960 it was noted that an increasing proportion of the thalassaemic patients in Britain were of Asian origin (Modell and Berdoukas 1984). Whereas 80 per cent of the Cypriot population were in London the Asian communities settled in other parts of the country, with about 60 per cent of British Pakistanis living in the north of England. The experience of Pakistani families affected by beta thalassaemia in one northern city has been documented in a sociological study by a Punjabi-speaking researcher, Aamra Darr (1990).

It had been noted that there had been a much lower uptake of prenatal diagnosis at 18 weeks by Pakistani Muslim couples than by Cypriots and Indians. Prior to this study:

assumptions about their low utilisation of prenatal diagnosis were based on social prejudice and influenced by language difficulties. Typical comments from health workers were 'Muslim families have a fatalistic attitude and do not take any initiatives, they are not interested in prenatal diagnosis, as it is against their religion – there is no point discussing it, they marry their cousins – if they didn't they wouldn't have genetic problems.' (Petrou *et al.* 1990)

The study by Darr (1990) involved 31 families (mostly originating from the Mirpur district) with a total of 45 thalassaemic children. In addition, 11 of these couples, all born in Pakistan, were intensively studied. At the time of the study none owned a car, six did not have a telephone and none of the homes was centrally heated. Darr (1990) states:

Virtually from the first contact in the homes the meetings became counselling sessions. This was the first opportunity the parents had to speak about their child and the disease with someone who spoke their language, gave them ample time and understood what they had to say. One of the most striking features during the initial visits was the isolation of the families due to their lack of awareness of the disease and of contact with other affected families.

(The researcher helped to establish a family support group in 1982)

The following case history has been chosen from Darr (1990) as an illustration of some of the experiences of the families:

Mrs O came to Britain in 1966 aged 16 years with her mother and brothers and sisters to join their father. She married her first cousin in 1974 – both originated from the same city in Pakistan where he had also graduated. The couple are fluent in English, Urdu and Punjabi, the latter being their mother tongue. Mrs O's youngest sister suffers from thalassaemia major. When she was diagnosed with the illness their G.P. had told Mrs O's mother that her children should not marry into the family otherwise the disease would appear again. The family disregarded this information as there were many couples in the family who were first cousins and whose children were all healthy. Other than this Mrs O does not remember any information being given about the disease and the family were therefore unaware of its inherited nature.

Their first son was born in 1975 and by four months began not to thrive. Several visits were made to the G.P. who was not very sympathetic and diagnosed the symptoms as being caused by teething. When the parents drew attention to their son's pale complexion the G.P. replied, 'Well, neither of you are exactly rosy-cheeked!' One year later, when the family moved to another county the child's condition was eventually diagnosed when Mr O wondered whether the child could have thalassaemia (at the time he only knew the name.)

At this time, in 1976, Mrs O was pregnant with her second child. Nothing was mentioned about prenatal diagnosis at the hospital or by their G.P. Mrs O learned about the disease and preventive service available at University College Hospital, London through a television programme on thalassaemia major. She contacted the centre and had the test when she was 18 weeks pregnant. It proved to be affected and she had a termination in her home town with an invasive and now outdated method called hysterotomy. She was on the waiting list for a few days, had a caesarean section under general anaesthetic and then had to remain in hospital for a week. It was an emotionally and physically distressing experience. On a follow-up visit to the outpatients clinic a doctor also told her that all her children would suffer from the same condition, which made her very angry as she knew this to be false information. She said 'I nearly hit him with my handbag. I didn't. Instead I got up and left and swore never to go back to him.'

In 1980, having moved back to her old town, Mrs O became pregnant for the third time. She again travelled to London for foetal blood sampling and returned the same day. The foetus was again affected and she underwent a termination of pregnancy. Although this was conducted in a sympathetic manner it nevertheless took three days because of the possible complications caused through a scar from the unnecessary procedure with the previous termination. With the next pregnancy in 1981, the couple made a conscious decision not to have the test. They felt a moral dilemma in relation to another possible termination of pregnancy and were emotionally and physically drained by their previous experiences. In addition, they had heard of a mistake with prenatal diagnosis. They had a healthy girl but had to wait over a year to have the result confirmed. In 1982 Mrs O miscarried a pregnancy that the couple had made a decision not to test. In 1983 the couple had a healthy child, Mrs O had been tempted to have new test available at nine weeks but, after conferring with her husband, decided to stand by their resolve and trust in God alone. Mrs O was pregnant again in 1986, did not request prenatal diagnosis and delivered a healthy child. This couple experienced seven pregnancies which had resulted in one thalassaemic child and three healthy children.

Darr (1990) noted that most of the families were not aware of the availability of prenatal diagnosis:

> When making an informed choice some couples rejected prenatal diagnosis totally either for religious reasons, or as a result of negative experiences. Some rejected prenatal diagnosis at 16 weeks but found it acceptable at nine weeks. Others accepted both at sixteen weeks and at nine weeks, particularly those couples who have experienced looking after a thalassaemic child over a long period in Pakistan.

She concludes that factors affecting uptake include: earlier availability of the test from sixteen to nine weeks in pregnancy; and a local service that avoided the necessity of travelling to London, with all the inherent financial and child care implications.

Darr noted a number of themes arising from the family studies. First, that there was insufficient knowledge of thalassaemia among the British Pakistani population. At the beginning of the study only two families understood the inherited nature of the condition.

Second, she noted that there was little or no stigma and blame directed towards parents themselves. This may be due to Islamic beliefs expressed by parents (that difficulties are an inevitable part of life and that some are willed by God to develop an individual's inner strength and capacity to cope; that God never puts a greater burden on a person than he or she has the capacity to bear). The lack of blame directed specifically at mothers may be due to the fact that many of the marriages were consanguineous (between relatives who have a common ancestor) and therefore to blame one's wife's family for 'bad blood' would be akin to blaming one's own family.

Third, virtually all were initially told that the condition was 'caused' by the couple being cousins. Darr states:

> This was not only false information, but in the process, correct information of their child's disease was denied to the parents . . . It also implies that the marriage pattern of the community has caused them to

have an affected child and the sole option available to them and the other people in their society is to change that marriage pattern. Coupled with the absence of information on the real options available, the result of such misinformation can only be to produce guilt and despair in the parents. As consanguineous marriage is highly favoured among Pakistanis, such statements are also seen as an attack on what is viewed as an established and positive social practice.

The researchers of the Newham sickle cell study (Black and Laws 1986) concluded their report with a chapter on the situation regarding to thalassaemia, especially in view of the estimated proportion of ethnic minorities in Newham (26.5 per cent), the majority of Asian origin. By word of mouth they became aware of 17 affected children and adults, mainly of Asian origin, the others being Cypriot and Chinese. A significant number of these attended hospitals outside of the district and it was therefore thought that this figure was an underestimate as the local hospital had not had a tradition for treating thalassaemics. The recent arrival of a haematologist (blood specialist) with an interest in the condition meant that more accurate figures became available for pregnant women screened in the local antenatal clinic. In a 15-month period (from 17 September 1984 to 11 February 1986), 104 women were found to have beta thalassaemia trait, which averages about 83 women per year (5.4 per cent of the total women attending the clinic).

They concluded: 'At present the situation in terms of service provision and of education work appears to be worse even than it is for sickle cell.' There is no voluntary organization with an active group in the borough, although there are individuals who work with the Thalassaemia Society.

In 1991 two descriptive studies were conducted by Jani *et al.* (1992) in relation to the level of knowledge and experience of beta thalassaemia within a Gujarati community in north London. In the first study, involving 15 families, they interviewed 29 parents of 17 thalassaemic children (one of whom had died). The children ranged between 2 and 25 years of age, with a mean of 11.5 years.

Of the 11 couples not detected as carriers, nine were not detected as carriers until the birth of the affected child, one woman was diagnosed as a carrier but the husband was not offered information and testing, and one child was adopted. Of the remaining four couples who had been tested, one husband had been diagnosed as 'normal', one couple had received a false negative prenatal diagnosis result and two couples only found out that they were carriers in the fourth month of pregnancy and refused prenatal diagnosis. They both accepted the earlier test at nine weeks in four subsequent pregnancies. One couple had two positive results and terminated those pregnancies and the other couple had four positive results and terminated all four pregnancies. In four out of the 15 families there had been a recurrence of the risk of a thalassaemic child in the extended family due to absent or ineffective counselling.

The second study was undertaken in a general practice where questionnaires were completed by 107 Gujaratis aged 18-44. Only 16 (15 per cent) had heard of beta thalassaemia and of these 11 had been tested either through the antenatal clinic or by their GP and six had been found to be carriers. Thus, in a population with a 10 per cent risk of being a carrier for beta thalassaemia 85 per cent had not even heard of the condition in 1991. Following information about the condition and its frequency within the Gujarati community, 70 were in favour of being tested, preferably through their general practitioner. If they and their partner were found to be carriers 63 would consider prenatal diagnosis, but selective termination was more likely to be favoured by Hindus than Jains.

Demands for better services

In 1981 the Sickle Cell Society set out why more centres similar to the one set up in Brent in 1979 were needed (Sickle Cell Society 1981). In addition, its 24 recommendations for improvements in services included that:

- Health Education Council and local health education units should make funds available for educational leaflets;
- professionals such as doctors and nurses receive more information on haemoglobinopathies in their basic and in-service training;
- there be a national policy to screen newborn babies;
- health authorities collect statistics about incidence and mortality rates for sickle cell desease (SCD);
- patients with inherited illnesses such as SCD be exempt from prescription charges;
- the government allocate funds for research and development related to SCD;
- that the DHSS take a lead in ensuring that all of the recommendations are implemented, including circulating updated information to all general practitioners and health authorities.

Over the next ten years reports emerged from a variety of sources setting out the need for better services for sickle cell disorders and thalassaemia. These included the Runnymede Trust (Prashar et al. 1985), WHO (1988), and the Royal College of Physicians (RCP 1989), and the National Association for Health Authorities and Trusts (NAHAT 1991). Points to emerge concerned the inequitable provision of service for SCD and thalassaemia in comparison with other conditions. The Runnymede report referred to the national screening programme of babies for phenylketonuria

(PKU) that occurs in 10–12 babies per every 100,000, compared to SCD that occurs in at least 500 in every 100,000 babies of Afro-Caribbean origin, and the network of Haemophilia Centres in Regional Health Authorities. There is a similar number of cases of haemophilia (5,000) to that for SCD.

More recently the discovery of the gene for cystic fibrosis (1 in 25 white British are carriers) has witnessed a great deal of interest concerning the need for appropriate information, screening and counselling. For example, the Medical Research Council organized a workshop in 1990 to explore key issues that it needed to take on board. It needs to be asked why it has not taken a similar interest in SCD and thalassaemia. Interestingly, the fact that cystic fibrosis also occurs in some Asian communities such as the Pakistani population has, until recently, been neglected. The Cystic Fibrosis Research Trust is presently conducting a study to try and establish how many such families there are in Britain (Spencer et al. 1993).

Response of the NHS

There is extremely little health service provision for haemoglobinopathy counselling in north-west Europe. The counselling centres that exist have been built up by motivated individuals, with moral backing from local support groups and insecure financial support provided for a few months or a year at a time, by research organisations, charities, or bodies concerned with race relations. The future of these services is precarious, and they are inadequate for the real and growing needs.

(WHO 1988: 41)

In 1979 the author and Dr Milica Brozovic (a consultant haematologist) established in Brent the first Sickle Cell Information, Screening and Counselling Centre in Britain (Anionwu 1989). It soon became clear that thalassaemia also needed to be incorporated into its activities. In 1984 the author was joined by two other counsellors, one of whom was a Gujarati-speaking health visitor with a special remit for thalassaemia. The success of this strategy in Brent attracted attention and was proposed as a possible model for other health authorities (Sickle Cell Society 1981; Prashar et al. 1985; Constantinides 1986; WHO 1988; RCP 1989). Ironically, the author left the centre when severe conflicts developed with some local doctors uncomfortable with an approach that flew in the face of traditional medical control. The impact within the NHS of black and minority ethnic nurse counsellors in the running of this and other centres is an aspect that has not yet been fully explored. Their presence has been unique in the NHS and has allowed a black, anti-racist perspective on issues such as community education, non-directive counselling for at-risk couples and the experiences

Table 5.2   Districts with sickle and thalassaemia counselling/development posts, March 1992

Greater London
 1 Brent
 2 Camberwell
 3 City & Hackney
 4 Croydon (Development post; no counselling)
 5 Greenwich (part-time)
 6 Haringey
 7 Islington
 8 Newham
 9 Waltham Forest
10 West Lambeth (part-time)

Outside London
11 Birmingham
12 Bristol (part-time)
13 Cardiff
14 Coventry
15 Derby (part-time)
16 Gloucester (part-time)
17 Liverpool (part-time)
18 Leeds
19 Manchester
20 Nottingham
21 Reading
22 Wolverhampton

of patients in hospitals. Currently (March 1992) there are 22 health authorities (see Table 5.2) employing approximately 40 full- or part-time sickle cell and thalassaemia counsellors, predominantly black nurses. The author is currently writing up the results of a survey to produce a profile of this group, their activities and funding as well as their views about current services.

While there have been some important developments within the NHS, the distribution and funding of existing services is causing alarm. It will be seen from Table 5.2 that many parts of Britain with significant black and minority ethnic populations are not listed as they have no designated information and counselling services for their local population. At the time of writing there are campaigns to set up such services by local groups and some health workers all over Britain – for example, in Preston, Southampton, Tower Hamlets, Riverside, Luton, Watford, Hammersmith and Fulham, Sheffield, Glasgow and Bloomsbury. In addition, there have been successful campaigns in Leicester, Bradford and Ealing that have resulted in a mixture of short-term and permanent funding for counselling posts in these districts as from April 1992. Information and counselling services must go hand in hand with sensitive hospital treatment for affected individuals. Recently, Camberwell Community Health Council has been active in responding to complaints by local sickle cell patients attending King's College Hospital (Camberwell CHC 1990; Pilger 1992). Two public meetings organized in 1990 and 1991 were attended by local patients, health workers and politicians. It resulted in a proposed Code of Good Practice for SCD patients and a set of ten national demands for SCD and thalassaemia. The latter received support from both the Greater London Association of Community Health Councils (GLACHC) and the national Association of Community Health Councils for England and Wales (ACHCEW) which have made representations to the Department of Health. In addition, Harriet Harman, the local Member of Parliament and at the time of writing Opposition Spokesperson on Health, raised the issue in the House of Commons. Shortly afterwards it was announced that the Standing Medical Advisory Committee (SMAC) had agreed to set up a working party on sickle cell disorders (Hansard 1992). The terms of reference were broadened to include thalassaemia, and the report was published in 1993.

Conclusion

This chapter has described how sickle cell and thalassaemia have been forcibly put on the NHS agenda despite apathy, financial constraints and organizational upheavals. It clearly demonstrates the resolve of the black communities and their abilities in developing more appropriate services which now serve as a possible model for genetic conditions such as cystic fibrosis.

However, the NHS has been slow to respond to the well-documented harrowing experiences of families affected by sickle cell disorders and thalassaemia. It is of interest that the gradual development of a network of services has occurred despite the purse-string holders being reluctant to accept the significance of these issues. The need for a co-ordinated national response is long overdue, and the setting up of the SMAC working party has clearly been in response to grassroots pressure.

The working party will have a large body of views and literature to draw from – the support groups now have a greater degree of confidence and will demand active involvement in their deliberations and recommendations. The various national sickle cell support groups, while wishing to retain some autonomy, also recognize the inherent dilution of efforts when different groups campaign on similar issues. They are now actively discussing the setting up of a confederation in order to co-ordinate their activities and lobbying. Constantinides (1986) sums up both the frustrations and the hopes of both sufferers and their carers, and health workers in this area:

> The more information that populations at risk for the haemoglobinopathies receive from home and abroad, the more intolerable it must seem to them that services are systematically provided for screening phenylketonuria or counselling haemophiliacs, but not for education, training, screening and counselling those at risk from thalassaemia and sickle cell disease.

6

Epidemiology, ethnicity and schizophrenia

S.P. SASHIDHARAN and E. FRANCIS

Introduction

The association between migration and hospital admission rate for mental illness (especially schizophrenia) is a well-known finding in psychiatric epidemiology. Various studies in England over the last twenty years have confirmed this trend and the focus of scientific enquiries has now moved on to the study of 'second generation' and their rate of psychiatric hospital admission. Most of these studies emphasize the significance of 'ethnicity' as an independent variable, defined and characterized uncritically and usually to the exclusion of other socio-demographic factors. Such epidemiological studies have generated much controversy over alleged findings that there exists an 'ethnic vulnerability' to mental illness, particularly schizophrenia. This chapter offers a critical examination of such studies and questions the methodological and theoretical validity of much of the work undertaken so far. We argue that the alignment of mental illness and ethnicity or race is indicative of underlying political ideologies rather than the product of empirical findings.

Within the European imagination, race and madness have a common history, at least in part, that denotes the significance of the 'Other', the need to strengthen the definition of self by denying the Other. For example, sanity and rationality are identified through the absence of madness and irrationality, and being white or European denotes the opposite of being black or African or Asian. At the same time, the approximation of rationality with being European is achieved more easily if irrationality is located as part of being non-European. Historically, the emergence of such cognitive forms was partly linked to the fashioning of 'race' sciences at a time when Europe and Europeans were increasingly coming into contact with the rest of the world in the context of geographical 'discovery' and political conquests. This new scientific enterprise, which was explicitly concerned with human variations and categorization invariably demarcated along racial and cultural lines, contributed to the reinforcement of the idea of race itself and the identification of racial differences as a scientific, biological question worthy of further enquiry. The increasing interest in 'race', transformed in the discourse of race science of the eighteenth and nineteenth centuries as a biological construct, was primarily fuelled by the barely concealed motive of establishing race differences, between Europeans and non-Europeans, which in turn was linked to notions of superiority and inferiority, the very substrate of political domination and subjugation. More than anything else, it was the idea of European superiority, not just in political terms but also as a scientifically established fact, that gave momentum to academic work in this area. In many ways, the historical legacy of such race science can be discerned in much of contemporary research and academic work in relation to ethnicity and culture in social and psychological sciences.

The psychological sciences, including psychiatry, have, of course, evolved and adapted since the days of anthropometry and racial categorizations and, in many ways, the crude measures and explicitly racist assumptions of an earlier era have been discredited and largely set aside with the increasing recognition that scientific activity, like most human activities, takes place in a social and political context. However, the idea of race and racial differences still maintains a salience and significance in contemporary culture, no doubt strengthened by an increasingly visible non-European presence within Europe. Such a presence and the experience of black people in their relationships with Europe and European people continue to be understood and articulated in largely negative terms and the messages and perceptions of immigrants and black people that are reinforced in contemporary culture are essentially a reworking of the earlier notions of racial difference, redesignated as ethnic differences. The marginality of black people, and the disadvantage and discrimination that is associated with such a status, find expression through a new vocabulary that invokes deviance instead of racial inferiority as an explanatory variable. Over the recent past, scientific interest in the area has been reawakened as a result.

It is within this context that contemporary psychiatry and the whole 'psychological complex' (Miller and Rose 1986) has assumed a relevance, particularly in relation to current black experience in Britain. Although the premises and practice of psychiatry and other psychological sciences, including social work, reveal their fundamental concern with deviance and disorder, it is in the area of scientific, in this case psychiatric, research that the approximation of ethnicity and deviance is most apparent and the reformulation of the irrational and therefore irresponsible African or Asian confirmed. Psychiatry, with its function of defining, monitoring and 'treating' psychological disorder, often identified in the context of social disorder, provides the scientific basis and the legislative and therapeutic justification for a particular approach in dealing with deviance. Furthermore, by asserting its expertise in dealing with madness, psychiatry provides the glue that binds the individually deviant behaviour in the socially sanctioned procedures for incarceration. Psychiatric research, especially studies concerned with ethnicity, accrues the evidence that links such deviance or madness to historically dictated hierarchies and divisions, currently fashioned on to ideas of ethnicity or race. Therefore, given the particular historical context of psychiatry and race within Europe, the approximation of race and madness, the enveloping of one within the other is easily accessible within the popular culture and continues to dominate academic thinking.

The major crisis within British psychiatry around the issue of race requires an analysis that brings in such a historical and cultural analysis. The crisis here is about psychiatry's inability to come to terms with what is happening in our psychiatric institutions and the nature of psychiatric practice that remains blind to the needs and aspirations of black people. The increasing numbers of black people, especially Afro-Caribbean people, who are inducted into a hostile psychiatric system, usually designated as suffering from schizophrenia, the reliance of psychiatric practice on coercion and control to deal with its black clients, the identification of psychiatry as a site of struggle by the black community and the increasing challenge posed to institutional psychiatry make such a crisis visible not only to those who are directly involved in this area but also to the community at large.

In this chapter, we attempt to challenge the 'scientific' basis of a particular professional position in explaining this crisis. The power of psychiatry here is vested in a professional argument that posits a direct relationship between being black and the propensity to madness. The 'ethnic vulnerability hypothesis' that explicitly argues that black people have a propensity to madness or that Afro-Caribbean people living in the United Kingdom have an increased vulnerability to developing a 'mental illness', namely schizophrenia, is critically examined on the basis of the empirical evidence that is made available through various studies over the last thirty years. Before an alternative analysis is possible, we believe it is important to challenge the methods and findings of such studies that, according to conventional psychiatric thinking, form the basis of currently influential professional position that the crisis here is largely a public health issue, namely an 'epidemic of schizophrenia' in the black community (Harrison 1990).

Ethnic vulnerability hypothesis

The increased risk of mental hospital admission for immigrant groups is one of the enduring findings in psychiatric epidemiology. In England, an examination of national statistics of hospital admission clearly shows that certain foreign-born groups are over-represented in mental hospital admissions. Those born in Ireland (Republic and Northern Ireland) and Scotland are followed by the Caribbean-born (both men and women) in such high risk groups for all admissions as well as first admissions. A closer study of the data also reveals that for the Caribbean-born, the risk of psychiatric hospital admission is highest for schizophrenia, and again this appears to be the case for both men and women and for first as well as all admissions. Hospital diagnosis of schizophrenia accounts for 40–52 per cent of all admissions for the Caribbean-born in England (compared to 12–14 per cent for the English-born) and over a third (33–35 per cent) of first admissions compared to one tenth (7–10 per cent) for the English born.

Although this pattern of psychiatric hospital admission has been known for nearly two decades, it is only in the last few years that ethnicity as a risk factor for schizophrenia has entered into scientific and more public discourse. In Britain there is, of course, a much longer history in social and behavioural sciences of race or racial difference being reified and abused in its descriptive and analytic models in a barely concealed attempt to bolster explicitly political ideologies. It is, however, the nature of the current discourse within British psychiatry, which posits a unique and direct relationship between being of Afro-Caribbean origin and the development of a particular type of 'mental illness', that demands careful scrutiny.

Before considering the epidemiological studies relevant to this question, it needs to be said that the observations relating to Afro-Caribbeans and mental hospital admissions may have multiple origins and need not in principle, be susceptible to any unifying explanation. Also, to paraphrase Kamin (1974), who was writing about intelligence and genetics, it would be an imprecise and scientifically meaningless statement to assert that there is no association between ethnicity and mental illness (schizophrenia). We cannot prove a null hypothesis, nor should we be asked to do so. The question is whether there exist data of merit and validity that require us to reject the null hypothesis. There should be no mistake here. As Kamin says, the burden of proof falls upon those who wish to assert the implausible proposition, in this case, that the variations that we observe for psychiatric hospital admissions and the attributions of descriptive and largely imprecise classificatory labels among loosely defined and essentially heterogeneous social groupings mean that an individual characteristic (being black) is specifically associated with developing a 'mental illness'. Such a proposition is still problematic even if conditional arguments about the levels of specificity are introduced or if we ignore theoretical notions about what constitutes mental illness or what we mean by schizophrenia.

This chapter is specifically concerned with the 'merit and validity' of existing data. The many substantive issues of ideology and meaning which the topic inevitably raises are only dealt with in a tangential way.

Methodological issues

Before considering the nature of the evidence linking schizophrenia and Afro-Caribbeans in the UK certain methodological issues relevant to epidemiological enquiries need to be emphasized. Since epidemiology is concerned with disease distribution and determinants, this approach entails comparison of rates and risks in different populations. Such comparisons (and calculations of rates) are crucially determined by a number of factors relating to both the numerator and the denominator.

Numerator problems

The most significant bias that could be introduced into the calculation of rates (of a particular disorder) stems from the choice and definition of the numerator. This involves case identification (whom we choose to identify as having the disorder) and case definition (how we choose to define the disorder). A unit change in the numerator can produce marked variation in the rate of disorder, especially when the number of cases available is fairly small.

Case definition in psychiatry is a problematic issue. The poor reliability of psychiatric diagnoses and the variability of clinical diagnosis among different clinicians is well acknowledged. The use of secondary data (such as hospital case note diagnoses, or based on case registry) thus heavily compromises the accuracy of the dependent variable in most studies concerned with calculating disease rates. If these biases inherent in case definition in comparative groups are equal or uniform, or if the extent of any bias could be quantified adequately, then the unreliability of a diagnosis such as schizophrenia would by itself not be a serious source of error. But all the evidence would appear to suggest that, first, overall clinical diagnosis of schizophrenia is unreliable (Cooper et al. 1972; Brockington et al. 1978); second, in secondary data, administrative errors or omissions could further vitiate case definition in this diagnostic group; and third, the diagnosis of schizophrenia in Afro-Caribbeans lacks reliability, stability (over time) and specificity (i.e. use of 'pseudo' categories such as 'cannabis psychosis'). These problems are likely to be of greater magnitude in black subjects than in white control populations (Carpenter and Brockington 1980; Rack 1980; Littlewood and Lipsedge 1981; Mukherjee *et al*. 1983). The greater variations in the clinical presentation of schizophrenia in non-white populations have also been recognized. Allied to this is the problem consequent upon the 'cultural gap' that exists between white practitioners and black clients than with white patients. If misdiagnosis of schizophrenia is a major problem, then calculation of rates based on such an unreliable method of case definition would introduce a significant bias in calculating relative risks for blacks over whites. In a recent study of hospital admissions for schizophrenia in England it was suggested that the apparent high rate of schizophrenia found among the Caribbean-born people 'could be regarded, in some part, as artefactual' because of the possibility of diagnostic inaccuracy (Cochrane and Bal 1987). Although others have disagreed that misdiagnosis accounts for the excess rates of schizophrenia found in hospital based studies (Leff 1988), doubts must remain about the comparability of a clinical diagnosis of schizophrenia in different ethnic groups (Littlewood and Lipsedge 1988).

The next issue is one of case identification. In calculating the incidence of a disease, the assumption is that all new cases of that disorder (or a specified proportion) are available within the particular sampling frame used by the investigator. If hospital admissions are used as a sampling frame then the calculation of disease rates is valid only if all the individuals are likely to be represented within it. It is recognized in psychiatry that hospital-based rates are better understood as statistics of administrative morbidity (Kramer 1976) and their relationship to true incidence (or prevalence) is a contentious area (Kraus 1954; Masai 1965). Variations in professional and patient behaviour, the availability of alternative provisions and the perceptions of illness and satisfaction with the care available could all influence hospital utilization and measures based on such nosocomial factors (Wennburg 1986; Morgan *et al*. 1991).

Some of the factors which crucially influence the ease with which individuals pass through the 'filters' that exist between the community and psychiatric treatment facilities have been identified (Goldberg and Huxley 1980). By no means is it clear whether black people who 'develop' 'schizophrenia' and their white counterparts traverse these filters with the same ease. The available evidence, however, suggests that black patients and white patients arrive at psychiatric hospitals through different channels (Rwegellera 1980; Ineichen *et al*. 1984; Moodley and Perkins 1987). Black patients are more likely to be admitted to hospital through coercive means than white patients (even when their diagnoses are comparable) and the usual methods of referral to the hospital, such as those involving GPs, are relatively rare for black psychiatric patients. Furthermore, there is evidence to show that recognition of psychiatric illness in black people and their referral to psychiatric services involves multiple agencies (such as the police, for example) more often than in the case of white patients (Hitch and Clegg 1980; Harrison et al. 1984). The eventual effect of all these powerful selection factors is such that when hospital statistics are considered there would be differences between groups both in terms of their absolute numbers and the nature of their constituent symptoms due to their different probabilities of being recognized, referred and admitted to hospital. This will be true even if the groups are diagnostically equivalent.

The relationship between first admissions and first psychiatric contact is also problematic when we consider schizophrenia which, according to most clinicians, is an illness of such severity that all those who develop the condition will be admitted to hospitals. Wing and Fryers (1976), in their comparison of two case registers (Salford and Camberwell for 1965–74), for example, show that the mean one-year inception rate for schizophrenia (that is, first contact with the Camberwell register – 40 per 100,000 population for men and women) consisted of 35 per cent first ever contact, 55 per cent first contact locally but not first ever, and 10 per cent first contact with no knowledge of previous contact. For the same period, the mean one-year first admission rate was 13.3 per 100,000 (out of 14 per 100,000 per year first ever contact) with first admission in whom previous contact was unknown making up another 1.1 per 100,000. Although it is obvious that a significant proportion of first contact with a local psychiatric service would consist of false positives, it can be seen that first admissions for schizophrenia represent 95 per cent of all first contact. This study was conducted nearly twenty years ago now but there is no reason to suspect that the pattern of psychiatric contact for those with schizophrenia has remained the same in the ensuing years because of the fundamental changes in service provision that have been introduced.

The incidence study of schizophrenia carried out in Nottingham in 1978–1980 presents a different picture (Cooper et al. 1987) and is perhaps illustrative of the impact of changes in service provision on the care of the mentally ill. Of the 108 new inceptions of schizophrenia, a quarter ($n = 27$) were identified as outpatients and 11 of these were never admitted to hospital at any time in the two-year follow-up period. More recently, in the World Health Organization (1987) pilot study of mental health services, Nottingham and Aberdeen were chosen as study areas. In both centres, cohorts of consecutive cases aged 15 and over without previous contact with services locally were chosen between January and April 1978. Out of a cohort of 200 such cases in Nottingham, eight achieved a diagnosis of schizophrenia or paranoid state and, at the time of entry into the study, none of them was an inpatient. Furthermore, when the cohort was followed up over a year, 75 per cent remained as outpatients with no admissions. In Aberdeen, the proportion of schizophrenia ($n = 13$) identified at first contact as outpatient was 70 per cent and those who remained as outpatients over the following year was 16 per cent. If all the patients with a diagnosis of schizophrenia are not being admitted to hospital (and, as has been shown, there is good reason to believe that a proportion of new cases of schizophrenia are being treated as outpatients, a trend that would be consistent with the current emphasis on community care and closure of hospital beds) then one would have to assume that blacks and whites with a diagnosis of schizophrenia have equal chances of being admitted to hospital before we can accept the validity of hospital admission statistics on which comparative morbidity estimates are being made. Because of the clear potential for differential selection that operates between blacks and whites in inception into care, particularly hospital inpatient care, we have good reason to doubt the validity of such a proposition.

Denominator problems

Most of the studies concerned with ethnic variation in hospital admission rates refer to problems in estimating the size of the at-risk population (interestingly, most of them ignore the numerator problems, except that of diagnosis). Briefly, there are four ways in which the calculation of the denominator could be subject to major error. Deficiencies of population census data and other estimations of at-risk population (such as those based on the electoral roll or other local authority figures) are well known. Lack of ethnicity information in such lists is a major problem, and only very few studies have even attempted to address this issue. Even when correction factors are incorporated into estimating the total black population in such studies, the final figure is nothing more than an informed guess. The findings of the Labour Force Survey carried out in selected areas of England in 1981 are sometimes extrapolated on local population estimation to give the best estimate according to ethnicity, although the numbers of ethnic minorities calculated thus are, at best, approximations of the actual figures (Smythe and Sashidharan 1990). Similarly, estimation of black population based on individuals in households with heads of households born in New Common-wealth countries and Pakistan belies certain untested assumptions about where and how black people live. Also, the complex relationship between ethnicity, nativity and age is overlooked in such calculations. A different kind of problem is that of Census undercount; black people are less likely to be counted at all in the decennial Census compared to white people for a variety of reasons. Figures from the USA suggest that the net undercount could be in the region of 4–18 per cent for black men (compared to 1–4 per cent for white men) and the magnitude of such underestimates could vary according to age (Siegel 1974).

The third source of error in estimating the denominator stems from the nature of the catchment areas where most of the studies on ethnic variations on hospital admission rates have been conducted. Most such studies have been carried out in hospitals serving inner-city catchment areas and invariably, such localities have a substantial resident black population. Also, people living in such areas tend to include many who are transient and highly mobile, and it can be postulated that this leads to both qualitative and quantitative changes in the estimation and characterization of the at-risk population. As those who are relatively well off and psychologically less vulnerable move out of such areas, their position will be taken up by those who are economically less able and arguably less resilient. If such inner-city shift or drift into predominantly black areas has an ethnic bias, as has been shown in Birmingham, then these changes are bound to have an effect on local hospital utilization.

The final source of error is in not recognizing certain special features of the at-risk population. The black population in Britain, particularly in inner-city areas, is much younger than the white population, and this introduces a bias in the estimation of incidence of a condition that is dependent on age unless appropriate corrections are made. Similarly, when control (white) groups are used, other salient demographic differences (such as social class, level of economic activity) require careful consideration before the populations from which 'cases' are derived are considered as similar.

Epidemiological studies

Epidemiological studies of psychiatric disorders among black people in the UK are largely based on hospital admissions. A brief review of such studies, which have estimated morbidity rates of schizophrenia for Afro-Caribbeans, is provided to emphasize the major problems in their conclusions.

These studies have involved examination of national statistics, admissions to all hospitals within particular geographic regions, case registries or admissions or referrals to local hospitals. Most of these studies, apart from two exceptions (Richards and Henryk-Gutt 1982; Harrison et al. 1988), relied on secondary data and all of them except the study carried out in Nottingham (Harrison et al. 1988) were based on hospital admissions alone.

Hemsi's (1967) analysis of first admissions to seven psychiatric hospitals serving the London boroughs of Camberwell and Lambeth was one of the first studies comparing West Indians and the native-born. The study was retrospective and was confined to admissions of individuals aged between 15 and 54 years. Diagnoses were based on author's criteria and these were applied to information obtained from case notes. Census data classified by nativity were used as the denominator. Interestingly, the overall first admission rates both for the major functional psychoses (namely, schizophrenia and manic depressive illness) and for personality and neurotic disorders were found to be higher in West Indians than in 'native-born'. Details about the selection of samples and the nature of their referrals are sparse and there is no comment about the precision with which numerators are linked to Census denominators. The author acknowledges that calculation of the denominator population was likely to be imprecise because of the pattern of migration to Britain from the Caribbean in the early 1960s. Reliance on case notes for arriving at diagnoses (the author acknowledges the 'atypical' nature of the West Indian sample) and the lack of socio-economic and other demographic data make the control group comparisons problematic. Similarly, whether the figures actually represent true incidence or hospital referral rates is difficult to establish. When the annual first admission rate for schizophrenia for Afro-Caribbeans in this study is compared with that reported in the study from Nottingham (Harrison et al. 1988), one can see how the estimates have increased threefold in 28 years (91 per 100,000 in Camberwell and Lambeth for the 15–54 age group in 1961 compared to 259 per 100,000 in Nottingham for 1984–6) while the rates for whites have remained much the same. Although the two studies differ in their methodology and design (the London study was retrospective, relied on case notes diagnosis and included only admissions, while the Nottingham study was prospective in design, used standardized clinical assessment and, most importantly, screened all psychiatric referrals) it is interesting to note that the incidence rates for schizophrenia calculated for whites have remained largely unaltered while rates for blacks show a substantial increase.

Similar problems in case selection and case definition undermine the validity of local hospital-based studies (Carpenter and Brockington 1980; Hitch and Clegg 1980; Littlewood and Lipsedge 1981; Harrison et al. 1984; McGovern and Cope 1987). The study by Hitch and Clegg (1980) was conducted in Bradford over three years (1968–70), and was primarily concerned with patterns of referral of first admissions to the local psychiatric hospital. The authors relied on hospital case data for diagnoses, country of birth, age, as well as a number of other variables. Census data were used as the denominator after dichotomizing the age range into 16–34 and 35–64 groups with the assumption that the dichotomous age distribution of the total local population was valid for all those born overseas. Thus the rates were calculated on the basis of a standard population after applying a weighing factor to the sample numbers. No tests were carried out to establish the validity of the assumption that different nativity groups had similar age distributions. Diagnoses were 'clinical diagnoses', subsequently aggregated into categories such as schizophrenia. Apart from the excess rates among patients born in the 'New Commonwealth' for schizophrenia (by a factor of 3.2) this study clearly pointed to the different referral routes taken by patients born in the UK and those born in the 'New Commonwealth' before they were incepted into care. Police and social workers were involved in the referral of those born in the 'New Commonwealth' to a significantly greater extent than with other groups. Interestingly, this applied across all diagnostic groups and was not necessarily associated with only 'compulsory' admissions.

The study by Carpenter and Brockington (1980) was carried out five years later, also in the North of England. Again, hospital admission records were used for case identification and clinical diagnoses were accepted as the dependent variable. The denominator was a 10 per cent census of Manchester conducted in 1974 to which the 1971 Census age distribution of a much larger area (the whole of South East Lancashire) was applied. The epidemiological aspect of the study confirmed the findings of others, that Caribbean-born people had a higher first admission rate for all categories of diagnoses (except alcohol/drug addiction and organic psychoses). When compared to the British-born, this excess was most marked for schizophrenia. This study thus confirmed the trends of earlier studies that when hospital admissions are used as a sampling frame, clinical diagnosis of schizophrenia is five to six times more likely to be attributed to those born in the Caribbean than native-born British people. An interesting finding of this study was the apparent excess of schizophrenia in the black groups of 'West Indians' and 'West Africans' but when this black group was compared to matched white controls most of the excess was accounted for by those with 'delusions of persecutions' and therefore, according to the authors, not suffering from 'true schizophrenia'.

The study by Littlewood and Lipsedge (1981) was not an epidemiological study as such since no information is available on how the numerators were related to the denominator population based on the 1971 Census. It is not clear, for example, whether all the 250 consecutive admissions that the authors studied came from the specified catchment area or not. The study used retrospective case note analysis and, on the basis of information thus collected, first admission rate for schizophrenia in patients born in the West Indies was given as 47 per 100,000 per year compared to 19 per 100,000 per year for UK-born residents. What was interesting about this study was the observation that 'psychotic illness' among the Caribbean-born patients was symptomatologically different from that found in white patients and there was much uncertainty associated with a diagnosis of schizophrenia in black patients.

Although the studies conducted in Bristol in 1978–81 (Ineichen et al. 1984; Harrison et al. 1984) were not primarily concerned with inception rates for schizophrenia according to ethnicity, they throw some light on the differential patterns of hospital admission for blacks and whites. The authors studied all admissions to three psychiatric hospitals which together served the whole of the city of Bristol, over a two-year period (1980–1). No diagnostic differentiation was sought within the sample which was categorized according to ethnicity that was established *post hoc*. The rates for compulsory admission in this two year sample were higher in the 'immigrant wards' (sic) of the city, that is to say, in those areas where there was a substantial black population. This ecological trend was confirmed when four-year compulsory admission data (1978–81) were compared with one-year voluntary admissions (1981) according to ethnicity. While 29 per cent of compulsory admission for men were for white UK residents, 58 per cent of such admissions consisted of West Indians. The comparable voluntary admission rates were 75 per cent for whites and 11 per cent for West Indians. There was a similar excess of black women in compulsory admissions.

The next study concerned with ethnic variations in inception rates of psychiatric illness and ethnicity comes from Birmingham, another metropolitan area in England with a multi-ethnic population (McGovern and Cope 1987). The Afro-Caribbean group in the study was separated into first and second generation according to nativity and age or time of migration. Again, like the earlier studies, this was a retrospective case note analysis of 'first admissions' to one psychiatric hospital serving an inner-city catchment area, over a period of four years (1980–3). A complex method, based on the findings of the Labour Force Survey and the National Housing and Dwelling Survey, was used to estimate the number of British-born Afro-Caribbeans. Such denominator calculation for British-born blacks was, at best, only an approximation of the true numbers, as many untested assumptions entered into the calculation. The authors were not able to specify the margin of error in such an estimate and this could seriously undermine the confidence with which the reported rates could be accepted as valid. Once again, hospital inceptions were based on first admissions as recorded in official hospital statistics (thus possibly overestimating first admissions) and case ascertainment was based on the examination of hospital records alone.

The results were consistent with earlier observations, the overall first admission rate as well as that for schizophrenia showing an excess among blacks compared to whites. The 'second generation' rates appeared to be the highest, although the lack of precision in calculating the denominator as well as the likely age association with first admission pose problems in interpretation. For example, the overall first admission rate for 'British-born Afro-Caribbeans' is estimated to be 246 per 100,000 per year, which would vary by 9 per cent if there is a change in the denominator by 100 or a unit change in the numerator.

The most influential study in this area is that of Harrison *et al.* (1988) from

Nottingham. In many ways, this study overcomes many of the methodological shortcomings of earlier work. This is the first epidemiologically based study in this area that used a prospective design involving face-to-face interviews with patients to collect symptom data using a standardized assessment instrument, the Present State Examination (PSE) (Wing *et al.* 1974), for case definition. The sampling frame included all new referrals, including both inpatients and outpatients. Clearly this study is an advance on earlier work. The control sample used, however, was from an earlier study (Cooper *et al.* 1987) also conducted in Nottingham but drawn from a more limited 'at-risk' population of 390,000, while the sample selected by Harrison *et al.* was drawn from a catchment population of 600,000. The results of this study show that the Afro-Caribbeans in Nottingham have one of the highest incidence rates of schizophrenia ever reported in the world literature (259 per 100,000 per year). If true, then one in every 300 Afro-Caribbeans in the 16–29 age group living in Nottingham will develop schizophrenia *every year*, in contrast to the overall *life-time risk* of schizophrenia which, according to all available evidence, is conventionally estimated as just under 1 per cent.

Any study that presents such a claim, entirely out of keeping with previous results of epidemiological studies of schizophrenia or of migrant communities, demands careful scrutiny and explanation. Risk ratios (or relative risk) of 12 to 18, as reported by these authors, if proved true, will be one of the most important findings in aetiological research of schizophrenia, far outstripping in magnitude the effect of most risk factors currently known to us.

What is compelling about this recent research on the epidemiology of mental disorders in Afro-Caribbeans living in England is the fact that this study from Nottingham has overcome many of the methodological problems that undermined the robustness of earlier findings. But, by adopting direct interviews of patients, did this study introduce a different kind of bias? In any detailed consideration of its methods and results, this research must be compared closely with the WHO study, also conducted in Nottingham (Cooper *et al.* 1987), and which was used as a control by Harrison and colleagues. When we do that, contrary to initial impression, a number of important differences become apparent.

The most important of these are in case finding and diagnosis. It is not clear whether the difference in the catchment population in the two studies, an increase of 50 per cent in six years (from 390,000 to 600,000), was associated with ecological changes of any significance. The case finding methods employed also differed in the two studies. In the WHO study, clinicians were asked to complete screening questionnaires which were later scrutinized by research staff to select the sample. Selection was based on symptoms as determined by treating clinicians. In the Harrison *et al.* study, in contrast, sample selection was primarily based on ethnicity and the researchers 'contacted . . . all medical staff . . . either personally or by telephone approximately every two weeks', and there was special screening of all Afro-Caribbean referrals. It is likely that such a case finding method, *screening by ethnicity as against symptoms*, and the use of regular reminders through personal contact, would increase the yield of likely Afro-Caribbean cases. Similarly, the supplementary case register search was based on the category 'likely ethnic origin', unlike in the WHO study, which sampled on the basis of particular diagnostic categories. There is the clear possibility that the attempt to select the sample by ethnicity (identifying all Afro-Caribbean patients who contacted the service) increased the number of black people being actively sampled and this, if true, introduces a potential source of bias in this study. The question of diagnosis also requires further examination. In both studies, consensus diagnosis was accepted on the basis of a structured clinical interview covering symptoms, syndrome checklist, and two other patient rating scales, along with the case notes and personal/family history and disability assessment schedule obtained through informants. Unlike in the WHO study, the patient interview and the informant interview were not blind to each other in the latter study. Most importantly, in the Afro-Caribbean study all information obtained over a period of one month following the entry into the study (including clinical data) was used in making the final diagnosis, while the WHO diagnoses were made on the basis of information available at the time of entry to the study.

Although a standardized diagnostic assessment was carried out using the PSE, the eventual diagnosis was more in keeping with an overall clinical diagnosis than with an operational one. Again, it is not clear whether the two teams achieved reliability in this procedure. Case definition is probably the most crucial aspect of a study such as this and it is interesting to note that in those designated as 'no schizophrenia' 50 per cent of the WHO sample had manic illness while only one in six Afro-Caribbeans achieved a similar diagnosis. It is also quite striking that the WHO sample and the Afro-Caribbean sample differed markedly in their constituent symptoms, as shown by the distribution of CATEGO syndromes.[1]

The age-specific and 'second generation' incidence rates reported by Harrison *et al.* are likely to have large margins of error given the small numbers in such groups and the imprecision inherent in estimating the denominator. Even in the overall rate, a unit change in the numerator or a denominator change of 200 produces a 4 per cent change in the incidence. Hence, the confidence attached to the absolute rates must be seen as unsatisfactory. It is also interesting to note that during the WHO study, six Afro-Caribbeans were identified in the inception sample as having definite schizophrenia. Using an at-risk population of 202,214 from that study and estimating the Afro-Caribbean group as comprising 1.9 per cent of the catchment population (on the basis of ethnic distributions reported in the paper by Harrison *et al.*) the incidence rate for Afro-Caribbeans can be calculated. Such a rate (7.8 per 10,000 per year) is considerably less than Harrison's results and more consistent with a risk ratio (when compared with whites) that would be expected on the basis of earlier studies. It is puzzling that two studies conducted at an interval of only six years, in the same area by researchers from the same institution and apparently using the same methodology, should report such varying rates for the incidence of schizophrenia among Afro-Caribbeans.

Clearly, this study from Nottingham needs to be replicated. In the meanwhile, its authors' observations that Afro-Caribbeans in Nottingham are up to 18 times more likely to develop schizophrenia than whites must be treated with extreme caution. It is highly likely that by using ethnicity as a screening index, by making efforts to include all Afro-Caribbeans in the initial screening sample and by their different case assessment methods to that of the WHO study, they may have contributed to increasing research recognition of schizophrenia in their psychotic group.

As has been shown, the choice of the study sample, especially if it is dependent on hospital admissions, could introduce powerful biases in calculating morbidity rates. We know little about the utilization of psychiatric services in Nottingham by various ethnic groups. In the Nottingham study, among those achieving definite schizophrenia diagnosis, 42 per cent in the Caribbean group were admitted compulsorily while only 23 per cent of whites in this diagnostic category were formal admissions. Another striking difference between the two groups was that while 85 per cent of the white sample were referred by general practitioners, only 33 per cent of the Afro-Caribbean group were referred by this agency. Thirty-eight per cent of the Afro-Caribbeans (as against 7.5 per cent of the whites) were referred by the police and 29 per cent involved a social worker/nurse or psychiatrist (compared to 7.5 per cent in the case of whites) (Harrison 1988).

Even after allowing for discrepancies in case selection and diagnosis, it is important to know the comparability of the Afro-Caribbean and white samples in Nottingham. If ethnicity was the independent variable of choice, then the samples should have been controlled for the effects of other socio-demographic factors which affect health service utilization and risk of schizophrenia. Except for age/sex matching, other factors that might influence incidence data (or more precisely inception into hospital care), including social class, level of economic activity and area of residence, are not mentioned in this study.

Apart from locally based hospital studies, epidemiological research of mental illness according to ethnicity has utilized official sources of data nationally and regionally (Cochrane 1977; Dean *et al.* 1981; Cochrane and Bal 1989). Case registries have also been used to estimate the incidence of psychiatric disorders among various groups according to nativity and ethnicity (Rwegellera 1977; Bebbington *et al.* 1981; Giggs 1986). These studies are not discussed here because the findings of such aggregate studies are even more greatly compromised by the errors and omission in data collection, diagnostic diversity inherent in such data and the lack of appropriate denominators. Their findings, however, appear to confirm the trend that Caribbean people are over-represented in first as well as all hospital admissions for schizophrenia.

Locally based case register studies are, however, of some interest in that they avoid many of the administrative errors inherent in national statistics, can be related to precise catchment population and, most importantly, include all types of psychiatric contact. The two studies based on the Camberwell register (Hemsi 1967; Bebbington *et al.* 1981) both used 10 per cent Census samples in a one-year population estimate although the patient data were derived from up to seven years. Apart from the observation that inception rate for schizophrenia for Caribbean-born patients appeared to be greater than in whites, two other findings of interest emerge from these studies. First, the overall inception rate recorded by the Camberwell case register (for both Caribbean-born and British-born) is in excess of rates found in other hospital admission studies; for example, the study by Bebbington *et al.* (1981) shows the annual inception rate for schizophrenia amongst UK-born males to be 110 per 100,000 for 1971 (five times the national average, and four times as great as the 27 per 100,000 (admission rate) reported from the same area (Hemsi 1967)). The age-corrected rate for black men remains high (over a seven-year period) while there is an excess of black women over white women (by a factor of 3). Second, there would appear to be an increased risk of inception for mania for both men and women born in the West Indies compared to UK-born patients.

This last point is worth emphasizing. The risk of hospital admission for Caribbean-born people is raised not just for schizophrenia but also for mania. Corroborative evidence is available from the cross-national study by Leff *et al.* (1976) which showed that the rate of first admission for mania was more than six times as high for Caribbean-born people living in Camberwell as for native-born people. The sample size in this study was rather small, but this observation is consistent with the results of other studies (Bebbington *et al.* 1981). Similarly, when Dean *et al.* (1981) studied first admissions to psychiatric hospitals in South East England they found that women born in the Caribbean had a higher rate than native-born women for schizophrenia as well as for the additional psychosis category 'other psychoses'.

Conclusion

The most consistent feature in the epidemiology of schizophrenia is the variability of rates in international comparison (Torrey 1980; Murphy 1982; Warner 1985). Such variations may be partly due to differences in case selection and diagnosis but all the discrepancies in reported rates cannot be adequately accounted for by methodological factors alone. It is also true to say that such reported variations in rates do not follow any recognizable pattern.

In studies conducted within the same population (ethnically homogeneous groups) variations in rates for schizophrenia according to social class, marital status, levels of economic activity and geographic location have been reported. Some of this variability may be accounted for by 'illness-related factors' but there appears to be robust evidence to suggest that the occurrence of schizophrenia is not independent of social and other cultural factors (Dohrenwend and Dohrenwend 1964; Cochrane 1984). In the last few years, however, much psychiatric research in relation to schizophrenia has moved away from detailed consideration of such potential sources of 'disease' variability, and instead there is a greater emphasis on genetic and biological factors in spite of the major conceptual and methodological problems in this area (Rose et al. 1984; Pam 1990).

This review of the epidemiology of schizophrenia according to ethnicity in England has emphasized the problems with much of the current data. Our contention is that the studies to date are seriously flawed in that they try to understand excess hospital admission rates for schizophrenia found in Afro-Caribbeans as indicative of individual pathology. With a few exceptions (Moodley and Perkins 1987), the process of hospitalization itself is rarely considered as meriting serious study. Methodological problems make the interpretation of these results difficult. The question of diagnosis (there can be little doubt that the diagnosis of schizophrenia means different things in black and white patients) and the issue of case selection are central to such problems. On the whole, case control designs employed in these studies have largely ignored the confounding effects of a variety of socio-demographic factors, including social class, on the dependent variable, that is, hospital admission or the likelihood of a diagnosis of psychosis. The choice of ethnicity (and ethnicity alone) as the independent variable signifies the ideological thrust of many of these studies but detracts from their scientific validity.

Issues of aetiology are also relevant in the consideration of present 'transcultural' or inter-ethnic research in psychiatry. Vulnerability to psychiatric disorders according to ethnicity has been a recurrent theme in psychiatric literature for a long time. The politics of such transcultural work has been commented upon previously (Black Health Workers and Patients Group 1983; Mercer 1986; Sashidharan 1986) and our conclusion is that much of the current research in the area of Afro-Caribbeans and schizophrenia is similarly undermined by the ideological legacy of the race science of the eighteenth and nineteenth centuries. The scientific credibility attached to such work can be contextualized in terms of the changing nature of British racial politics and it is no surprise that the pathologization of black people in the UK is taken a step further by the 'racialization' of schizophrenia.

This chapter, however is not meant to be a full exploration of the politics and ideology of transculturalism. Our aim has been to provide a critique of the current status of transcultural epidemiology from a rather limited perspective, that of scientific methodology and conventional academic discourse. The problem here is not whether rates of mental illness or schizophrenia vary across populations but how such variations are understood and articulated in scientific papers. Our conclusion is that by choosing an arbitrary and theoretically unsound division across 'ethnicity' as the independent variable in research in this area, much of which is unsatisfactory and invalid, psychiatry has become a powerful vehicle for articulating ideas about race rather than distress, disease or illness.

Note

1 CATEGO refers to syndromal categorization based on constitutent symptoms elicited by using a standardized interview and derived through a computer algorithm.

7

Healthy margins: black elders' care – models, policies and prospects

NAINA PATEL

Introduction

Ageing is not a matter of choice. But how it is experienced is dependent upon many factors. To notice that in Britain there are today a substantial and increasing number of older people (approximately 9 million aged 60 or over) would be a good start, since being aware may lead us to assess how our society values the old and provides for their needs. Changing current attitudes towards older people necessitates a change in the equation, 'retirement from work equals retirement from life'. It is not surprising that this view has given rise to expressions such as 'the grannie boom' or the 'greying explosion' and the perception of the old as a burden. And if the plight of the UK's elders is poor (King's Fund 1992), that of black[1] elders is arguably even worse.

This chapter first considers the overall characteristics of black elders and then looks at some of the major issues in the provision of health and social services. Inevitably the politics of 'race' cannot be divorced from the wider changes, such as the NHS reforms and the NHS and Community Care Act 1990. The implications of these will be briefly examined.

Although the 1980s witnessed several locally based empirical studies into the needs and demands of the black elderly, research into specific health provision issues is still in its infancy. The under-researching of this area may be due to a number of reasons: the general 'invisibility' of black people in welfare services; the assumption of insignificant numbers of black older people; the notion that black families 'care for their own'; or simply that the topic does not have the same 'attraction' for researchers as, say, black people and schizophrenia.

Nevertheless, the relative absence of health research[2] into issues for black elders does not (and should not) invalidate their experience of another welfare sector, the social services. It is generally accepted that the NHS has been less responsive to the needs of black and minority ethnic groups than the social services (Johnson 1987). Bowl and Barnes (1990: 15), in considering joint health and social service professionals' working relationships, state that 'relations with health authorities were often seen as problematic. Even when they were good, and this was easier at the planning level than on the ground, race and mental health was not seen as a fundamental issue' by health authorities. So reference to social services developments and their critique would be instructive for our purpose. Other complementary studies in health and 'race' will also be referred to in order to make specific deductions.

The demography of the black elderly population

The number of over-65s in the UK has increased from 5.5 million in 1951 to about 9 million in 1990 and is expected to rise to 11.3 million by 2025. A similar trend follows for those over 80; accounting for 2.8 per cent (1.6 million) of the population in 1981, and projected to 4.2 per cent (2.5 million) by 2001 (Central Statistical Office (CSO) 1991: Table 1.2). Add to this the dependency costs of the very old and the consequences for social policy and health care expenditure are considerable. According to the Association of British Pharmaceutical Industry, between 1991 and 2001, a 5 per cent increase in hospital and community health spending and a 17 per cent increasing on spending on long-term care (estimated rise of £1.4 billion in real terms, since current costs approximate £8 billion a year) will be required (*Guardian*, 30 September 1991).

Within this context, the black minority elderly currently number over 100,000. Contrasting ageing in the black and white populations, about one-fifth were aged over 45 compared to two-fifths of the white population (Shaw 1988b). By 1988 about 4 per cent of the black population had reached retirement age. Table 7.1 indicates the distribution of the population by age and ethnicity.

With the 'approaching' elderly group (45–59-year-olds), it is clear that within the next decade the number of black elders will more than double. According to *Social Trends* (CSO 1992), 13 per cent of the black population will be in this category. Moreover, there will be variations among the black elderly groups regarding age distribution and location. So while the demographic profile indicates that overall the Asian elders will increase three

Table 7.1   Black elderly population by ethnicity

Total ethnic minority population	2,580,000
Those aged 60 or over	
Indian	39,350
West Indian or Guyanese	34,650
Pakistani	8,560
Bangladeshi	2,160
Chinese	6,250
African	3,360
Arab	4,380
Mixed	8,610
Total	117,320

Source: Annual Labour Force Survey 1986–88, cited in Local
Government Information Unit (1991).

to seven times in the next 15 years, in some geographical areas this is
unlikely. For example, given the relative youth of the Nottingham Asian
community, the number of Asian elders is very small (Fenton 1987; Ebrahim
et al. 1991). Numbers are important in needs assessment and planning, but
this importance should not be exaggerated. Contrary to those who quibble
about 'precise' numbers of black elders, it is worth citing Fenton (1987): 'the
1991 elderly will not only be a larger group, but will also include many more
older elderly people in their 70s and 80s (rather than 60s)' (1987: 13) 'where
questions of care become very much more urgent'(1987: 30).

Black elders: poverty and health

Historical and social factors have determined the economic and social
position of black elders in Britain today. These factors have affected them as
a group throughout the process of migration and settlement, frequently in
the context of a struggle against racism and poverty. Black elders' health and
health needs cannot be understood without reference to their experience of
employment, housing and income.

Although black people have been in Britain for over 500 years (File and
Power 1981; Fryer 1984), most of today's black elders in Britain arrived from
the Indian sub-continent, the Caribbean, East Africa and Hong Kong in their
twenties and thirties as postwar migrants. The state was engaged in their
active recruitment (London Transport, the British Hotels and Restaurants
Association, not to mention Enoch Powell, who as a Health Minister openly
welcomed Caribbean nurses!).

Figure 7.1 shows the unequal distribution of black workers by sector and
industry in the 1970s. The unevenness is explained by differences in labour

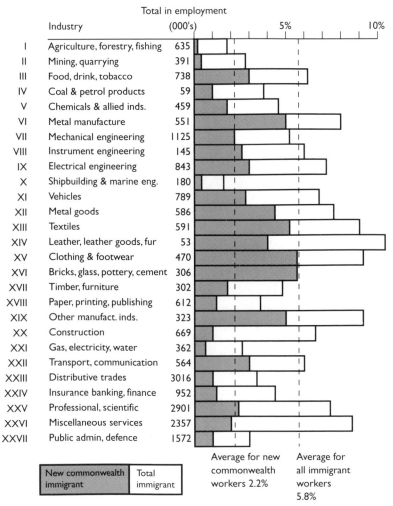

	Industry	Total in employment (000's)
I	Agriculture, forestry, fishing	635
II	Mining, quarrying	391
III	Food, drink, tobacco	738
IV	Coal & petrol products	59
V	Chemicals & allied inds.	459
VI	Metal manufacture	551
VII	Mechanical engineering	1125
VIII	Instrument engineering	145
IX	Electrical engineering	843
X	Shipbuilding & marine eng.	180
XI	Vehicles	789
XII	Metal goods	586
XIII	Textiles	591
XIV	Leather, leather goods, fur	53
XV	Clothing & footwear	470
XVI	Bricks, glass, pottery, cement	306
XVII	Timber, furniture	302
XVIII	Paper, printing, publishing	612
XIX	Other manufact. inds.	323
XX	Construction	669
XXI	Gas, electricity, water	362
XXII	Transport, communication	564
XXIII	Distributive trades	3016
XXIV	Insurance banking, finance	952
XXV	Professional, scientific	2901
XXVI	Miscellaneous services	2357
XXVII	Public admin, defence	1572

New commonwealth immigrant / Total immigrant

Average for new commonwealth workers 2.2%

Average for all immigrant workers 5.8%

Figure 7.1 'Immigrant' workers as a percentage of the total workforce by industry
Source: Runnymede Trust (1980).

requirements between various industries and discrimination by employers and unions (Smith 1977; 1981; Brown 1984). Once obtaining jobs, black workers also bore the brunt of discrimination in earnings, as Smith (1977: 11) states:

in the case of non-manual workers, earnings for white workers were £52.4 compared to £40.5 for black workers; for skilled manual workers were £39.3 compared with £35.6 for black workers; while earnings of semi-skilled and unskilled manual workers are exactly the same.

Moreover, there is a greater range of earnings at different job levels among white workers than among the minorities.

This disparity in earnings in the 'working period' as well as the *length* of working life, directly accounts for differences in pensionable income. Black elders' pensionable income is further reduced by the level of National Insurance contributions; by the type of and access to occupational pension schemes; by the levels and period of unemployment experienced; and, in many cases, by their status as 'dependants', thereby reducing their entitlement to state income benefits.[3] The current experience of poverty for many black elders is determined by the above factors. Their poverty is further compounded by the state's failure to remove racial barriers to claiming welfare benefits, such as attendance allowance, income support and heating allowances (Farrah 1986; Holland and Lewando-Hundt 1986).[4]

Material deprivation is a major factor in explaining inequalities in health (Townsend and Davidson 1982; Whitehead 1987). As Townsend (1990: 386) states: 'this conclusion carried a powerful implication for the construction of poverty. The elimination or reduction of material deprivation and not just the organisation of more efficient health care services had to become a national objective for action.'

Victor (1991), in a recent study, using data from the General Household Surveys of 1980 and 1985 and Mortality Statistics, noted that about 71 per cent of deaths of the elderly (65 +) are due to heart disease, stroke, cancer and respiratory diseases. She shows (Victor 1991: 33) that:

in both 1980 and 1985, there were statistically significant differences between social classes in the prevalence of chronic ill health and in perceived health status. Consistently those elderly from the professional and managerial classes experience better health than their contemporaries from the manual occupational groups . . . The prevalence of chronic illness of those aged 75–79 from the semi-skilled and unskilled classes is higher than that for those aged 80 and over from classes I and II. Within each social class I and II there is a clear trend for women to experience poorer health than their male counterparts.

As Figure 7.1 shows, black elders have occupied a vulnerable position in Britain, being largely concentrated in working-class occupations. Consequently, they have faced health hazards through high concentration of employment in foundries, textiles, transport and nightshift work. Looking at the other side of the equation, several writers (Kushnick 1988; Ahmad 1989; Torkington 1991) have argued about the nature of health care services and the ideology surrounding them in relation to black patients. This inevitably requires us to examine the NHS *per se* as the major provider of health care in Britain.

Moreover, black elders are one section of black patients – the individual and institutional racism explained by those writers is also part of the continuum working against black elders' health care. For example, linguistic and cultural barriers, use of racial and cultural stereotypes, professional and medical ideology and scientific racism are applied to *all* black patients – though clearly there will be variations according to gender, class, age and disability since their respective ideologies intersect with 'race' to reproduce differential outcomes.

However, the focus on individuals and their 'cultures' produces a reductionist process which, by using the individual and his/her culture as the central unit of analysis, in turn produce racist explanations and effects. Critiques of such culture-blaming approaches to the health issues facing black populations are presented elsewhere in this volume (see chapters by Ahmad, Stubbs, Sashidharan and Francis).

Health problems and characteristics

Black elders face a range of health problems and the mainstream health and social services have been inadequate in meeting their needs[5] (Bhalla and Blakemore 1981; Farrah 1986; Bowling 1990). Where developments have taken place, they have largely depended on black self-help projects attempting to meet the basic needs of black elders, particularly in day care centre provision. We shall return to this point later.

Regarding common health problems treated in day and health centres, the findings of two significant surveys by Bhalla and Blakemore (1981), a Birmingham-based survey which was also the first of its kind on black elders, and by Farrah (1986), a Leicester based study, are summarized in Table 7.2.

Table 7.2   Health problems reported by the elders, by 'ethnic' group (per cent)

Problem	Afro-Caribbean		Asian Birmingham only (N = 169)	European Birmingham only (N = 52)
	Birmingham (N = 179)	Leicester (N = 109)		
Sight	61	89	53	52
Feet/walking	50	28	36	48
Hearing	7	12	22	31
Dental	15	30	21	10
Depression	na	26	na	na
Forgetfulness	na	34	na	na

Sources: Bhalla and Blakemore (1981); Farrah (1986).

A more recent survey by Ebrahim *et al.* (1991) of Gujarati elders in North London found them to be more prone to diabetes, asthma, gastro-intestinal bleeding, cataracts, heart disease and strokes than white groups. Table 7.3 shows the prevalence of diagnoses, while Table 7.4 demonstrates the common problems of Asian elders. These findings suggest little differences between the 'Asian' and 'indigenous' subjects. However, Ebrahim *et al.* (1991: 60) suggest that the higher use of prescribed medications by Asian elders may be 'due to the increased frequency of diagnosed disease'. Similarly, the higher levels of life satisfaction are explained by 'the need to maintain an optimistic state of mind in the face of getting older in a foreign country. High life satisfaction may be related to a more spiritual dimension in the life of Asian elders; a subject commented that he felt that old age was a time of coming to terms with one's self and with God' (1991: 60). Alternatively, the Asian elders may have simply come to expect *less* from life: lower expectations result in assessing the current state of life as satisfactory.

It is necessary to emphasize here that the sample consisted predominantly of one section of Asians, the Gujaratis; commenting on their class position, the authors state that their 'findings relate to a relatively wealthy group of Gujarati Asians living in north London' (1991: 61). Such studies indicate the importance of not regarding black people as a homogeneous group and of the relationship between 'race' and class.

The Bhalla and Blakemore and Ebrahim *et al.*'s studies provide evidence for a relatively higher use of health services, including general practitioners, by elderly Afro-Caribbean and Asians compared to white groups. However, frequency of contact with GPs and hospitals (Table 7.5) does not indicate the quality of treatment received, as shown by Table 7.6. For instance, why is it that for all three ethnic groups, hearing problems were largely untreated? Bhalla and Blakemore (1981: 27) emphasize the need for further examination to explain the reasons for lack of treatment: 'Are the problems caused by language and cultural factors, or are they a result of GPs not asking the right questions? The cost of treatment if compared to the expense of hospitalisation of an elderly patient would be minimal and a saving for the National Health Service.' Sadly, these questions have remained unanswered for over a decade.

Effective communication is a prerequisite to gaining access to services. Information on the system of benefits and services (such as Department of Health guidance on growing old and health; advice and education leaflets on health promotion) is disseminated through leaflets and application forms with the assumption that the potential recipients speak, read and write English, an assumption which should not even be made for all white clients (Stimson and Webb 1975). The inability to communicate in English disadvantages recipients. Indeed, even when leaflets are translated into appropriate community languages, one should not assume that *all* elderly

Table 7.3 Prevalence of diagnoses in Asian and indigenous subjects (per cent)

	Asian		Indigenous	
	Men (n = 34)	Women (n = 25)	Men (n = 34)	Women (n = 25)
Myocardial infarction	21	0	9	0
Diabetes mellitus	6	16	9	0
Hypertension	12	16	24	16
Stroke	9	4	3	0
Chronic bronchitis	3	8	18*	12
Asthma	9	12	0	4
Peptic ulcer	6	12	0	8

Note: * $p < 0.05$ (Asian men versus indigenous men).
Source: Ebrahim et al. (1991: 59).

Table 7.4 Common problems of old age in Asian and indigenous subjects (per cent)

	Asian		Indigenous	
	Men (n = 34)	Women (n = 25)	Men (n = 34)	Women (n = 25)
Visual impairment	15	8	15	4
Hearing impairment	35	24	26	20
Depressed mood	6	8	0	16
Low life satisfaction	53	64	79	80*
Falls	6	16	18	24
Incontinence of urine	3	8	9	12
Use of walking stick	25	8	6	4*
On prescribed medication	68	72	41	40**

Notes:
* $p < 0.05$ (Asian men versus indigenous men)
** $p < 0.05$ (Both groups).
Source: Ebrahim et al. (1991: 59).

Table 7.5a Contact with GP and hospital (per cent)

Contact	Afro-Caribbean	Asians	Europeans
Seen GP within last month	68	57	57
Visited hospital because of ill health in past 12 months	42	25	29
Been an inpatient in hospital in past 12 months	20	13	15

Source: Bhalla and Blakemore (1981: 26).

Table 7.5b

Contact[1]	Asian		Indigenous	
	Men (n = 34)	Women (n = 25)	Men (n = 34)	Women (n = 25)
Seen GP within last month	26	44	24	24
Visited hospital because of ill health in past 12 months	41	52	41	48
Been an inpatient in hospital in past 12 months	24	12	6	4*
Seen nurse within last month	0	8	6	0
Seen chiropodist within last 6 months	3	4	6	24*
Seen dentist within last year	44	32	56	60*
Seen optician within last year	65	56	59	68
Seen alternative practitioner within last year	3	20	0	8
Hospital inpatient	24	12	6	4*

Notes:
* $p < 0.05$ (Asian women versus indigenous women)
[1] Author's adaptation of categories.
Source: Ebrahim *et al.* (1991: 60).

Table 7.6   (a) Percentage of elders reporting ailments; (b) Percentage of elders reporting ailments who are not receiving treatment

Ailments	Afro-Caribbean	Asians	Europeans	Total
(a)				
Poor eyesight	61	53	52	57
Feet/walking difficulties	50	36	48	44
Poor hearing	7	22	31	17
Dental problems	15	21	10	17
(b)				
Poor eyesight	43	32	41	38
Feet/walking difficulties	32	48	32	38
Poor hearing	85	70	56	70
Dental problems	65	40	40	50

Source: Bhalla and Blakemore (1981: 26).

speakers of such languages are necessarily literate in those languages. Minorities other than Asians and Afro-Caribbeans also experience problems in communication (Lim 1979; Norman 1985). Table 7.7 illustrates this point by comparing level of knowledge of and potential take-up of services by Asian and white users.

It is clear from the above and other studies (Bhalla and Blakemore 1981;

Table 7.7   The level of knowledge and potential use of services (per cent)

Service	Service unknown[*]		Potential use[*]	
	Asian	White	Asian	White
District nurse	57	14	80	78
Bath nurse	76	32	66	69
Chiropody	64	9	75	82
Home help	62	1	54	78
Meals on wheels	58	0	54	62
Social workers	44	6	69	74
Day care	60	18	54	59
(N)	(81)	(55)		

Note: [*]Author's modification in title
Table excludes those who already receive services, so N varies by service.
Source: Atkin et al. (1989: 441).

Farrah 1986; Holland and Lewando-Hundt 1986) that if sufficient information about services were made available it would be used by black elders. It is necessary to note that even where services for ethnic minorities are developed, for example – link-workers and health visitors – they are limited to 'maternity or child health services . . . but no schemes involving health visitors for elderly people have been reported' (Pharoah and Redmond 1991). But qualifications are in order: for example, meals must reflect the elders' religious and cultural beliefs, and the preference for male nurses to bathe men should be respected. And yet in an era where women's preference for female doctors/nurses is increasingly seen as acceptable, and consumer choice is regarded as an indication of individual rights, we still hear of many personal denials and tragedies relating to black elders (Rooney 1987). In a case highlighted recently, a 90-year-old Hindu man, a strict vegetarian, was forced to eat meat in a residential home. This happened in a London borough where 25 per cent of the population is Asian (Moore 1991). Translation and interpretation facilities, though important, do not in themselves address the problem of appropriateness of services.

What, then, prevents health and social services from making the necessary changes to ensure that services are accessible, appropriate and geared to meeting the growing demands? In the example just highlighted, the authority's response ranged from 'lack of provision on the difficulties of catering for Hindu dietary needs and recruiting Guj[a]rati-speaking staff' to 'no demand for residential care of Asian older people because traditionally families looked after their own relatives' (Moore 1991).

Let us examine this latter point in detail. It is indeed a popular image that an extended network of 'families within families' provides care and social-psychological support. Strangely, such virtues are married to a stereotype of 'overcrowded households'. Family structures are continually changing as they adjust to internal and external conditions; black families are not immune from this process (Westwood and Bachu 1988). According to Bhalla and Blakemore (1981), the extended family played a more prominent part in the care of Asian elders than of Afro-Caribbean and European elders, when discharged from hospital. However they comment that 'very little help was obtained from the community resources' (1981: 27). The important question is not whether extended family structures exist, but whether black elders are receiving the necessary forms of care from the health and social care system according to their requirements, irrespective of the nature of the family structure. 'They look after their own' is a useful myth and constitutes a cost-effective evasion, maintaining the status quo in services. This myth is sadly operationalized by many professional staff, including black GPs, who do not refer black older people to existing services, believing that their needs are best provided for by the presence of extended families. In the absence of such families, for black older people *no referrals* to services means *no assessment* of their needs, hence *no services*. The myth essentially determines the eligibility criteria for services, not the rights or needs of black older people.

Since health care is a public good (meaning that it is notionally available to *all*), it is often said that 'we treat everyone the same'; 'our service is open to all'; 'providing for special needs is discriminatory – it is racism in reverse'. Given the preceding information on inadequate provision of health and social services and consistent evidence that services would be used if they were accessible and appropriate, it is necessary to explain the continued neglect of unmet collective needs of black elders.

Racisms and service delivery

Figure 7.2 provides the basis for understanding the responses from health and social services to the care of black elders. As Figure 7.2a shows, the need for health and social services is determined by the material and structural conditions in wider society. Since racism is fully integrated into the economic core of society it will inevitably interact with a range of cultural, social, political and ideological agendas (see segment 2, in Figure 7.2b).

Take *individual racism*, for example. People are not born racist, but years of exploitation and racial subordination justified by racist claims (through scientific theories of racial superiority or 'new racism' based on socio-biology) influence people's conciousness and the individual sense of 'self' which is expressed in their normal behaviour and practice.[6] So ordinary problems of care are solved (or not solved) in the context of staff's judgements influenced, in part, by racist perceptions (see also the chapters by Ahmad, Stubbs, and Sashidharan and Francis in this volume). In Atkin *et al.* (1989: 442), a nurse

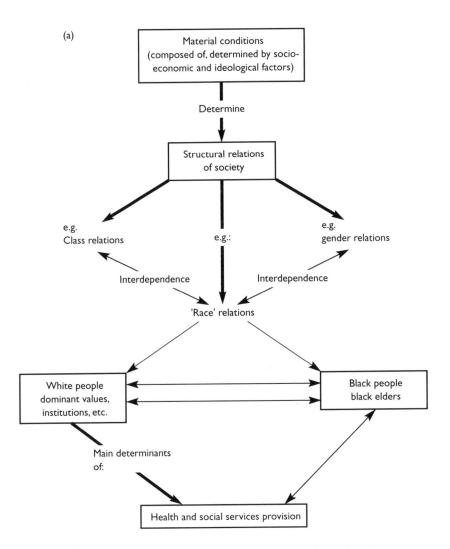

Figure 7.2(a) The position of black elders in the structure of British society

reporting on elderly Asian men said 'they expect you to do it all; you have to bully them. They are very stubborn'. Another district nurse said 'they come to the surgery with trivial things . . . it is because they have a lower pain threshold'. The issue here is how ordinary problems are interpreted and dealt with through inappropriately based or preconceived ideas of racial identity and stereotypes. As for GPs, Ahmad *et al.*'s (1991) study on their perception of Asian and 'non-Asian' patients found them more frequently holding negative attitudes towards Asians than towards other patients. 'Consultations with Asians were felt to be less satisfying; they were thought

(b)

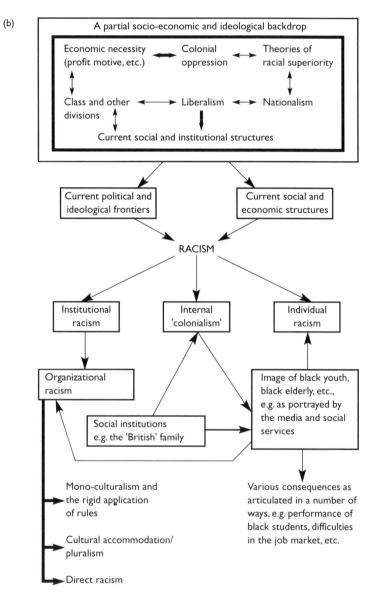

Figure 7.2(b)   A conceptual framework for the analysis of British racism and its consequences, particularly at the organizational level
Source: Patel (1990: 37, 50).

to require longer consultations, to be less compliant and perceived to make excessive use of health care' (1991: 54). These attitudes highlight the role of 'influential professions' in affecting service provision and the nature of 'care', often to those who are in greatest need and least effective in exercising their rights.

The second aspect of racism, in Figure 7.2b, refers to *internal colonialism*. Carmichael and Hamilton (1967) first suggested broad similarities between institutional racism and colonialism, with the former operating *internally* in the USA and resulting in the exploitation of black Americans in the economic, political and social spheres. This concept need not refer only to white–black relations, but can also include the exploitation of women, working-class and other groups. In the context of the NHS, the employment of black staff illustrates the operation of internal colonialism at its sharpest (see also Ward, this volume).

The CRE, in its study of 14 regional health authorities in England in 1987, found that 'four out of ten white doctors and five out of ten ethnic minority doctors felt that there was discrimination in the Health Service' (Kushnick 1988: 75). Six months later, another report confirmed that race discrimination affected all NHS workers from ancillary workers to consultants (Mohammed 1987). These issues are discussed in detail by Ward (this volume).

Institutional racism

'Institutional racism' is a popular term, particularly in health and social services authorities attempting to introduce or implement equal opportunities and/or anti-racist policies. Jones defines institutional racism as 'those established laws, customs, and practices which systematically reflect and produce racial inequalities . . . if racist consequences accrue to institutional laws, customs or practices the institution is racist whether or not the individuals maintaining those practices have racist intentions' (cited in Williams 1985). Viewing institutional racism in the context of organizations (referred to as 'organizational racism'), we can further sub-divide this for our analysis into: mono-culturalism and the rigid application of rules; cultural accomodation/cultural pluralism; and direct racism.

Mono-culturalism and the rigid application of rules

Professional staff are guided by specific professional ideologies. The dominant method of conceptualizing needs is based on notions of dependency, passivity and compliance of patients (particularly accentuated for older patients). Black elders have been 'inserted' into a concept of care which views *all* elders as a homogeneous group entitled to services on the basis of established practices. But to receive these established services requires information about their existence; awareness of *how* to obtain them; and assessment of entitlement by 'professional' staff. This shows that although the organizational system may not deliberately discriminate, the very system of established practices precludes black patients, as we saw earlier, from obtaining community services (Bhalla and Blakemore 1981; Atkin *et al.* 1989).[7] Consider also the increasing withdrawal of health resources (for example, through closures) from inner cities. It is most unlikely that health authorities deliberately strive to withdraw these resources because black people are concentrated in inner cities (Grant 1988). We know, however, that inner cities and poverty accompany each other. Inner cities are characterized by poor housing stock and previous low availability of health resources. Given the black elders' housing and income situation, the withdrawal of health resources would have an adverse effect on them and compound problems in access to services.

An organization's propensity to change or be flexible generally determines whether services can be 'client-oriented'. The institutional belief that the efficient functioning of a service is through a strict adherence to rules and regulations which take precedence over the rights and needs of clients is likely to ensure 'inertial racism'. Also, the operation of 'professionalism' by a range of personnel mitigates against organizational change. This may be true also of black health professionals. Commenting on negative attitudes of Asian doctors towards their Asian patients, Ahmad *et al.* (1991: 150) state:

> although linguistic barriers between the doctor and patient are not present, there are others of class, educational snobbery, and status. Like all professionals, doctors are socialised into particular ways of perceiving patients; internalisation of racist stereotypes of patients, therefore, is not entirely surprising.

Cultural accommodation/cultural pluralism

The health authorities which have introduced interpretation services, provide information on community services via translation of leaflets, employ link-workers or cater for diverse dietary needs have largely responded to pressures from black groups and committed individual staff. These 'culturally sound' services are important and may make considerable difference to the individual black elders' experience of health care. But is this sufficient? If the treatment elsewhere is unchanged, leaving staff's perceptions of black people intact and mainstream services remaining mono-cultural, the 'culturally sound' service, though necessary, is only a peripheral accommodation reflecting black people's relegation to the margins of society.

Direct racism

The emergence of equal opportunities policies in many health authorities is in part due to a recognition of the existence of direct discrimination[8] in employment and services. The values and practices mentioned in our explanation of individual and organizational racism, underlie the ideas and practice of direct racism: a denial of the black presence or, alternatively, a recognition of the black presence but denial of equal rights and entitlement to different services. Either way, marginalization remains. The following case illustrates this:

> In 1981 when lawyers acting for Ibrahim Khan, who had been thrown out of a window by three youths, wrote to St Mary's Hospital in London to request a letter from the hospital so that a claim for criminal compensation could be made on his behalf, they received the following reply.
>
> No one here is prepared to write a report for you about this patient . . . Mr Khan has been extremely fortunate to receive treatment that exceeds the cost of a heart transplant. There is absolutely no reason why this patient should receive preferential treatment or become a burden on the tax payers here. I find it immoral to use public money allowing Mr Khan to become a burden on their dwindling resources. Signed: Orthopaedic secretary and over-burdened tax payer. (Kushnick 1988: 467)

Such attitudes and practices are not isolated. They reflect and justify the treatment of black people as second-class citizens – and would have particularly negative consequences for black elders. As shown above, different forms of racisms (individual, direct, organizational) are inextricably interlinked and legitimate a general marginalization of black people – old and young, women and men.

Black elders' care

In the meantime, who has been caring for black elders when they require it? The simplest answer is black elders themselves: they are not passive by any means. First, family, community or religious-centre gatherings become the source of mutual exchange for traditional forms of health information and solutions.[9] Second, black elders undertake a whole range of responsibilities in order to care for the young and old within the family, as do other black carers – relatives and friends (Bhalla and Blakemore 1981). Third, self-help projects in the black voluntary sector, in the absence of health and social services provision, meet black elders' obvious needs. Day centres, for example, are an essential lifeline for black elders, not only receiving services the centres provide but also in reducing acute levels of isolation. In a recent study of four projects in Berkshire, Lancashire, Northampton and Southall, Bowling (1990: 43), commenting on existing service provision, noted:

more often project workers found themselves in a 'service provision vacuum' and faced with a 'bottomless need' for immediate and on-going services. It was consistently found that prior to the projects being set up, very few or no resources had been passed from voluntary or statutory agencies to minority community organisations for care of the elderly. In many cases this lack of resources meant that there was no pre-existing service provision to this group.

This ties in with Norman's (1985) extensive study of black voluntary projects and has led Lalljie (quoted in Glendenning and Pearson 1988: 55) to comment that 'it is the existence of such facilities that have rendered black elders visible: without them, these elders would have remained scattered and invisible'. Pharoah and Redmond (1991) cite the potential for success when mainstream services (through health visitors) link up with day centres in the black voluntary sector in setting up *Look After Yourself* (LAY) programmes as part of health promotion and prevention of heart disease. Their particular case study illustrates further:

1 that health visitors 'in helping elderly people are a particularly valuable resource to the Asian community because, with the exception of GPs, Asian elders are very isolated from community health and social services' and 'the specific health risks of this group lie in preventable diseases' (1991: 22);
2 the additional role played by the co-ordinator's insight and rapport with the community at the day centre made up for resource deficits of the concerned health authority when it came to interpretation service;
3 that the success of the LAY programme depended upon the very existence of the day centre which provided the channel between mainstream health service and black elders.

However, sadly most such projects are small-scale, existing on shoestring and temporary budgets (Blakemore 1985; Bowling 1990; Patel 1990; Jeyasingham 1992). They cannot be expected to provide comprehensive services for *all* black elders in the community. Nor can they reach all sections such as frail elders and the disabled – particularly critical when the incidence of diabetes and arthritis is reported to be high among black groups (Torkington 1991). Bowling (1990: 50) raises a critical question in the conclusion to his study, in which all four projects shared the problem of short-term funding:

to what extent is it possible for Central Government, Local Government, Age Concern and other voluntary organisations to retain credibility for their claims of 'commitment' to 'helping the community to care' when low cost, community-based initiatives which are up and running, demonstrating consistent support for elderly people within the community, are allowed to die through lack of long-term funds?

It is important to note here that despite the crucial role of the black voluntary sector in the care of black elders in the absence of mainstream services, they *are* playing a *substitute* role (not complementary as in the traditional white voluntary sector). In essence black self-help projects have become the *primary* providers of care. Such projects are often financially supported and positively viewed by mainstream health and social services because they provide a 'buffer' against direct criticism of failure to provide mainstream services. Since they are characterized by small budgets, often on short-term basis, a 'fringe' provision is created which in a climate of financial stringencies can be trimmed, cut or stopped, as shown by Bowling (1990). Arguments about autonomy and effectiveness cannot be sustained when such groups are marginalized (in their resource base) but are required to be the primary providers of care at the same time. The functioning of such an arrangement simply assigns black elders to a marginal existence in the overall marginalization of black people.

The future in the 'community care' society

Looking to this decade (the 1990s), the NHS and Community Care Act 1990, with its market-orientated approach and unwillingness to recognize structural barriers to services to black elders, threatens to exacerbate their situation within an increasingly chaotic and shrinking welfare society. In considering joint working between community nursing and social services, Bebbington and Charnley (1990: 424), in their survey of 176 elders receiving both community health and social services, comment:

> most government and academic reports focus on the problems created by organisation fragmentation. However, we shall focus on three specific difficulties relating to staff and field practice: these stem from the continuing low priority given to work with the elderly; the different traditions and professional paradigms of health and social care; and the pressure that is put on field working as a result of resource constraints.

Add to this the stereotyping, gatekeeping, organizational, individual and direct racisms, and one begins to appreciate how effectively these work to keep black elders 'out of the market' – according to the market dynamic, if they cannot register demand for services, it follows that they *do not* have need for such a provision! Will, therefore, the inverse care law continue to apply, that is, those with greatest need get least in quantity and quality of care from the NHS? The fact that there is now a reference in the legislation concerning 'particular care needs and problems' of 'minority communities' and that 'good community care will take account of the circumstances of minority communities and will be planned in consultation with them' (Secretary of State for Health 1989: 10–11) should be regarded as progress. At least 'minority communities' are now recognized and the need to provide specific services is legitimized. At present the reference would only be meaningful to black people, if we assumed the following:

1 Appropriate services are already developed and *exist* – the question that would remain then is *who* provides them.
2 Service staff have the necessary skills and knowledge to make an appropriate assessment of 'needs', and these are set within a system which acknowledges the prevalence of racism and poverty. Services can then be designed, planned, developed and delivered with appropriate resources.
3 Existing information on black people's usage of mainstream and voluntary services is sufficient. This information is necessary to build a profile of the 'specific local market' for services and in assessing the potential demand for these for making future plans.

The reality, however, suggests otherwise: a cursory glance at some community care plans suggests that only a few authorities still wish to undertake surveys in needs assessment or establish pilot studies for the development of services. As mentioned earlier, information on the health of black older people nationally is unavailable: there may, therefore, be good reasons for undertaking needs assessment surveys. Nevertheless, the important point here is whether such exercises delay the provision of services unnecessarily. If health care services to black elders were regarded with some urgency, needs surveys (if required) would be undertaken quickly or deductions made from existing information (for example the local surveys cited in this chapter). The crucial point, it would seem from anecdotal evidence, is a general lack of urgency as far as authorities are concerned on the issue of specific services to black elders: those that are doing something are doing too little; the others are not doing anything at all. In the language of the 'market', the demand is there – but not the supply. Over and above the general arguments concerning major changes and the resultant chaos and shrinkage of resources experienced by health and social services sectors, if the underlying view is that black elders do not have specific needs within health care (the colour-blind approach) it then follows that there is no need for targeting of resources for developments, including education and training on 'race' and anti-racism, to alter the current situation of inappropriate and inaccessible services, use (or misuse) of interpreters, link-workers as 'intermediaries' and so on.

In these circumstances, health professionals can use their considerable power to bring about changes in staff training and health policy, with resource shifts to ensure the appropriateness of services for the rapid rise in the growth of black elders. For example, it is recognized that black elders make frequent visits to their GPs. Are such GPs aware of interpreting, catering, social services and other benefits which they inform their patients to call upon? If GPs lack such information (as is suggested by the experience of some of the black elders known personally to the author), the low level of referrals is in part explained. In these circumstances, GPs are not aware of their power as 'gatekeepers' to other services in the process of making (or not making) referrals and may be failing their black 'customers'. The new requirements of health checks for those over 75 are important in potentially improving referral rates to services as well as identifying particular needs issues. But this assumes that health professionals start from a view that current *take-up of services is low*. It is therefore not surprising that when faced with labels like 'home help', – 'carers' or 'respite care', for example, black elders frequently respond with 'who knows – will these help me?'.

Education and training specifically on issues concerning black elders (see, for example, Ahmad-Aziz *et al.* 1992) for health professionals would make some difference. Responding to these different needs may well improve the services for all elders; after all, if a service is flexible and democratic in principle, it would in practice be able to cater for diverse needs with a quality range of services in keeping with users' rights. Health professionals cannot remain on the sidelines[10]: to do nothing would be to accept racism, the marginalization of communities and the consequent ill-health of black elders – along with other disadvantaged groups. At the same time, work must focus on raising black elders' expectations of health and social services rather than accepting their tolerance of problems 'as normal'.[11]

Notes

1 'Black' is used throughout this chapter to express the political sense of collective experience of those communities, visibly identified, in contemporary Britain, ie, people originating from Asia, Africa, the Caribbean and Middle East.

2 The current study being undertaken by the Age Concern Institute of Gerontology (ACIOG) into existing services to black elderly and their specific needs is to be welcomed (Pharoah 1991).

3 For further details, including housing, see Brown (1984); Bowling (1990); Lewando-Hundt and Grant (1987); Patel (1990: 13).

4 This is not to say that *all* black elders face poverty. Like white elders, black elders are a heterogeneous group, requiring different levels and forms of support.

5 Daily papers frequently report on the deficiencies and effects on old patients, following the NHS reforms. This does suggest that currently services are far from

satisfactory for older people.

6 This is why it is not necessary for black people to be present in a particular location for racism to exist. To insist that it does, apart from being incorrect, suggests that it is black people who cause racism.

7 In targeting services to black elders it is often argued that there are insufficient numbers – since in organizational terms a service can only be provided if a need is established. However, for black elders how can a need be demonstrated in the absence of appropriate and accessible service?

8 A glance at the Annual Reports of the Commission for Racial Equality would indicate the type of discrimination cases in employment and services, in health and social services, brought by individuals, and sometimes formal investigation by the CRE itself.

9 We should not underestimate the sophistication of analysis of ailments and their remedies. Substantial anecdotal evidence suggests that such remedies have positive effect, physically and psychologically – particularly since it is suggested that specific health risks of black elders lie in preventable diseases (Pharoah and Redmond 1991).

10 For suggestions, ideas and further analysis, see a practical guide on 'Improving Practice with Elders' (Ahmad-Aziz et al. 1992).

11 This tolerance may also be due to the need to adopt an optimistic view in the face of growing old in Britain (Ebrahim et al. 1991). Fenton's (1986) work suggests how many 'approaching' elderly regret not being able to return to their original home in their old age.

Part 3

HEALTH POLICY

8

Health promotion for ethnic minorities: past, present and future

Raj Bhopal and Martin White

Introduction

An analysis of past and current efforts to promote health among ethnic minority groups in Britain is long overdue and, in view of the current development of a national health strategy in England, timely (Department of Health 1991b).

The fields of health promotion and ethnic minority health are confused by differences of definition and philosophical and ideological stances. We therefore start by defining our own terms of reference. Next we ask whether the foundation for effective health promotion of ethnic minorities exists. This is followed by an analysis of the role and focus of health promotion for ethnic minorities in Britain. Following this, we outline basic principles for a future strategy and make recommendations for research, policy and practice.

Issues of definition and meaning

We use 'health promotion' in the sense described below. However, as our focus is largely on areas of health promotion engaged in by professional groups we use the term 'health promoters' to refer to individuals who are professionally involved in health promotion (health promotion officers, nurses, doctors and so on). This is not to ignore the important role of 'lay' people in health promotion, but signifies the limits of our knowledge base for this analysis. We shall, however, refer to the principles which may foster a partnership between 'lay' and professional people involved in health promotion. The term 'practice of health promotion' is used with similar limitations. We acknowledge that there are individuals and organizations outside the health sector who have an important role in promoting health – e.g. workers in education, transport and recreation in the public sector, manufacturing and service industries in the commercial sector, and voluntary, charitable and community organizations.

The overwhelming majority of 'health promoters' in Britain belong to the ethnic majority and hence ours is largely an analysis of their work. The implications of this will be referred to throughout the text.

A perspective on health promotion

Our perspective is that of public health medicine. While no simplistic scheme aptly describes the world view of public health practice, it is a perspective in which the social and environmental influences on health are given heavy emphasis.

Health promotion has been repeatedly defined without leading to a single, agreed definition. Some have provided a classification of relevant types of activity, such as the separation of 'health promotion' from 'disease prevention', which is in widespread usage (see, for example Pledger and Watson 1986; Abelin 1987; Breslow 1987). One definition is that health promotion 'comprises both efforts to enhance positive health and prevent ill-health' (Downie *et al.* 1990). A wider definition is 'the process of enabling people to increase control over, and to improve, their health' (WHO, Working Group on the Concepts and Principles of Health Promotion 1984). None of these is entirely satisfactory and we make explicit our own working definition below.

Our view is that health promotion *includes those activities undertaken by professionals from the health and other sectors, and by lay people, aimed at enhancing the health status of individuals and communities.* We exclude from these activities, as Noack (1987) and Pledger and Watson (1986) have, the *medical treatment* of established disease, though this does not deny that clinical doctors and other professionals engage in valuable health promotion.

Figure 8.1 summarizes these relationships: health promotion is seen as overlapping both clinical medicine and public health. Public health is defined here as 'the science and art of preventing disease, prolonging life and promoting health, through organised efforts of society' (Department of Health and Social Security (DHSS) (1989). This definition, based upon that produced by the World Health Organization in 1952, describes a public health function which includes the provision of appropriate health care services as well as measures to protect and enhance the health of the public. This is reflected by the overlap between public health and clinical medicine, which would include, for example, the activities of public health doctors in assessing

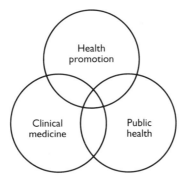

Figure 8.1   The spheres of action to improve and maintain health

the need for, planning, monitoring and evaluating of health care services. We do not see health promotion as synonymous with public health, as Tannahill (1988) does. Much activity to promote health takes place informally within families and communities which is not initiated, though it may be influenced by, organized public health activity. The overlap between health promotion and clinical medicine includes, for example, *ad hoc* advice on health given by health professionals to their patients during normal consultations.

The notion of 'empowerment' is central to our working definition and this places a clear onus on professionals who practice health promotion to seek to enhance the knowledge and skills of their clients in order that they can determine their own pathway to better health. This knowledge may disturb the traditional balance of power but is essential for effective collaboration between different sectors and between public and professionals (WHO Working Group on the Concepts and Principles of Health Promotion 1984).

Health promotion is directed at achieving change (Ashton and Seymour 1988). Following Tannahill (1985), we group the activities of health promotion into three broad, but overlapping spheres of health education, prevention and health protection (Figure 8.2). Health promotion activities may be initiated by either professionals or the public, individually or collectively. The balance of activities is strongly influenced by the dominant concerns of society and, moreover, will reflect the needs and demands of the dominant groups in society. This issue is of particular relevance to the theme of this chapter.

Prerequisites for effective health promotion

In the Ottawa Charter for Health Promotion (WHO/Health and Welfare Canada/Canadian Public Health Association 1986) nine prerequisites for health are described: peace; shelter; education; food; income; a stable

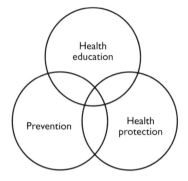

Figure 8.2 The spheres of activity in health promotion
Source: Reproduced, with permission, from the Health Education Journal (Tannahill 1985).

economic system; sustainable resources; social justice and equity. Here we concentrate on three of these – education, social justice and equity – which we perceive to be most specifically relevant. A brief discussion of the relevance of the other six follows.

Peace is an important prerequisite for health. However, racism remains a major threat to both local, national and international peace and has a bearing on many other prerequisites. Similarly, economic stability and sustainability of resources are important to all population groups. Both are linked and, as we move towards a new era where sustainability of resources will inevitably become a critical social and political issue, economic stability may be less assured. The association between low income and poor health is established, and the fact that the income of ethnic minority groups is both lower than that of the general population, and within ethnic minority communities is unequally distributed, is thus a matter of public health concern.

Next to peace, food and shelter are the most essential prerequisites, not only for health promotion, but also for survival (Ashton and Seymour 1988). Access to nutritious, palatable food is linked not only to income but also to policies on agriculture, importation and exportation of food, and local supply. Food which accords with current guidelines on healthy nutrition may, for the general population, be more expensive and less accessible than diets generally followed. Food to the taste of ethnic minority groups may be even less easily available, and exhortations to eat 'healthy' food may, therefore, be both inappropriate and ineffective.

Lastly, both the importance of good housing in promoting health and the fact that ethnic minority groups tend to have less adequate housing, are established. Availability and tenancy of housing by ethnic minority groups may be affected by economic factors, local housing policy and the socio-political circumstances in any locality.

All six of these prerequisites need to be met if the health of ethnic minority groups is to be promoted. Our more detailed analysis of the three remaining prerequisites will exemplify the obstacles and problems to be faced in meeting all prerequisites for health.

Education

Professionals

Health promoters need to understand the social history of ethnic minorities including their culture; changing circumstances; current social, economic and political problems, of which racism, which is agreed to be a 'fact of life' by whites and non-whites alike (Runnymede Trust 1991), is perhaps the greatest concern; health related knowledge, attitudes and behaviour; and health status. Here, there are several problems. First, such understanding is hard to acquire. Consider, for example, the extensive factual material required to understand the background circumstances of one such group, 'Asians' (Henley 1979) or the problem of mastering one issue, the naming system of 'Asians' (Henley and Clayton 1982). Becoming attuned to the history, circumstances, needs and hopes of one's own community is itself a difficult task; achieving this for a number of unfamiliar ethnic minority groups whose circumstances are changing is nigh impossible.

Second, for various reasons the teaching of issues concerning both ethnicity and health promotion to professionals has been weak. The curricula of many health care courses are already replete (General Medical Council Education Committee 1991) and few staff have the skills or commitment to teach these complex issues. Most educational materials, including recent textbooks, provide simplified information relating not to the contemporary issues of British ethnic minorities, but to the cultures of their countries of origin. New textbooks are emerging which combine empirical data from British research with information based on general principles and these exemplify the complex nature of the health issues (Cruickshank and Beevers 1989; McAvoy and Donaldson 1990).

Equally, there are few studies of the knowledge base, attitudes and behaviour of health promoters. These corroborate anecdotal evidence that health promoters are not well equipped with the requisite knowledge or attitudes. For example, health visitors were poorly informed about the customs of ethnic minority groups (While and Godfrey 1984) and general practitioners' attitudes were not found to be conducive to a partnership based on mutual respect (Ahmad *et al.* 1991).

Bhopal (1988) was concerned that the perceptions of health professionals on the health care priorities of ethnic minority groups were ill focused. In the course of teaching postgraduate and continuing education seminars to disparate groups of interested professionals he asked a number of questions to assess their understanding of relevant health issues (about 100 people had attended such seminars). One question was: 'Is immunization uptake among "Asian" children higher or lower than the average? Why?' The ratio of those incorrectly (Baker *et al.* 1984; Bhopal and Samim 1988) responding 'lower' was about three to one. Another question asked: 'What role do traditional and folk systems of medicine play in the health and care of "Asians" in Britain?' There is no 'correct' answer to this question, although the balance of recent research (Johnson *et al.* 1983; Bhopal 1986a) suggests that the role of traditional systems of health care may have been exaggerated (Aslam 1979). However, the ratio of responses indicating that role of traditional and folk medicine was important, compared to those indicating it as of little importance, was about four to one.

Tables 8.1 and 8.2 present the results of two other open questions. The low rankings for racism, discrimination and prejudice, and for coronary heart disease and tobacco/alcohol, are particularly striking as, from a public health perspective, these are of central importance (Bhopal and Donaldson 1988; Bhopal 1991). In Table 8.2 the high rank enjoyed by immunization, and the low ranks of tobacco, alcohol and staff training are similarly noteworthy.

More research of this nature, on representative samples of health professionals (including policy makers) may shed light on the process of priority setting. While these data need cautious interpretation they suggest that health professionals' perceptions of health priorities of ethnic minorities are at odds with epidemiological information (Bhopal 1988; Bhopal and Donaldson 1988; Bhopal 1991); that they have insufficient knowledge to generalize from first principles; and that their knowledge of the relevant literature is poor. Research has shown a disappointingly poor level of understanding and highly negative attitudes to teaching health promotion in general, particularly at a medical school (Weare 1986), with some encouraging exceptions (Tannahill and Robertson 1986; Joffe and Farrant 1989; Amos *et al.* 1990).

To conclude, we have two proposals which warrant evaluation. First, the education of health promoters on ethnicity and health should not be based on a catalogue of facts, but on a set of principles and skills which in turn could allow health promoters to discover, in a local context, those facts which are pertinent to the population they serve. The principles would span the issues of migration, social change and cross-cultural understanding, while the skills would include the ability to gather and interpret information on ethnic minority groups locally, both from individual interactions and from social surveys.

Second, with regard to education on the subject of health promotion, there is a need for educators to develop a clearer understanding of its

Table 8.1 Perceptions of postgraduate students and health professionals of the health and health care of 'Asian' ethnic minority groups (responses in rank order of frequency)

Instruction: Write down the first three thoughts which come to mind on thinking about the health problems of the ethnic minorities who originate in the Indian sub-continent

Rank	Topics	(Frequency)
1	Communication/language problems	(48)
2	Service utilization problems	(24)
3	Lifestyle, cultural differences	(22)
4	Housing problems and related environmental issues	(17)
5	Nutritional problems	(14)
6	Diet/food preferences	(14)
7	Tuberculosis	(14)
8	Mental illness (stress/depression)	(13)
9	Women's needs/problems (isolation, modesty)	(11)
10	Rickets	(10)
11	Racism, discrimination, prejudice	(9)
12	Migration-related health issues	(9)
13	Infections	(8)
14	Coronary heart disease	(7)
15	Poverty-related disease	(7)
16	Diabetes	(6)
17	Infant health	(6)
18	Large families	(5)
19	Family planning	(3)
20	Genetic differences	(3)
21	Tobacco/alcohol	(3)

concepts and, in particular, the importance of its empowering, participative and multidisciplinary nature. Educators need skills in developing strategy and policy, and in conducting research.

The public

The educational needs of ethnic minority communities are also poorly defined. Several small-scale studies have indicated that, for example, the health-related knowledge of the 'Asian' community (Bhopal 1986b; Firdous and Bhopal 1989; Kay *et al.* 1990; McAvoy and Raza 1991) and knowledge of aspects of health and social services is poor (Smith and McCulloch 1977). Their attitudes towards preventive health issues have generally been favourable, as in many repects is their health-related behaviour (Bhopal 1986b; Firdous and Bhopal 1989; Kay *et al.* 1990).

However, the greatest obstacle is perhaps the generally lower educational

Table 8.2   Priorities for health education for the 'Asian' community (responses in rank order of frequency)

Instruction: If you were given £100,000 to spend on a health education campaign for the 'Asian' community in your region, what would be your three priorities?

Rank	Topics	(Frequency)
1	Health care services (including preventive care)	(27)
2	Nutrition	(20)
3	Appropriate health education material	(18)
4	Immunization	(15)
5	People to act as link-workers between services and community	(14)
6	Research on needs	(12)
7	Other specific diseases (including mental health)	(12)
8	Coronary heart disease	(10)
9	Identify community leaders and resources	(8)
10	Teach English/communication	(8)
11	Antenatal care	(8)
12	Women's health	(6)
13	Tobacco	(6)
14	Child care services	(6)
15	Family planning	(6)
16	Housing and other environmental issues	(5)
17	Staff training	(5)
18	Other disease-orientated care	(4)
19	Infant health	(3)
20	Alcohol	(3)

status of members of ethnic minority groups educated outside Britain. A substantial minority of 'Asians', for example, will be entering old age with a poor grasp of English (although they may be familiar with several other languages) and using health services of which they know little (Donaldson and Odell 1986), and where they will find, in the main, inadequate help from trained interpreters or link-workers. While it is a statutory obligation of health authorities to provide services meeting the needs of all their population, the fact is that most have been unable to meet this ideal. With current economic constraints in the NHS, it seems unlikely that this will change.

Health promotion in a multilingual setting poses challenges which are extremely difficult to surmount, except perhaps in the context of well-resourced, small-scale projects and specific problems, particularly where members of the ethnic minority group concerned are involved in a professional capacity (McAvoy and Raza 1991). The teaching of English may need to become integral to health promotion endeavours. Health promotion issues may provide attractive themes for language education. Mastery of the English language may itself promote self-esteem and empower individuals and communities. Vigour, innovative research and resources are also essential to promote health effectively in a multilingual setting (Bhopal and Donaldson 1988; Bhopal 1991).

Equally, the life circumstances of the majority community need to be understood by ethnic minority groups for several good reasons. First, for most ethnic minority groups the process of acculturation appears to be both rapid and irreversible. Understanding the majority's culture may help ethnic minorities to control better the changes which are occurring within their communities. Second, mutual understanding is needed for the partnership between the public and health promoters which is so important to success in health promotion. Third, many of the messages of health promoters are deeply rooted in Western ideology (for example, the pursuit of individual health or personal choice as a priority, rather than, say, religious or family duties) (Research Unit in Health and Behavioural Change (RUHBC) 1989). Without understanding of the underlying principles and rationale of the majority community's life circumstances, ethnic minority groups may find health promotion messages irrelevant or even confusing and hence fail to derive full benefit. The argument that 'if this occurs then health promoters have failed in their professional duties' may be correct but, in terms of achieving the goal of better health, it is negative and unhelpful. More effective means of achieving mutual understanding in the context of health promotion should be actively sought.

Social justice and equity

The law both reflects and determines society's position with respect to individual and social actions by providing a formal framework for acceptable and unacceptable actions. Many laws are of fundamental relevance to health promotion and a comprehensive review would be impossible here. However, it is important to recognize that laws on housing, immigration, employment, food and nutrition, water, pollution, health and other services, religion, equal opportunities and many other aspects of everyday life affect health, and that in their racially biased application lies an impediment to health promotion. Legislation on the National Health Service will be explored here to illustrate the issue of equity.

The law permits the medical examination of immigrants both on entry and subsequently on settlement (McNaught 1985b). One objective of such laws is to control tuberculosis. Tuberculosis notification rates in Indian origin minorities in Britain remain extremely high (Medical Research Council 1985). Many cases of tuberculosis are, without doubt, acquired after immigration to Britain (Grenville-Mathers and Clark 1979). History is clearly repeating itself: in the mid-nineteenth century Irish immigrants to

Scotland were scapegoated as the harbingers of disease, but evidence shows that their health deteriorated *after* immigration (Williams 1992). The health gain derived from the laws permitting medical screening of immigrants is small, the costs are high and they diminish the potential for equal partnership. Yet 'Port Health' remains an integral part of the immigration service (McNaught 1985b).

The NHS Acts (1948) are explicit in defining the fundamental principles of the health service (see Box 8.1). The principle of equity is enshrined in the NHS Acts and defined in terms of equality of entitlement, access and cost at time of use. Equity in this context has too often been perceived as the provision of a single service based on one model and standard of care to be used by all. The fallibility of this approach has been demonstrated in Tudor Hart's (1971) exposition of the 'inverse care law'. Equity requires that the equal needs of all are met with equal effectiveness. A uniform service, therefore, cannot meet with equal effectiveness the needs of ethnic minorities and the ethnic majority. Special projects cannot meet more than a fraction of the needs of ethnic minorities (Bhopal 1988). Therefore, all services should be planned with the needs of ethnic minorities considered in advance. The NHS reforms (Secretary of State for Health 1990a, 1990b) provide the potential to veer away from the uniformity of service provision of the past, but it remains to be seen whether the reforms will lead to more equity or less.

Law does not exist in a vacuum. The interpretation and application of the law will vary in accordance with the values of those in influential positions. Successful health promotion requires equality in the eye of the law; just, fair and effective laws; laws which allow clear interpretation; and, above all, the application of law which is not racially biased. Not all of our actions are governed by law; many are governed by tradition, convention, or even informal agreement. It is self-evident that the arguments made in respect of law also apply to these forms of social enforcement.

Box 8.1 The objectives of the NHS

1 To encourage and assist individuals to remain healthy.
2 To provide equality of entitlement to health services.
3 To provide a broad range of health services of a high standard.
4 To provide equality of access to health services.
5 To provide health services which are free at the time of use.
6 To satisfy the reasonable expectations of the population.
7 To provide a National Health Service which is, nevertheless, responsive to local need.

Recent and current approaches to health promotion for ethnic minority groups

Our interpretation of the published material emphasizes the similarities in disease patterns between ethnic minority and majority groups, in epidemiological assessments of the need for health promotion and with respect to the strategic approaches which should be adopted. The differences lie largely in the understanding of people's circumstances required by the health promoter in adapting or developing appropriate programmes. Examples might include mastering the difficulties of health promotion in a multilingual context or gaining access to, and the trust of, community groups to facilitate community participation and developmental action. Clearly, in these circumstances the approaches and methods will be different, though the ultimate health goals are the same.

Although, for simplicity, we discuss empowerment, community participation and collective action/community development under the heading of 'Education' below, it is clear that they are central to all approaches to health promotion for ethnic minorities, whether at a policy level, in the context of preventive screening or in one-to-one health education. Ethnic minority groups need to be actively involved in the process of health promotion at all levels in order that what is 'provided' meets their real needs and not merely those perceived by professionals.

Strategy development

The methods for health promotion strategy development should not differ in principle from those more generally applicable. However, the prerequisites for health promotion among ethnic minorities need to be taken into account, in particular, in so far as they will affect the choice of methods, settings, actors and targets for health promotion. Figure 8.3 shows a strategic framework derived from a logical series of steps common to much rational planning. This is an ideal planning cycle, which could be useful in the field but would require adaptation. In addition, although community aspirations and perceptions of need are highlighted at the 'needs assessment' stage of this framework, it is important that communities are actively involved at all the stages of health promotion, planning and implementation described. Such participation is uncommon at present but, we feel, an essential prerequisite for effective health promotion.

We do not wish to dwell on the details of this framework. However, it is important to point out that each stage of the cycle is dependent on the availability of accurate, comprehensive and timely information; such information is the cornerstone of effective strategy development. In order to

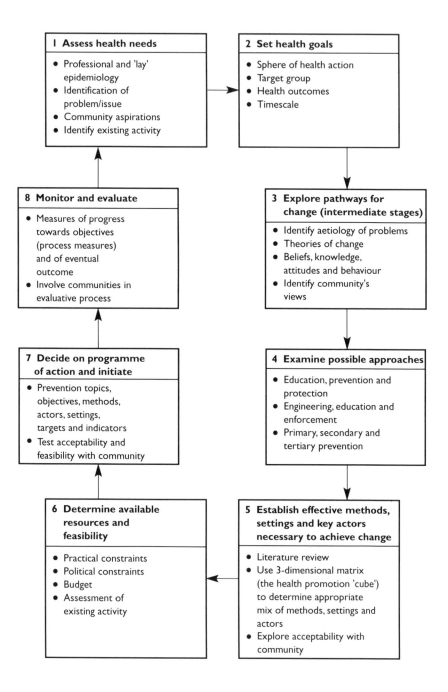

Figure 8.3   A proposed cycle for health promotion strategy development and action

set our analysis of current approaches to health promotion in context, we discuss the current information on health promotion for ethnic minorities.

Information for assessing health needs

A rational health promotion strategy requires appropriate data in each of the classes of information shown in Table 8.3. As the table indicates, much of the information required is currently unavailable with appropriate ethnic classification either nationally or locally. Furthermore, the information base is particularly poor for some groups (such as Chinese or Afro-Caribbeans). Information is dominated by 'hard' data – on deaths, hospital admissions, episodes of illness, or on health-damaging behaviours. As both Table 8.3 and Figure 8.3 illustrate, for the development and implementation of health promotion, much more information is required on the community's views and aspirations; on their reactions to and intuition regarding proposed methods, actors and settings; and on the effects of interventions, not only in terms of changes in the target behaviour, knowledge or ill health, but also in terms of their effects on wider social and cultural aspects of the community's life.

The move towards 'consumerism' in the NHS, as evident from the launch of the 'Patient's Charter' (Department of Health 1991c) and other initiatives (NHSME DHA Project 1992) should, in theory, help to support a more participative style of needs assessment and service provision. Increasing public consultation should empower and enable communities to contribute to decision-making.

In the following discussion we draw heavily upon published work on 'Asians', for research on them has been relatively abundant; lessons may be generalizable to other communities.

The health and health care needs of ethnic minority groups are, arguably, similar to those of the majority community (Bhopal 1988; Bhopal and Donaldson 1988; Bhopal 1991). Rankings of causes of death, hospitalization, and general practice morbidity in 'Asians' are dramatically similar to those of the general population (Bhopal and Donaldson 1988). Such an analysis is clearly crude, ignoring the social class and other demographic differences between the minority and majority groups. However, the pattern of disease among ethnic minority groups is so similar to that of the majority population, with chronic diseases such as coronary heart disease, stroke and cancer most common (Balarajan et al. 1984; Marmot et al. 1984; Bhopal and Donaldson 1988), that it is unlikely that the key issues of interest in health promotion will be different for ethnic minorities.

Studies of the health status of ethnic minorities have been rare, except in the context of research into a single health problem. The Glasgow MRC Medical Sociology Unit's comparative survey of 173 'Asian' adults (aged

Table 8.3 Information required to plan health promotion for ethnic minority groups

Class of information[1]	Examples of types of data	Availability National	Availability Local (district level)	Notes
Health outcomes[1]	Mortality (rates, SMRs, YOLL)	Limited[2]	Limited[2]	[1] Information in these categories ideally should be standardized for age, sex and social class/income.
	Morbidity (incidence, prevalence, admissions, etc.)	No	Limited[3]	[2] Mortality rates only available by 'country of birth', not by ethnicity or race (Marmot et al. 1984)
	Perceived health status	No	Limited[3]	[3] Some local databases include ethnicity as a demographic factor: for example, Birmingham Births Register (Griffiths et al. 1989)
Risk factors[1,4]	Smoking, diet, alcohol, exercise and stress	Limited[5]	Limited[6]	[4] Includes data on behaviours, beliefs, knowledge and attitudes.
	Sexual behaviour[7]	Yes[8]	Limited[6]	[5] Cox (1987) included ethnic origin and provisional published data available (Howlett et al. 1992). Other surveys, such as the General Household Survey (OPCS 1990), have no ethnic breakdown available.
	Occupation	Yes[5,9]	Limited[6,9]	[6] Many local 'health and lifestyle'-type surveys. Some with ethnicity recorded, most without (Killoran 1990; Popay and White 1993).
	Social class, education, marital status, housing and other demographic factors	Yes[5,8]	Limited[6,8]	[7] Including family planning practices.
				[8] National Survey of Sexual Attitudes and Lifestyles has ethnic coding (Johnson et al. 1993).

Current health promotion activity	Objectives Methods Key actors Settings Targets and indicators	No[10]	No[11]
Public and professional views on priorities for action	'Consumer'-type information[12] from surveys using qualitative methods (community aspirations versus professional priorities)	No[13]	No[13]

[9] Data available from decennial Census, but only by 'country of birth' up to 1981, not ethnic origin. From 1991 census, available by ethnic origin (Sillitoe 1987).

[10] As yet, no agreed national health promotion strategy or targets for ethnic minorities. Work on target-setting is available from WHO HFA 2000 Programme (WHO Regional Office for Europe 1985; 1992), Faculty of Public Health Medicine (1991) and Department of Health (1991b).

[11] No comprehensively documented local health strategies for ethnic minorities have been published.

[12] Essential in order to adopt a rational, participative and equitable approach to resource allocation.

[13] Very few national or local studies addressing ethnic minority issues have been pubished.

Notes: SMRs = Standardized mortality ratios; YOLL = Years of life lost.

30–40 years) and 319 members of the general population living in Glasgow (aged 35 years) is a notable exception. The health status of 'Asians' is similar to that of the general population, but there are some differences in health status, both favourable and unfavourable to the majority group (Williams *et al.* 1993). When publicly available, the data from this study and from the survey sponsored by the Health Education Authority, of 5,000 members of ethnic minority groups and 5,000 whites, will be of much benefit. (For examples of local level initiatives see Johnson, this volume.)

With this background, we now analyse the current state of health promotion for ethnic minorities using the framework for health promotion described earlier (Tannahill 1985). For simplicity, we address the three main spheres of activity (education, prevention and protection) in isolation, though many of the examples we use clearly straddle more than one sphere.

Education

French and Adams (1986) describe health education as having three main approaches for achieving its goal: information giving; empowerment; and collective action leading to community development. Though not mutually exclusive, they reflect, respectively, the ethos that information leads to knowledge and knowledge to rational choices in behaviour; that the skills and confidence to change behaviour are more important than knowledge; that behaviour takes place in a social context; and that individual behaviour change both leads to and is accelerated by a shift in societal attitude and behaviour patterns. A valid analysis of health education for ethnic minorities would require detailed review of all three types of activity. However, most published work has described information-giving approaches, which reflects both an imbalance of formal health education activities and the difficulties of evaluating and reporting self-empowerment and community development approaches.

Information giving

Table 8.4 presents an analysis of health education materials available at four different times, derived from published catalogues (Bhopal and Donaldson 1988; Bhopal 1991). The pattern reflects the perceived need for health education materials for ethnic minority groups. However, on closer examination of the materials, particularly in relation to needs, cross-cultural understanding, equity and patterns of health, a rather unbalanced collection is apparent. Bhopal (1988; 1991) and Bhopal and Donaldson (1988) have argued that this imbalance of health education topics reflects a conflict between demand, need and provision. This conflict encapsulates, first, the

Table 8.4   Pamphlets and leaflets on health education topics available in four time periods

	Number (%) available on each topic			
	1977 (n=41)	1984 (n=115)	1987 (n=151)	1990 (n=179)
Infant care and feeding	12(29)	20(17)	20(13)	17 (9)
Diet (including vitamin D)	6(15)	11(10)	13 (9)	16 (9)
Occupational hazards (and legislation)			3 (2)	14 (8)
Birth control	3 (7)	24(21)	29(19)	12 (7)
Sickle cell anaemia		7 (6)	13 (9)	12 (7)
Pregnancy/MCH	2 (5)	11(10)	13 (9)	10 (6)
Using health services	2 (5)	5 (4)	5 (3)	8 (4)
Infectious diseases (and immunization)		2 (2)	7 (5)	5 (3)
Dental health			6 (4)	5 (3)
Diabetes			4 (3)	5 (3)
Lice	1 (2)		3 (2)	5 (3)
Cervical smears	1 (2)	2 (2)	1 (1)	5 (3)
Language or phrase books	3 (7)	3 (3)	1 (1)	5 (3)
Food hygiene	3 (7)	3 (3)	5 (3)	4 (2)
Breast examination or problems		6 (7)	1 (1)	4 (2)
Heart disease				4 (2)
Traditional mineral remedies (surma, sikar)	1 (2)	2 (2)	1 (1)	4 (2)
Medicines			2 (1)	4 (2)
Alcohol		1 (1)	1 (1)	3 (2)
Accidents	5(12)	6 (7)	5 (3)	2 (2)
Social Security	2 (5)	1 (1)	5 (3)	2 (2)
Others		11(13)*	13 (9)†	33(18)‡

Notes:
* Colostomy, race relations (3), spina bifida, skin and hair, general health, background information on ethnic minorities (4).
† Adoption, antibiotics, colostomy, foot care, race relations (2), spina bifida (2), skin and hair (2), school (1), warmth (2).
‡ Racism, equality, and immigration (4), spina bifida (3), foster care, Caesarean section, gender of babies, footcare, patients' rights, malaria, warmth (4), general health, asthma, tuberculosis and immunization with BCG, bronchitis and emphysema, legionnaires' disease, skin care (2), back problems, physical education, marriage and separation, mental health (2), genetic disorder (2)
Sources: 1977 figures, Wandsworth Council for Community Relations; others, Health Education Authority. First published in *British Medical Journal* Bhopal (1991). Reproduced with permission

problem of health promoters from the ethnic majority controlling health promotion for ethnic minorities whom they understand poorly; second, paying insufficient regard both to epidemiological information and to the observations of ethnic minorities; and third, a failure to involve, in a participative way, ethnic minority communities themselves. Why, for example, is there so much material concerning birth control, and yet so little on health service utilization, heart disease, smoking and alcohol? The following are some possible explanations:

1 Birth control is indeed a dominant health problem of ethnic minority groups.
2 It is perceived as a dominant health problem by health promoters, but not necessarily by ethnic minority groups themselves.
3 It is perceived as the dominant health problem by ethnic minority groups themselves, and health promoters act upon this information.
4 It is (or is perceived as) a culture-specific problem, while the other problems are (or are perceived as) 'culture-free'.
5 Health education materials on birth control for the general population are unsuitable for ethnic minority groups, but those on the other topics for which few materials have been prepared (such as smoking and heart disease) are quite suitable.
6 Topics such as heart disease are (or are perceived as) unimportant.
7 Those health professionals who have a major health education responsibility are particularly interested in birth control and related matters.
8 The provision of birth control material reflects society's concerns about the rising immigrant population.

Reflection on these explanations is warranted bearing in mind the following: that among some ethnic minorities preferred family size is apparently larger than that chosen by the general population and, therefore, we might expect the demand for birth control measures to be lower; that matters such as the prevention of heart disease are extremely complex and require subtle and detailed education; that most deaths in all ethnic minority groups are from cardiovascular disease, with the figure approaching 50 per cent for South Asian men and women (Marmot *et al.* 1984); that lung cancer is common in ethnic minority groups (Donaldson and Clayton 1984); that there are powerful cultural taboos against smoking, drinking alcohol (Bhopal 1986b) and against the consumption of certain categories of food (Henley 1979); and that smoking and drinking are common in sub-groups of South Asian males (Jackson *et al.* 1981; Bhopal 1986b; Ahmad *et al.* 1988).

Currently available health education materials match neither the priorities for health promotion based upon epidemiological analysis, nor the likely priorities of ethnic minority groups themselves (Webb 1981, 1982; Pearson 1989). We shall return to this theme in the concluding section of this chapter.

Empowerment

Self-empowerment approaches to health education aim to help individuals to develop the confidence, skills and knowledge necessary to make their own decisions about health. In theory, the decision taken is not the concern of the educator. In practice, however, self-empowerment approaches emphasize knowledge as the basis of decision-making, and the values of the educator often inform and even direct the educational process (McEwan and Bhopal 1991).

One example of an initiative which aimed to empower ethnic minorities was an experiment with patients' advocates in the maternal care setting (Parsons and Day 1992). Well-informed lay persons were employed to act as intermediaries between the health service providers and patients. By providing the patients with knowledge and permitting them to negotiate (albeit sometimes through the advocate), patients were to be empowered. This experiment has been widely judged to be successful, though the formal evaluation of its impact on pregnancy outcome remains unclear, partly because of problems with the research design (Parsons and Day 1992). Nevertheless, the study suggested that the advocacy project favourably affected antenatal length of stay, rate of induction of labour and mode of delivery. Much has already been written on a similar, but broader initiative, the Asian Mother and Baby Campaign (Alibhai 1984; Rocheron and Dickinson 1990). The overall impact and value of this project, however, was diminished by the health professional's use of the link workers as, largely, interpreters (Mason 1990).

A local, though unpublished, example illustrates the use of such an approach. It was recognized by community health workers in Newcastle upon Tyne that Bangladeshi, Pakistani and Chinese mothers were less likely to breastfeed their babies than their counterparts in their countries of origin or local white mothers. The preference for bottle feeding was greater among recent immigrants. A project was established initially to identify the attitudes and behaviour of women in the three ethnic groups. Interview surveys were conducted, together with a number of focus group discussions. Sampling was performed using the 'snowball' method which, apart from overcoming the difficulties of having no population sampling frame for ethnic minorities, encouraged the introduction of local women by word of mouth, thus gaining their trust and ensuring participation. The surveys and focus groups identified inconsistencies in, and misinterpretation of, messages given by health professionals and also identified the unavailability of halal baby foods as an obstacle to appropriate weaning practices (Lin 1991; Shahjahan 1991). The women were thus involved in identifying their needs and have remained involved in the development of the subsequent health promotion programme.

By a process of joint professional and community planning a number of initiatives have been developed. Continued community participation in these initiatives will be essential to ensure their continued responsiveness to ethnic minority needs (Barbara Wallace, personal communication).

The empowerment approach has much appeal, particularly for ethnic minority groups. However, it is comparatively costly and time-consuming and, by its very nature, cannot reach large numbers of people (McEwan and Bhopal 1991). The development and use of empowering techniques by all health promoters in their everyday practice is thus highly desirable.

Collective action

The emphasis here is on group action, whereby communities are empowered and motivated to act in order to alter existing socio-economic conditions so as to make healthy solutions easier (French and Adams 1986; McEwan and Bhopal 1991). The community development (CD) approach is one way of initiating collective action at a local level. Its main features are outlined in Box 8.2.

The CD approach has been used extensively in less developed countries, in both community health and other spheres of action. It has also become more common in the last fifteen years in Britain, predominantly in deprived areas, as small scale projects mainly funded from charitable sources and urban development funds (RUHBC 1989). While the ultimate aim of a community health project may be to improve the health of a local community, the focus

---

Box 8.2 The features of community development (adapted from UKHFAN-CPG (1991))

1 Focuses on collective rather than individual change.
2 Actively counters prejudice and discrimination through positive action for equal opportunities.
3 Work with disadvantaged and oppressed groups is a priority.
4 Method of working is held to be important in itself and should be health-enhancing in its own right.
5 A holistic approach that encompasses all aspects of people's lives that affect their health and health potential.
6 Recognizes the central importance of formal and informal social support and networks in bringing about change.
7 Seeks to enable people to identify common needs and concerns and to facilitate collective action in ways agreed on and prioritized by people themselves.
8 Opens up access to resources, services and information to assist people to make realistic, informed decisions and choices in relation to their individual and collective health and welfare.
9 Precise outcomes cannot be predicted, so ongoing participative evaluation is needed which focuses on processes and outcomes.

of the CD approach is determined by the community itself and may be very different from that of health professionals, commonly concerning issues such as inadequate housing, lack of work, feelings of powerlessness, living and environmental conditions (Watt and Rodmell 1987).

The number of local/geographically based CD projects in Britain is small, though there are a larger number of community health projects employing CD approaches, some aimed specifically at ethnic minority groups (Blenner-hassett *et al.* 1989; RUHBC 1989). Jeyasingham (1992) provides an account of ethnic minority initiatives in this area.

Because approaches to health promotion involving empowerment and collective action are directed at underlying causes of ill health, largely unremediable by medical means, and encourage people to take control of their health, such approaches present a significant challenge to medical dominance (Watt and Rodmell 1987). This is an obstacle to the wider adoption and funding of such approaches by health authorities, though there are now some encouraging signs of change.

Among ethnic minority groups the ethos of self-help based on community support is strong and the collective action approach is one which may well be fruitful. For example, the development of temples, mosques and the black churches has been largely accomplished by collective endeavour. These now provide one forum for bringing people together. Similarly, community centres for ethnic minority groups, often developed entirely by shared community resources, not only contribute in a general sense to community well-being but also make possible the opportunity to take collective action on health issues. These grassroots-level developments provide the foundations for participative health promotion. Professional health promoters should key into such networks and identify their potential for health promotion by building partnerships based on equality. Where information is not easily available the local Racial Equality Council should be able to provide advice.

Organizations which join together can increase their sphere of influence. An example of this is the Confederation of Indian Organizations (CIO) to which 59 non-political organizations (representing 250,000 members) are affiliated, but which has, among its aims, clear political goals. The CIO includes research and the assembly and dissemination of health information as part of its remit. The CIO's (1986) report, *Coronary Heart Disease and Asians in Britain*, commissioned by the Coronary Prevention Group, was influential in bringing to wider attention a massive, but hitherto largely ignored health problem (CIO 1989). It is likely that there are many more unpublished examples of health promotion involving collective action initiated by ethnic minority groups without the involvement of professional health promoters. (The *Share* project, based at the King's Fund Centre, London, houses useful information on community health initiatives.)

Prevention

Many examples of prevention involve elements of health education and cannot, therefore, be examined in isolation. However, the performance of a preventive service can be assessed provided this is done in the knowledge that this performance may depend on effective health education.

Tannahill (1985) and Downie *et al.* (1990) have classified prevention into four types of activity, similar to the more traditional classification into primary, secondary and tertiary prevention:

1 Prevention of the onset or first manifestation of a disease process, or some other first occurrence through risk reduction.
2 Prevention of the progression of a disease process or other unwanted state, through early detection when this favourably affects outcome.
3 Prevention of avoidable complications of an irreversible, manifest disease or other unwanted state.
4 Prevention of the recurrence of an illness or other unwanted phenomenon.

Immunization and the early detection of disease by screening will be used here as examples of two of these four types of preventive activity in relation to ethnic minority groups.

In view of language and cultural differences, relatively poor knowledge on a range of health issues, comparatively low socio-economic status, and the paucity of adaptive change by the NHS to meet the needs of ethnic minorities, one would predict their immunization rates to be lower (Bhopal and Samim 1988). The false perception that they are lower is common (see for example, p. 142 and Table 8.2). In fact, immunization rates are about the same or higher in ethnic minority groups (Baker *et al.* 1984; Bhopal and Samim 1988). The lessons from this research for preventive health programmes are these: the prediction of the behaviour of ethnic minority groups on the basis of common sense, first principles, or on the scientific knowledge acquired from the study of the majority population is not advisable; language barriers may, occasionally, be an aid to health promotion, for the community may be unaware of controversy about certain preventive procedures (Bhopal and Samim 1988); the attitudes of ethnic minority groups towards prevention are favourable and not in conflict with their preventive health behaviour (Bhopal 1986b; Bhopal and Samim 1988; Kay *et al.* 1990); the popular statement that 'the NHS is not meeting the needs of ethnic minority groups' is too simplistic, for in some regards it is and in others it is not.

Screening is a vast field, with procedures as varied as blood tests to detect foetal abnormality, and mammography for breast cancer. There are two main issues to be examined. First, what are the responses of ethnic minority groups to invitations to be screened? Second, do existing programmes reflect the priorities for screening ethnic minority groups?

The evidence on the response to screening of ethnic minority groups is confined to a few screening services and a number of research projects based on screening. Overall, their response is comparatively poor. For example, studies show that 'Asian' women attend for antenatal care later and more erratically than their ethnic majority counterparts (Clarke and Clayton 1983), and that both pregnant and non-pregnant 'Asian' women are less likely to be screened for cervical cancer (Firdous and Bhopal 1989; McAvoy and Raza 1988). While a full discussion of the reasons is beyond the scope of this chapter, we note that the evidence from Clarke and Clayton's study suggests that the services for 'Asian' women were not of the quality available to white women.

In the context of research, however, response rates for screening among ethnic minorities are usually comparable with ethnic majority groups. For example, in an intensive community based screening study in London the response rates to an invitation to screening for coronary heart disease in 'Asians' and 'non-Asians' were 62 per cent and 66 per cent, respectively (McKeigue *et al.* 1991). This is a paradox with a clear policy implication: in the context of routine services, ethnic minorities are less likely to come forward, but in the context of research they do so. It is likely that in the latter circumstances special efforts, including the appointment of staff from appropriate minorities, are made to ensure that ethnic minority groups understand the purpose and value of screening.

Although the health care needs of ethnic minority groups are similar to those of the majority, one specific screening programme, for tuberculosis, will be discussed here. (See Box 8.3 on criteria for evaluating screening programmes.)

Box 8.3 Seven criteria for deciding whether a screening program does more good than harm. Reproduced with permission: Little, Brown and Company, Boston (Sackett *et al.* 1985)

1 Has the program's effectiveness been demonstrated in a randomized trial?
  If an effectiveness trial with a positive result has not been carried out:
2 Are there efficacious treatments for the primary disorder and/or efficacious preventive measures for its sequelae?
3 Does the current burden of suffering warrant screening?
4 Is there a good screening test?
5 Does the program reach those who could benefit from it?
6 Can the health system cope with the screening program?
7 Will positive screens comply with subsequent advice and interventions?

The control of tuberculosis in the UK has depended on socio-economic improvements, a curative treatment for tuberculosis, screening by mass miniature radiography (MMR), contact tracing and BCG immunization. Mass miniature radiography has been an effective component of the strategy for control. When tuberculosis declined sharply in the 1970s, MMR was abandoned, though X-ray units were generally stored for occasional use in the context of large outbreaks. In the current attempts to control tuberculosis among Asian migrants MMR has found no place. The issue is not whether MMR is needed, but that it has not been debated and MMR has not been considered as having a place in the control of tuberculosis among ethnic minority groups. Once again, is this because screening policies are based on the needs only of the ethnic majority?

There is no effective forum for consideration of the relevance and applicability of national screening programmes to ethnic minorities, or for their evaluation. This is a matter which requires urgent attention.

Protection

Protection embraces legal or fiscal controls, regulations and policies, or codes of practice which aim to promote health (Tannahill 1985). Other than laws governing the health screening of immigrants, there are no specific national protective measures to promote the health of ethnic minorities.

Within the NHS, in response to the problem of racial discrimination and, in particular, institutionalized racism, there have been a number of initiatives. The Training in Race and Health Project aimed to raise awareness of the health needs of ethnic minorities, including the effects and circumstances of racial discrimination, and hence to motivate staff to seek personal and organizational change (Training in Health and Race 1984). Since the mid-1980s there has been a steady increase in the development of health authority policies for the health care of ethnic minorities and in the implementation of equal opportunity and ethnic monitoring policies. These have been facilitated in some cases by the appointment of equal opportunity advisers, though their role has often been seriously undermined by adherence to a 'colour-blind' approach by health authority members and senior managers (Whelan 1988). If only lip service is paid to codes of practice or policies for ethnic minority groups, it will lead to ineffective policies which may be a greater obstacle to progress (see also Ward, this volume).

The National Assocation of Health Authorities (1988) report *Action Not Words* suggested realistic objectives for health authorities to improve access to, and delivery of, services for ethnic minority groups and advocated further training and information for NHS staff. The report stressed that this should be a broad policy issue, irrespective of the ethnic minority composition of each authority's local population. Unfortunately, particularly in areas with a small ethnic minority population, it is unlikely that these objectives will be realized (Brown 1991).

At present, policy measures on racial discrimination in the NHS are unlikely to be a panacea. Nevertheless, there is some evidence of a shift in attitudes. The Commission for Racial Equality, currently preparing codes of practice on the care of ethnic minorities, may have some impact, as may an increasing emphasis on 'consumerism' in the NHS, and the introduction of the 'Patient's Charter' with an accreditation or 'chartermark' scheme for health authority policies and procedures (Department of Health 1991c).

The wider inadequacies of legislation and social policies affecting the health of ethnic minority groups, however, represent a greater and more significant challenge. Legislation is at the root of much effective health promotion, for example, that on drinking and driving, wearing of seat belts and crash helmets, food quality and safety, the sale of alcohol, cigarettes and drugs, limits on advertising and, of course, legislation on the health and social services. It is unclear if the legislative base, and the implementation of such legislation, is as effective in promoting the health of ethnic minority groups as it is for the ethnic majority.

Changes in law and policy which increase the chances of equal opportunity in employment, allocation of housing and educational places, may have greater health promoting effects than much of the professional health promotion activity proposed in this chapter. Health, and in particular the health of ethnic minorities, is a political issue; to achieve health promoting change at this level will require political will.

A strategy for the future

Future strategy for the development of health promotion for ethnic minorities in Britain needs to be based on broad thinking in at least three spheres: social, economic and legislative; research; and health promotion practice. Strategy also needs to be informed by a strong moral and ethical stance.

The social, economic and legislative environment

As already argued, the promotion of health does not occur in a vacuum and, as members of society, professional health promoters need to strive to create the conditions in which health improvement can occur. The political dimension to this has been alluded to above.

On a more immediate front, health promoters need to be fully aware of the relatively disadvantageous position occupied by many ethnic minority groups. This awareness will permit them to understand better the relative importance of the many forces impinging on ethnic minority health, including cultural and genetic factors, and socio-economic, political and environmental factors. Too often, the assumption has been made that health problems are the result of biological or cultural factors when they are as likely to have a political or economic basis (Johnson 1984; Ahmad 1989). Health promoters may need to adapt their activities to meet the needs of ethnic minorities in the same way as they may adjust their work to make it more relevant to, say, social classes 4 and 5, rather than social classes 1 and 2, or women rather than men. Moreover, health promotion must meet this challenge in the face of structural disadvantages in society, of which racial discrimination is perhaps the most important.

It is also essential that health promoters make bold efforts to achieve a fundamental shift in the power base of health promotion. While this is important for all disadvantaged groups, empowerment of ethnic minorities is an absolute prerequisite for progress in this field. Health promotion is at present at risk of being hijacked by a political agenda which dictates that it is something which professionals do to people. The types of activity encouraged in GP health promotion clinics (Department of Health 1989a; Secretary of State for Health 1990b) and the largely disease-orientated personal behaviour-based strategy set out in *Health of the Nation* (Department of Health 1991b) are good examples of this emphasis. Whether or not this wider view of health promotion is taken into account nationally, the critical test will be its translation into action at a local level.

Research

The research base of health promotion activities needs to be strengthened, and the field of health promotion for ethnic minority groups is unexceptional. Three main types of research are needed:

1 Studies of the impact of social policy and social circumstances on the health of ethnic minorities.
2 Epidemiological studies of the health status, including risk factors and the determinants of health, of ethnic minority groups.
3 Research to establish the appropriate principles and information base to guide the development and evaluation of health promotion interventions for ethnic minorities.

Discussion of the first type of research is beyond our expertise; nevertheless, it is clearly an important and much needed part of the agenda. One problem is that there is insufficient collaboration between public health, epidemiology, health promotion and social policy researchers. There are clear differences in both methods and philosophical approaches, but these will need to be bridged. Some of the key areas we would like to highlight are the relationship between ethnicity, socio-economic deprivation and health; the effects of housing, employment and education policies on health; and the relationship between health gain and access to health services in different ethnic groups (see also chapters by Ahmad and Stubbs in this volume).

The second type of research, epidemiological, is now fully established for 'Asians'. In order to seek causal understanding of diseases, many comparative epidemiological studies have been reported, and databases have been, or are being, established to permit new work. These data can be useful to health promoters. For health care planning (including health promotion) simple data based on absolute risks is necessary, and data based on relative risk (so vital for developing hypotheses on disease causation) can mislead (Bhopal 1988). Health promoters must thus take great care in selecting and interpreting information to assess the likely health status of 'Asians'. For most other groups the data are scant, except in regard to specific diseases (such as hypertension and stroke in Afro-Caribbeans). Data on minority ethnic groups in other countries (for example Japanese, Chinese and South Asians in USA) must be interpreted with caution. The priorities for epidemiological research for health planning in Britain are, first, to develop sound methodology (Bhopal 1992), and second, to study ethnic minority groups from the Far East (Hong Kong Chinese in particular), Africa and the Caribbean.

The third area of research, into the practice of health promotion, is the most urgent priority. Broadly speaking, two types of research are needed: needs assessments and evaluation. Essentially, health promotion initiatives should be based on information on what individuals know, think and do (McEwan and Bhopal 1991), together with information on what is effective and practically possible (see again Table 8.3 and Figure 8.3). Clear and measurable objectives, sensitive to both individual and group differences, can be set using such information.

In the context of health promotion for the general population, this type of research base is weak, though developing rapidly (Killoran 1990; Popay and White 1993). There is a growing interest in the methods of market research, in particular qualitative techniques such as focus groups (Luck *et al.* 1988), found to be particularly useful in health promotion (Luck 1991). Research on the beliefs, knowledge, attitudes and behaviour of ethnic minority groups is not merely desirable but essential. Furthermore, because of changing lifestyles within migrant communities, principles derived from research will need to be continually reviewed.

Except in a few locations, where the proportion of the ethnic minority population is high, health surveys of the general population will not succeed in recruiting sufficient numbers of ethnic minority people (Ecob and Williams 1990). Studies in areas where the density of the ethnic minority population is high may not be generalizable to the areas where such population is scattered (Ecob and Williams 1990). Further, because of the technical difficulties of translation of questions, the problems of validity and comparability of questions, the difficulties in identifying ethnic minorities and the vexed issue of non-response, particularly in postal surveys, carefully done specific studies will be needed. Evaluation research, aimed at the structure, process and outcome of initiatives, is an equally high priority. Few evaluations of initiatives to promote the health of ethnic minority groups have been published (Peach 1984a; 1984b; Rocheron, Khan and Dickinson 1989; McAvoy and Raza 1991; Parsons and Day 1992), but the need for such research is self-evident.

To paraphrase Bhopal and Donaldson (1988): without the guidance of a research effort, health promotion services for ethnic minority groups are unlikely to overcome the continuing challenge.

The practice of health promotion

The challenge of rationally planning effective health promotion services for extremely heterogeneous ethnic minority populations, together comprising some 5–6 per cent of the total British population, is immense and probably impossible without clear principles, an appropriate strategic framework and adequate resources.

Health promoters need to be informed, and passive learning from textbooks, reviews or scientific papers is inadequate. They need to acquire local knowledge by building appropriate alliances which will then permit personal, local enquiry. Here, interviewing and moderating skills (with individuals and groups) in a cross-cultural setting are possibly the most vital needs. The following principles may be helpful to health promoters:

1 Priorities should be based on careful analysis of information on the health status of the ethnic minority groups, and not simply on a 'first principles' approach or on general perceptions of health needs.
2 The priorities should not simply be those health problems which are specific to an ethnic group.
3 Where possible, potential well-recognized problems should be pre-empted to aid prevention (for example, smoking among women).
4 Services for the general population will usually need to be adapted to meet the needs of ethnic minority groups.
5 The materials and methods will be similar in principle, but often different in detail, to those used for the general population.
6 Health promotion practice needs to be underpinned by research.
7 Health promotion for ethnic minorities requires a co-ordinated approach. In the absence of a national strategy, a local strategy will be needed to avoid a piecemeal approach.

8 Effective work with ethnic minority groups requires the development of a partnership which permits the sharing of expertise and knowledge.
9 Methods adopted, whether educational, preventive, protective or a combination of these, should embody the principles of empowerment and community participation. The CD and collective action approaches should be considered where applicable.

There are additional costs of intiatives aimed at ethnic minority groups, for example translation (Fuller 1987). Unnecessary duplication of work, therefore, needs to be avoided.

Recommendations

Below we make a number of recommendations for policy, research and practice in the development of health promotion for ethnic minorities in Britain. This is not an exhaustive list and reflects the analysis we have performed for this chapter.

Policy

1 Health promoters should work for the achievement of a social milieu where the pre-requisites for health are met for all ethnic groups.
2 Policy formulation and implementation needs to be based firmly on the principles of equity, community participation and multi-sector collaboration.
3 Policy should be based on analysis of objective information and not on general principles, for general principles may not apply.
4 Specific needs, when applicable, should be met in addition to, rather than instead of, those needs which are shared in common with the ethnic majority group.
5 The health needs of all minority groups, including ethnic minorities, should be explicitly addressed in national and local policy documents.

Research

1 Research is essential to guide the development of health promotion and, therefore, should, wherever possible, form a component of all health promotion strategies and programmes.
2 The priorities for health promotion research are studies of:
   (i) the relationship between socio-economic environment, social policy, culture and health;
   (ii) health-related beliefs, knowledge, attitudes and behaviour;
   (iii) the effectiveness and cost-effectiveness of interventions.

3 Local research needs to be supplemented by regional and national research.
4 The research base should broaden to take account of all ethnic minority groups.
5 The ethnic minority groups to be studied, and the methods of analysis and presentation, should be determined in accordance with the principles of health needs research rather than aetiological research. This will lead to a de-emphasis on the quest for differences between groups and an increasing emphasis on the use of qualitative methods to gain deeper understanding. (See also chapters by Ahmad, Stubbs, and Sashidharan and Francis in this volume).

Practice

1 Health promoters should develop the skills to acquire, actively, information in cross-cultural settings and to work collaboratively with ethnic minority communities. Training courses need to be devised to provide these skills.
2 Members of ethnic minorities should be actively involved in the development of health promotion at a local level, and empowered to do so by health promoters.
3 National and local strategies are required to guide health promotion activities.
4 Priorities should take into account both the views and aspirations of ethnic minority communities and objectively acquired information. These can be agreed by a negotiated process involving local people, within a rational approach to planning using an appropriate framework.
5 Techniques and methods demonstrated to be effective with ethnic minority groups need to be used, others need to be evaluated.
6 Additional resources should be made available to foster and support good practice.
7 Health promotion for ethnic minority groups requires an ethnic minority voice; ideally one representing both lay people and professionals. Members of ethnic minority communities should be represented among the staff and members of health authorities and community health councils. In particular, many more professional health promoters are needed from relevant ethnic minority groups.

9

Race equality and employment in the National Health Service

Laurence Ward

Introduction

In the field of health and 'race' much is heard about black people but little is heard from them. Black people have been the object of numerous papers by people who, in the words of one of the interviewees in *Black Testimony* (Cottle 1978: 172) 'sit in their little offices all day long writing reports about us, and telling the government what the policy about us should be. That may be even worse than any National Front' (see also Lawrence 1982a; 1982b; and Bourne and Sivanandan 1981).

These inadequacies at the research level have been mirrored in race equality policy-making and implementation, and have led to a failure in many cases to express black people's experiences in their own terms. Many of the studies on employment opportunities for black people concentrate on what happens to them in the system, and there is a regrettable lack of information about the subjective experience of discrimination in employment, and its effects on the lives and opportunities of black people (cf. Baxter and Baxter 1988). Today the situation has changed little from the position fifteen years ago, when Cottle (1978: 80) remarked:

No amount of discussion on the sociology of work or any recounting of employment statistics could ever convey the meaning and value of work to a man or woman, or to their society. To work is to believe in one's fundamental worth . . . They [the black families he visited] knew as experts about social stratification; how high they could rise in society, how low they could sink, and where they would never find work. They told me about the subtle and not so subtle ways they were excluded from certain jobs, and how absurd and degrading they found these exclusions to be. Nothing seemed to convince these families of their second class status and their meagre chance of improving their station in life as much as their jobs.

This chapter gives an account of the main policy initiatives and practical programmes in the National Health Service over the past twenty years which relate to the employment and deployment of black people. The Department of Health and the health authorities have been reluctant to admit to discrimination against black people, and have collected little information on the problems of institutional racism. The Department of Health has failed to ensure that health authorities implement its circulars and exhortations with respect to equal opportunities. The result is that it is not possible to present a comprehensive and systematic picture of either the state of the service with respect to discrimination, or a clear definition and evaluation of the effectiveness of initiatives to rectify the problems. This lack of national information is problematic but there are many local surveys and individuals' testimonies that allow the presentation of a reasonably clear picture of the state of the service to emerge. A survey of public policy in the area will allow us to match the gains against the expectations.

This chapter is therefore divided into three main parts. The first part will look at how discrimination presented itself in the 1970s and 1980s. By 'discrimination' we mean that individuals have been denied employment, promotion and deployment opportunities on the basis of skin colour, ethnicity or place of origin rather than genuine occupational reasons of ability, training and so on. It will focus upon two professional groups, doctors and nurses, and only tangentially refer to other health care professionals and workers. In the space available any wider coverage would only be superficial, though this does not deny the need for attention to these areas (see, for example, Commission for Racial Equality (CRE) 1984).

In the second part of the chapter I wish to show how the development of equal opportunities in the National Health Service has been hampered by failings at both the national level by the Department of Health, and at the local level by district and regional health authorities. The national failings can be summarized as a refusal by politicians with health service responsibilities to accept the reality and prevalence of discrimination, and the subsequent collusion of senior civil servants in the Department of Health in ensuring that any policy developed was not implemented. The local failings were multifarious, but rest on the fact that local managers were unlikely to divert resources to policies that seemed politically problematic, when funding for even routine patient services appeared to be inadequate. The national initiatives, like the King's Fund Equal Opportunities Task Force, were largely public relations exercises that concealed a failure in the Department of Health to take racial equality seriously, while local initiatives were invariably patchy and poorly resourced, and generally the result of individual initiative usually in spite of, rather than because of, pressure from above (Gibbon 1990).

The 1980s in particular saw major changes in health service organization and service development, and many of these initiatives were driven from the centre. The adoption of performance indicators, of resource management, and of devolved business units, whether they became trusts or were directly managed, were all Departmental initiatives that were well resourced from a policy and implementation point of view. Equal opportunities was a case of a policy without the implementation.

In the final part of this chapter I shall assess prospects of future employment opportunities for black people in the NHS, and comment on how the market for health care will benefit or disadvantage black people in the future.

Black workers in the National Health Service

The NHS is the biggest employer in Europe and the largest employer of people from black and minority ethnic communities in Britain. The existence of a large number of black people within the NHS, and the problems they have encountered and are encountering, is the first point that needs to be understood before we look at the various initiatives which constitute the health service's attempt to deal with these problems. Many of the criticisms levelled at the NHS in relation to black communities seem to be predicated on the assumption that an essentially white-dominated system is failing to provide an appropriate service to black people, and that many of the problems stem from just this white dominance (see Littlewood and Lipsedge 1982: 85).

The issue of the lack of appropriateness of the system to black people's needs must be separated from criticisms about the white dominance of the system, for the paradox is that the areas where the system is regarded as least appropriate for black people, for example mental health and geriatrics, are often the areas where black professionals are most prevalent (Smith 1980: 197; Rashid 1990: 41). Many NHS managers see the various policy initiatives around race equality as occurring in a vacuum, as if the mere existence of large numbers of black staff in the system of itself constituted a refutation of any claims about a lack of equality, or legitimized the rhetoric that 'we can't be racist because we employ so many black people'.

Racism in the nursing profession

With the exception of individuals like Mary Seacole, the history of black nurses in the NHS started after the Second World War. An acute labour shortage in Britain forced the Department of Health to recruit nurses in the British ex-colonies, so that the emerging NHS would have sufficient personnel to meet its needs. The strict controls on immigration introduced in 1962 and 1965 were waived for the NHS (Pearson 1987: 25; Lee-Cunin 1989: 4–5). Enoch Powell was one of the ministers responsible for this recruitment programme, and the result was that many black auxiliary and trainee nurses arrived in Britain from its ex-colonies.

In the 1960s and 1970s most overseas nurses were channelled into State Enrolled Nurse (SEN) courses, as opposed to the more highly regarded State Registered Nurse (SRN) course. Nine per cent of all NHS nurses came from overseas, but they made up 20 per cent of the total number of SENs working in the NHS (Thomas and Williams 1972: 6). The results of this channelling of nurses into the respective courses were significant, for the career prospects of many nurses were limited before they emerged from basic training (Brent Community Health Council 1981: 6).

After basic training the health service lost no time in channelling the nurses into the least glamourous and consequently understaffed areas of psychiatry, mental 'handicap' and geriatrics, where one-third of overseas-born nurses were working in 1977. The general situation of overseas nurses has been described by Pearson (1987: 26):

> They are still over-represented on the roll [as SENs] as opposed to the register [as SRNs], in the least attractive specialisms, undertaking the least rewarding and menial tasks, working unsocial hours on night duty, and grossly under-represented in the community and in management.

As one of the West Yorkshire nurses interviewed in *Daughters of Seacole* (Lee-Cunin 1989: 11) stated:

> I've only worked on the psychiatric ward. They said that that was the only post available. Geriatrics and psychiatrics are dead end spots and the white people don't want them . . . You think, this is my kind of job . . . But what else can I do? Everyone has to work in order to eat and live.

Racism in the nursing profession took many other forms after people were accepted into basic training. These ranged from demands about the clothes people wear, to policies which channel black nurses into unpopular specialities. Some health authorities, and in particular some nursing schools, did not even get as far as allowing black people to train for enrolment. At one teaching hospital in Liverpool, of the 170 students training to be SRNs only two were black. Of the 136 training for enrolment only one was black. There were no black nurses above the post of ward sister, and out of 92 ward sisters only two were black. Of the 146 staff nurses none were black (Torkington 1983: 14). As late as 1986 only 4 per cent of Leicester's nursing school students were of Asian backgroud, while the city itself has an Asian population of 22 per cent (Rashid 1990: 51). London fares no better; in some nursing schools less than 1 per cent of the students are Asians while the proportion of Asians in the city itself is around 15 per cent.

In nursing the solutions to these problems of black under-representation in high quality nurse training, and over-representation in unpopular specialities in undesirable locations, is made doubly difficult by major general reforms that are taking place. Project 2000 is a major initiative in the nursing career structure that will eliminate the distinction between the 'roll' and the 'register' by creating a single registered nurse qualification. Current SENs are required to go on conversion courses to upgrade their qualifications, and there is some evidence that racial discrimination is operating in selection for these conversion courses (Lee-Cunin 1989: 40).

Apart from this, however the plan for a unified qualification will cause problems for those students who would have previously worked their way up from SEN to SRN, for the new course will require higher initial qualifications than the current SEN course, and this higher requirement will indirectly discriminate against communities who are made to fail academically.

However, even black students whose academic performance is better than that of their white counterparts are discriminated against when they consider nursing as a career. Much has been made of the important opportunities currently available for recruiting Asian nurses, and even more has been made of the problems arising from this, and the all too quickly presumed 'cultural' reasons why Asian women in particular do not go into nursing (Karseras and Hopkins 1987: 27; Rashid 1990: 52–3). No one in this debate has so far questioned why Asian men do not go into nursing, for most of the religious and cultural factors frequently cited do not apply to them, and many of the so called 'cultural' factors are only relevant to racially discriminatory practices in nursing that have no relation to nursing competence. The 1980 case of Tajwinder Kaur against Kingston and Richmond Area Health Authority is a clear example of this.

Notwithstanding this there have been the fairly standard attempts to make Asian families themselves responsible for the lack of attractiveness of nursing. In their book on Asian populations and the health service, Karseras and Hopkins (1987: 27) ask why health care professions in general, and nursing in particular, seem to be so unattractive to potential Asian entrants.

. . . Firstly, parents are reluctant to allow their daughters to enter a profession which requires its practitioners to have extremely close contact with members of the opposite sex . . . Secondly, nurses in the subcontinent are usually untrained women of low status and they form the role models for parents who, if their children are to have careers, will want 'something better'.

Thirdly, marriage is central to career planning . . . Fourthly, prospective employees could be forgiven for assuming that career prospects are bleak for non-white workers. Finally, there are fears that cultural beliefs will not be respected, particularly with regard to dress.

The first two suggestions here make fairly major generalizations about a group of people who differ enormously in culture, beliefs, place of origin and religion, and take many of these beliefs as static and homogeneous (Barker 1984). They fail to acknowledge that the views people have of a service or institution, in this case the National Health Service, are not merely a product of cultural beliefs but also relate to their experiences of and within those institutions.

The third suggestion does not bear empirical analysis, because the reality is that many married women with children are in full time employment, and the problem is in any event not a family one but a question of the degree to which employers are willing to be flexible in providing support to parents, male or female, who are in this position.

The tragedy waiting to happen in nursing would be if Project 2000 and the Community Care Programme resulted in a new apartheid in nursing, where Asian nurses are cultivated and promoted to do the nursing on a more equal basis with white colleagues, and Afro-Caribbeans were employed to become the new helpers/support workers. Many Afro-Caribbean nurses, for example, are found in the old Victorian asylums rather than the prestigious modern hospitals, and the Community Care Programme will disproportionately affect these nurses, as historical discrimination in graduate and postgraduate training will not have equipped them for working in the community (CRE 1983b).

Racism and black doctors

A National Health Service needs doctors as well as nurses. The West Indies were targeted for nurse recruitment, and India and Pakistan, and other former colonies, were called on to provide doctors. The process for this, until the early 1970s, allowed accredited colleges in former colonies to train students as doctors who could practice in Britain without further qualification as 'fully registered practitioners'.

In 1972, after leaving the Commonwealth, accreditation was withdrawn from Pakistan. However, the report by Merrison (1975) was a more significant limiting factor in overseas doctors' access to Britain. This report, on 'the Regulation of the Medical Profession', used 'objective' and 'subjective' evidence to call into question the standards of qualification for overseas black doctors. Merrison cited the data shown in Table 9.1 on pass rates for the Royal College of Psychiatrists examinations to show that the performance of doctors from the Indian subcontinent was significantly lower than that of doctors from the United Kingdom, Australasia and South Africa – that is, white doctors. What concerned Merrison's committee was that these discrepancies occurred in a speciality with a high percentage of black doctors; the Department of Health had provided evidence to the committee that 60 per cent of registrars, 34 per cent of senior registrars, and 16 per cent of consultants in the area of mental illness were 'born outside the U.K. or Ireland' (Merrison 1975).

Merrison (1975) also cites what seems little more than glorified gossip to defend the restrictions which he proposed the General Medical Council should adopt for black doctors from overseas. He states:

184 We could not fail to be aware of a widespread conviction that the standard of overseas-educated doctors allowed to practice in this country is lower than that of home-educated doctors. Expressions of this belief can be found regularly in the correspondence columns of the medical journals . . .

187 We believe that this unsatisfactory situation is principally to be attributed to a willingness on the part of the GMC to allow its duty as the protector of medical standards to be compromised by the manpower requirements of the NHS.

The staffing requirements of the NHS for overseas doctors were considerable. One report on medical staffing estimated the level of inflow of overseas doctors to be about 1,600 per year in the late 1970s, but expected this to fall

Table 9.1   Pass rates for three Royal College of Psychiatrists Examinations

	Exam			Average per cent
	1	2	3	
United Kingdom, Australasia	80	84	79	81
South Africa, United African Republic,				
Indian Sub-continent	47	44	48	47

by 40 per cent in the following decade (Department of Health and Social Security 1985: 7). The main reasons for the high dependence on foreign-born doctors have been the savings on training costs and the fact that 'the immigrant is a cheap source of doctor labour' (Maynard and Walker 1978: 8; Smith 1980: 196–8).

The solution to the perceived problem was to create a new body called the Temporary Registration Assessment Board (TRAB) which would ensure that black doctors were suitably qualified. The racism of the tests is clearly shown by the fact that they were aimed at doctors' immigrant status rather than at their medical competence. As Maynard and Walker (1978: 8) observed:

> The TRAB tests, if they were really concerned with protecting the public interest by ensuring competence in doctors, should be applied to all doctors not just new immigrants. Many of those already registered might well fail the TRAB tests. It is unfortunate that the logic of the competence tests is not taken to its logical conclusion.

The facts about the recruitment and deployment of black doctors around this period are quickly summarized. In 1977 about a third of all doctors in the UK came from overseas, the majority of overseas doctors (about 80 per cent) were black, and doctors from the Indian subcontinent made up the largest proportion of this group (about 18.5 per cent of all doctors) (Smith 1980).

There was a higher proportion of doctors from overseas working in hospitals (38 per cent) than in general practice (20 per cent), and within hospitals the general pattern was that overseas doctors were over-represented in the lower medical grades (registrar, senior house officer) and under-represented in the higher grades (senior registrar, consultant). It should be noted that in the 1960s, when general practice was unpopular, many Asian doctors were channelled into this area, and many of these doctors are now in unattractive single practices in undesirable inner-city areas. (see Rashid 1990: 43; Smith 1980: 194). In the 1960s black doctors were often forced into general practice because of discrimination in the teaching hospitals, as a last resort as it were; while in the 1970s and 1980s, when general practice became popular, black doctors were denied the opportunity to work in it. The outcome in both cases was the marginalization of black doctors into unattractive specialities within medicine.

In hospitals, doctors were over-represented in the least popular specialities and under-represented in rural areas and in teaching hospitals. Geographically most of these doctors were found in Yorkshire and the North West of England (Maynard and Walker 1978: 32).

The Merrison Report, with its subjective and objective 'evidence', seems to suggest that much of the discrimination relating to the employment and deployment of overseas doctors can be explained with reference to inadequacies in medical education in their 'places of origin' and is unrelated to racial discrimination. This argument is accepted by most white doctors, and Merrison can be seen as a less than eloquent articulator of the prevailing prejudices (Smith 1980: 194). The solutions proposed thus post the problem with the overseas doctors rather than with the system that discriminates against them (King's Fund 1990a: 43–44).

This colour-blind use of the evidence is not convincing. The important statistical point about the 1970s data is that it is primarily about 'overseas doctors', and we have to extrapolate conclusions about race and ethnicity to assess the ways and degrees to which discrimination operated. The complexity arises from the fact that there are many overseas doctors who are white, many British-born doctors who are black, and many overseas born doctors, black and white, who have received their medical training in Britain.

In the 1980s a number of studies were carried out on 'ethnic minority' or black doctors to find out the degree to which discrimination operated on the basis of colour or ethnic origin (Smith 1980; Anwar and Ali 1987; Smith 1987; McKeigue et al. 1990). These demonstrated that 'race', rather than one's place of qualification, was the real reason why black doctors were employed and deployed in the way they were, although some studies have sought to qualify this (McKeigue et al. 1990).

The problem seems to result from a mixture of direct and indirect discrimination. On the one hand we have the admission of a former president of the Royal College of Physicians that: 'much – but certainly not all – of the apparent discrimination against overseas doctors is based on a not-unexpected tendency to favour graduates of one's own medical schools' (Hoffenberg 1985: 4). Allied to this is the fact that many of the prestigious teaching hospitals discriminate against black students, from whatever place of origin, when they apply for basic training (Smith 1987).

The 'subjective evidence' that discrimination is the reason for the way black doctors are employed and deployed is much more convincing than the occasional muttering in the medical press that so impressed Merrison. A white doctor admitted to Allen (1988: 253):

> I know Asians better at the job than me who never get above Senior House Officer (SHO) level – wandering around the country with very little opportunity to get to be consultants. They have to stay in geriatrics or psychiatry and finally move out of England.

This information is straightforward, but there are many other features of medical appointments that have not been comprehensively studied but which give cause for concern about possible discrimination. Consultants' merit awards, by which doctors award their colleagues substantial salary increases, have long been cited as an example of the 'old boy network', or 'old middle-class white boy network'. In a 1986 study of the North Western Regional Health Authority, for example, black doctors rarely got the awards (8 per cent of black consultants as against 30 per cent of white) or sat on the committees that awarded them (2 per cent as opposed to 10 per cent) (Smith 1987: 328). The national picture contains similar statistics, with further discrimination evident in the class of award people receive (Anwar and Ali 1987: 54–6).

Tackling NHS racism – policy and implementation

Over the years numerous industrial tribunal cases have been brought against district and regional health authorities for alleged racial discrimination (CRE 1984; Anwar and Ali 1987). These cases involved considerable resource and time costs for the authorities concerned. Indeed, it is possible that more senior personnel management time was taken up with defending these cases and painting a favourable picture of their employment practices than with actually implementing anti-discrimination policies.

The Department of Health has responsibility for ensuring that health authorities implemented the various anti-discriminatory policy objectives agreed by the Minister of Health. In the 1970s, under a Labour government, the Department's original response was to seek to get health authorities to end discrimination through the adoption of equal opportunity policies. Since then a number of initiatives have emanated from the Department of Health and other agencies, as indicated in Table 9.2.

Table 9.2   Equal Opportunity Employment Initiatives

Date	Initiative
Oct 1978	DHSS Circular (78)36: *Personnel – The Race Relations Act*
April 1984	Commission for Racial Equality issues Code of Practice
Nov 1985	London Association of Community Relations Councils (LACRC) report: *In a Critical Condition*
May 1986	DHSS Press Release. 'Minister welcomes Task Force for Ethnic Minority Jobs in the NHS'
May 1986	DOH Circular (86)12: *Equal Opportunities in Employment for Ethnic Minorities*
July 1987	DHSS Press Release: 'Tony Newton announces NHS seminar on Services for Ethnic Minorities'
August 1991	Commission for Racial Equality publishes *NHS Contracts and Racial Equality: A Guide*

The first circular in October 1978 is an explanation of the Race Relations Act, which was introduced in June 1977, and details the consequences of the Act for regional and what were then area health authorities. The document is quite comprehensive, both in outlining the Race Relations Act and in suggesting that existing recruitment practices be reviewed to ensure that equality of opportunity becomes a reality.

This circular is noteworthy for a number of reasons. It shows that a policy framework was in place as early as 1978 to begin to seek to eliminate discrimination from the NHS. It also outlines the areas where discrimination in the health service can operate, particularly with respect to training, the recruitment of nurses from overseas, and the treatment of visitors from overseas. Finally, the circular combines exhortation with direction and specifically advises authorities to take the following action:

- Review existing policies to ensure that they conform to the general criteria indicated.
- Review selection, training, transfer, promotion and discharge policies to ensure that no direct or indirect discrimination takes place.
- Examine job specifications and criteria for entry to posts to ensure that no element of unjustifiable discrimination has been introduced.
- Consider the desirability of arranging for English language training for any staff, especially those in regular direct contact with patients, who may need it.

The circular was also supplemented by detailed guidance, issued by the Commission for Racial Equality in 1984, on how to implement equal opportunities policies (see, for example London Association of Community Relations Councils (LACRC) 1985; CRE 1987).

In November 1985, seven years after this first circular was issued, the London Association of Community Relations Councils commissioned a survey to find out to what degree health authorities had complied with the circular. The LACRC (1985) report, like so many others, is best seen as a snapshot of how things were in a particular place (London), at a particular time (1985), but it is useful in that it provides a fairly comprehensive assessment of the degree to which London's 31 district health authorities had complied with the Department of Health's 1977 request.

Twenty-seven health authorities (out of a total 31) responded to the survey which showed that six had no policy, seven had developed a statement of intent, nine had developed a programme of action which had yet to be ratified, and only five had programmes agreed and in the process of implementation.

Within these health authorities there were many variations, and there were possibly cases where good equal opportunity practices were occurring without the formal policy framework being in place. However, the overall picture is of little concerted effort or action on the 1978 Code of Practice. Indeed, it is noteworthy that one of the main recommendations of the report, i.e. that the Department of Health recommend that health authorities 'maintain and analyse records of the ethnic origin of employees and applicants for employment' was not implemented until 1992 (LACRC 1985: 35).

The Department of Health did not issue further guidance as a result of the Code of Practice in 1984, and employed no resources in determining to what degree, if any, health authorities were complying with the initial circular and subsequent Code of Practice. In 1986 Edwina Currie unequivocally stated that the DHSS had no central information on the degree to which individual health authorities had implemented equal opportunities policies, and that the department did not consider further guidance necessary. The response of the Department to the Code of Practice and the LACRC (1985) report was to maintain that the problem was one of information rather than commitment, and that health authorities were more than willing to ensure equality of access to employment but they needed someone to advise them on how to achieve it.

The King's Fund Equal Opportunities Task Force and the review system

The Department funded the King Edward's Hospital Fund for London to set up an Equal Opportunities Task Force. At the time 'task forces' were seen as the solution to everything from the problems of Liverpool to the Falkland Islands, and creating a task force for equal opportunities gave the Department a public relations victory. At a stroke the Department was seen to be doing something. The Task Force, being outside the Department, was outside the monitoring framework by which the Department assessed performance on its priorities. Many of the pronouncements regarding the Task Force also give the impression that the view inside the Department was that the lack of progress was due to a lack of knowledge and information rather than commitment. To verify this one simply has to compare the 'equal opportunities initiatives' with other initiatives in service provision, such as resource management or medical audit, or in personnel, such as clinical regrading, which were occurring at the same time.

The usual management principles with respect to the implementation of policy were ignored in respect of equal opportunities policies. There is no evidence that any action was taken by the Department between 1977 and 1986 with respect to its circular on personnel, despite the fact that the Department was expending massive resources in ensuring that its circulars were implemented. There are arguments about the degree to which circulars have any significance in influencing local action, but it is commonly accepted that when circulars are supplemented by action through the regional and district review system then action does take place (McNaught 1988: ch. 1). This occurred with the introduction of general management, it did not occur with the introduction of equal opportunities policies.

Nineteen seventy-nine saw the election of a Conservative government in Britain, and in the following seven years massive changes to health authority management took place. Essentially these changes brought in the concept of general management (in place of administration), where individual managers were given responsibility for the performance of their authorities, and were remunerated accordingly.

Health authorities were never subjected to the pressures that local authorities experienced in the 1970s and 1980s with regard to eliminating discrimination, and this must be attributed to their lack of accountability (members were appointed rather than elected). When black workers organized themselves it was mainly for reasons of self-advancement, as with the Overseas Doctors Association, and only indirectly as a challenge to discrimination against black staff in the system as a whole. Mainstream health service unions have never given equal opportunity policies a priority (King's Fund 1989).

However, a more basic reason why improvements in equality were difficult to monitor or gain was the complex consensus management that existed in the NHS prior to the first series of Griffiths's general management reforms. The National Health Service, according to Best (1987), was a:

> classic administrative bureaucracy characterized by uniform structures and procedures, an internal focus with a consequent insensitivity to the consumer, an administrative rather than managerial approach to change, and a reactive rather than proactive stance in relation to the external environment.

With the allocation of funding to the NHS went a system whereby the Minister of Health or a deputy, accompanied by appropriate civil servants, visited each of the 14 regional health authorities of England and Wales to decide service priorities over the coming year, and to examine progress on the previously set priorities. Usually regions were given about ten main priorities – for action – and a number of desirable priorities. Equal opportunities did not appear as a priority until 1988, and then it was generally spoken of as a limited priority. Also it appeared problematically at the same time the massive clinical regrading exercise was introduced, which overwhelmed personnel departments for about two years. During these two years little or nothing was done on race equality in employment by personnel managers, and what was done occurred in the teeth of opposition from managers who believed that race was not a priority (McNaught 1988: ch. 4). Race equality, in either employment or service provision, was never a major nationally set objective for the service, and when it did get on the agenda other priorities took precedence. All the objectives that health authorities were set related to policy development and programme implementation, none actually set targets for employing black people.

Achieving race equality in the health care market

Most of the Codes of Practice and advice on implementing equal opportunities in employment in the NHS that have emerged initially from the CRE and subsequently from the King's Fund Task Force are geared to centralist hierarchical organizations with top-down approaches to planning, and bureaucratic personnel systems (CRE 1983a; King's Fund 1989). Furthermore, the advocates of this approach, in arguing for equality of opportunity in employment and equality in service provision, usually seek to advise employers not merely what services to provide but also how to provide them. The most recent CRE publication on the NHS, for example, uses the language of contracts but essentially fails to understand the actual purpose of the NHS reforms (CRE 1991a). On page 19 we read that:

> In some circumstances, racial equality standards should be met immediately by the provider. For example where a service is to be provided to a substantially non-English speaking population by medical staff who are largely unable to speak the relevant language(s), it will be important to have a fully resourced interpreting service, and to provide translated information materials on services.

It is precisely this type of injunction that the health service will be able to avoid, for one can think of many ways in which the service requirements could be met without using interpreters. A number of health authorities in close proximity, each with a relatively minor black population but collectively possessing a substantial one, might choose to contract together to create the appropriate medical or paramedical teams, or alternatively might contract with the private sector to provide the service.

This example reveals an interesting limitation to the policy development. The importance given in the emerging contract culture to needs analysis, contract specifications and quality assurance provides an opportunity for those concerned about race equality to ensure that services are appropriate to actual multi-cultural needs, but will seriously limit their capacity to stipulate how these services are organized or staffed. The fragmentation of district health authorities into purchasers and providers, and the subsequent creation of a mixed economy of care, will allow more specific needs-led provision to emerge.

How this will impact on employment opportunities is not yet clear. The freedom purchasers have to determine priorities is countered by a new freedom of providers in determining how they meet the specifications that arise from the priorities. Figure 9.1 is a representation of the relation between some of the elements in the equation. Inputs are the resources an organization possesses. In health-based organizations these will include doctors, nurses, paramedical and hospital staff, as well as capital and other assets. Outputs refer to the way these services are configured in order to produce quasi-medical events like operations, psychotherapy sessions, ambulance trips, and so on; while outcomes are the consequences the deployment of these resources has on the health of the local population – the health gain, as it were.

In race equality terms inputs relating to employment opportunities would consist of training, policy development, information systems and other organizational resources related to the personnel function; while outcomes are the actual improvements that happen as a result of putting policy into place.

The Department of Health's demands from health authorities in relation to equal opportunities, influenced by the CRE's view of organizational development, are more about the 'inputs' of equal opportunity policies than about 'outcomes'. Because of lack of ethnic monitoring of staff most health authorities did not know how many black staff they had in what positions, and therefore could not be asked to improve on this but only to introduce policies that were believed to improve the employment opportunities for black staff (Gibbon 1990).

No health authority has yet been asked to increase the numbers of black people employed and to improve their conditions of employment. Indeed, to some degree the early obsession with policy and implementation has led to people forgetting what the purpose of the whole process is, that is to end discrimination and ensure black people are employed and deployed on the basis of their abilities rather than of the colour of their skin, and to concentrate on the policy and programme side rather than on outcomes. It had still to be demonstrated that equal opportunity policies lead to the best outcomes as far as black people's employment opportunities are concerned. As with the field of service provision, the health service prefers to spend

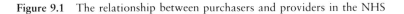

Inputs produce Output lead to Outcomes

Efficiency relation Effectiveness relation

Figure 9.1 The relationship between purchasers and providers in the NHS

money and resources on the research and bureaucracy related to race rather than on improving conditions for black people either as employees or as clients.

Purchasers are ultimately responsible for the ends, while providers are responsible for the means. In old-style NHS planning the district held the contracts of employment and could thereby influence recruitment decisions. With the emergence of self-governing trusts and the demarcation that is emerging between purchasers and providers, this situation will no longer obtain. Self-governing trusts employ their own staff, and it is difficult to see how purchasers will be able to influence this, except indirectly.

In the long run it may be the case that equal opportunities makes good business sense as well as furthering social justice. It may equally be the case that demography will play a greater part in influencing recruitment decisions than hitherto. For example, many nurse recruitment initiatives, particularly among Asian women, stem from an awareness that the supply of middle-class white women is drying up.

The role of central planning will diminish under the NHS reforms, and no single body will be able to demand or ensure that race equality in employment practices becomes a priority for the health service as a whole. However, the network of rewards and benefits that the new system has brought with it will enable, at least at a theoretical level, purchasers to specify rewards for achievements in outcomes.

Part of the problem about race equality is that people have hitherto been rewarded for what they have attempted to do rather than what they have achieved. We have to move away from the position of congratulating people for what they are attempting in race equality and progress towards a situation where actual success is rewarded.

10

Equal opportunities in service delivery: responses to a changing population?

Mark R.D. Johnson

Introduction

The founding fathers of the National Health Service had a simple vision of a health service which would be 'free at the point of use' and would ensure that 'for every citizen there is available whatever medical treatment he requires, in whatever form he requires it . . .' (Beveridge 1942: 158). Have we indeed made progress towards that better brighter society of equality of access envisaged by the parents of the welfare state and indeed the hopeful incomers of the 1950s? And if so, in what ways – what models of good practice can we draw on and promote to ensure that black and ethnic minority patients throughout Britain can all enjoy that 'universal' and sensitive service? For even if locally there have been developments, the NHS nationally still resembles closely the social services whose progress towards multi-cultural sensitivity was described over a decade ago as 'patchy, piecemeal and lacking in strategy' (Association of Directors of Social Services 1978).

As has been well publicized in recent years during the political debate about its future, the NHS was born in July 1948, barely a fortnight after the *Empire Windrush* docked in London. While the landing of 22 June 1948 was not the beginning of settlement in Britain by ethnic minority groups (perhaps better dated to the Roman period!), it is frequently taken as emblematic of that process. All too frequently in discussing 'race relations' in Britain, television film directors resort to those clips of immigrant hopefuls arriving to seek their fortunes in the 'mother country'. Academics and political commentators also have found it hard to lay to rest the notion of 'the immigrant' and the belief that migrant settlers are attracted by the benefits of a benevolent welfare state, even if that notion was countered very early on by a classic economic study (Jones and Smith 1970). Indeed, it may be argued that in some respects the health service is less well positioned to meet the needs of Britain's black and ethnic minority citizens now than it was then.

While the old 'immigrant reception' services have been replaced by 'transcultural clinics', and the language of 'assimilation' replaced by that of 'special needs', consideration of the needs of British black and ethnic minority citizens remains a subsidiary rather than a 'mainstream' issue. That said, there have been changes and will continue to be so. Black and ethnic minority communities have themselves, in their struggles for increased sensitivity, made no small contribution to the development of the welfare state. However, while the NHS has relied heavily upon the contribution made to its fortunes by that population, it is less certain that the minority communities have benefited proportionately from developments in the health service.

A changing population

The birth and development of the NHS has coincided with the postwar growth of Britain's black and ethnic minority population; these two crucial elements of modern British society have grown up together – and been intimately related. Migrants did not abandon their homelands to seek an easy life supported by a philanthropic state, as has been alleged: they came to Britain at the behest of that state, the 'head of the Commonwealth', in order to serve and preserve it. Once engaged and exploited in that service, they became settlers, contributing as both labour and taxpayers to its maintenance.

It is therefore perhaps important to reflect upon the changes that have taken place in the British population since that first vision of a postwar 'land fit for heroes'. In that war many volunteers from the Commonwealth gave their lives and their contribution to the war effort brought some of them from Asia, Africa and the Caribbean to the 'mother country' for the first time, to work as part of the national industrial effort alongside white British workers. Most of the wartime black workers in Britain were men, and although the majority were in civilian positions they hardly formed a significant part of the community: there were indeed, neither resources nor demands for 'special treatment'. Even where there were, largely in certain seaports with significant numbers of settlers of minority origin, little was known of their medical needs and indeed the technology of the day had little to offer. By the last decade of this century, however, both medicine and population have changed immeasurably.

After the war, and the repatriation of most of the war workers, the 'coloured population' of Great Britain (as it was then known) numbered only a few thousands: fifty years later, following the 'most striking change to occur to the population of Great Britain since the turn of the century' (Peach *et al.*, 1988: 561), more than one in 20 of the residents and citizens of Britain trace their ancestry back to the African, Caribbean and Asian lands of the Commonwealth and former Empire. While much of the population movement which fuelled this change was voluntary (at least in principle, even if the economic and political pressures signalled a different imperative) the migrants included significant numbers of refugees (most notably from East Africa and South East Asia). There were also those who were directly recruited (many by the National Health Service itself) from Jamaica, Barbados, Pakistan and India. The data from the 'ethnic question' in the 1991 Census, which became available in 1993,[1] will illustrate just how significant a proportion of the population it is that chooses to describe its ancestry as belonging to one or other 'ethnic minority'.

The earliest evidence available for the size of the black and ethnic minority population after the war is in the 1951 Census, which recorded 218,000 individuals born 'in the New Commonwealth', or 0.4 per cent of the population of the UK. However, significant numbers of these, perhaps as many as one-fifth, were white people born to families involved in trade, missionary work and administration in the Empire, largely in India. Perhaps half of the remainder (about 17,000) were born in the West Indies of 'African-Caribbean' descent. The numbers of 'Commonwealth immigrants' were also small in comparison to the numbers of settlers and refugees from eastern Europe, many displaced by the same world war and eagerly recruited to fill the needs of the British industrial economy. By the 1961 Census the number of West Indian-born had increased tenfold, and the total New Commonwealth-born risen to 541,000; just over 1 per cent of the total population. With the bringing down of the 'iron curtain' and the recovery of mainland European economies, the supply of white migrants from that source had effectively ceased.

Following 'Africanization' in East Africa, which stimulated a flow of refugees of Asian origin during the early 1960s, and further migration in an attempt to 'beat the ban' heralded by the 1962 Commonwealth Immigrants Act and 1965 White Paper on immigration from the Commonwealth, the population of New Commonwealth origin rose to 853,000 in the 1966 (sample) Census. For the first time, this figure is believed to have underestimated the black and ethnic minority population, which was probably just over 1 million as families with British-born children began to develop. This process, of course, had its implications for the provision of NHS facilities.

The 1971 Census, recognizing the presence of 'second generation' citizens of New Commonwealth origin, asked about the place of birth of parents, and recorded a significant increase in the minority population. Around one in three of the population of Asian, African and Caribbean origin had been born in Britain (Table 10.1), and because of the Immigration Act 1971, the flow of 'non-patrial' settlers was virtually closed off. Thus, while the 'immigrant' population had now peaked at just under 1 million, about 2.7 per cent of the national population was of black (African, Asian and Caribbean) or ethnic minority origin.

Despite the increasing flow of 'return migration' after 1970 attributable to earlier migrants retiring to their birthplaces or seeking better conditions overseas, the minority population has continued to grow. In this way, perhaps, they have solved the conundrum faced by Beveridge and underlying his design of the NHS: 'With its present rate of reproduction, the British race cannot continue: means of reversing this recent course of the birth rate must be found . . .' (Beveridge 1942: 154).

That is to say, the 'invention' of the NHS was in no way an act of unconcerned philanthropy, any more than had been the welcome afforded to the early migrant settlers. Both owed their *raison d'être* to the economic imperative of maintaining an adequately large, dynamic and healthy workforce to keep the (pre-automation) wheels of industry turning. Had the modern arts of robotics been then available, it is possible that Beveridge and his Royal Commission might have been content to let the birthrate continue to fall in the hope that rising standards of living would have reversed the outflow of (white) emigration to the 'new worlds' of the Americas and Dominions.

By 1981, and using yet another Census definition, the 'black/minority

Table 10.1 Estimates of 'New Commonwealth' minority population in the 1971 census

Birthplace of self or parent	Self born (thousands)	Parents (UK-born) (thousands)	Percentage of total UK-born
India	255	129	33
Pakistan/Bangladesh	133	36	21
West Indies	302	246	49
Africa	122	36	23
Other NCW	131	96	42
Total NCW	943	543	36

Note: Overall population of New Commonwealth origin: 1,486,000.
Source: House of Commons Library Research Division; Background Paper 56, 1976.

population' was estimated to have reached 2,171,000 or 4.6 per cent of the UK total. Increasingly, and in all ethnic groups, this underestimated the population because of its reliance on birthplace: present data can only give a partial estimate of fertility among ethnic minority groups because of their reliance on birthplace (Jones, C. 1991). Even in 1977, 5 per cent of the 'Indian' heads of household identified by the ethnic question of the National Dwelling and Household Survey had been born in Britain. By 1984, over half of the Afro-Caribbean population had been born in Britain (Peach *et al.* 1988: 578). Subsequent data therefore must be derived from a direct question on ethnic origin. The most recent figures available (until the Census data of 1991 have been fully processed) are those of the regular Labour Force Survey, which in 1987 estimated a total national minority working-age population of 1,600,000, or 4.7 per cent of the total population of 33,740,000. Of that number, 514,000 were of Indian origin, 342,000 West Indian or Guyanese in origin, about 290,000 of Pakistani or Bangladeshi origin, and the remainder gave their ethnic background as Chinese, African, Arab or a mixture of origins. However, 7.9 per cent of the population aged under 16, and only 0.9 per cent of those over state retirement age, fell into one of these minority groups (*Employment Gazette* 1991).

As Peach *et al.* (1988: 593) observe, however, while the migration process has brought rewards to some, for many:

> migration has served only to transfer them from poverty in one country to poverty in another, whilst the colour of their skin has ensured that they are subjected to institutionalised differential treatment, racial harassment and abuse, and attacks upon their property and person.

Among the refugee populations, while there have been signs of economic prosperity shown by some of the East African Asian community, the Vietnamese have encountered problem after problem, being settled with government aid, according to Peach *et al.* (1988: 608), in:

> areas which the local population was abandoning because of lack of economic opportunities. With few transferable skills and in many cases no English, the Vietnamese were unlikely to succeed where British people had failed ... Many Vietnamese are frustrated and isolated, and some commentators suggest that this will manifest itself in mental disorders.

From this it may be seen that despite the effective ending of mass migration in the 1970s, and the transformation of a once migrant population into a settler population, smaller groups of ethnic minority origin have continued to be added to the diversity of the British population. Each has then experienced afresh the problems of 'newness' which were believed to be the key issues that faced their predecessors. However, the ability to 'integrate' or be 'assimilated' was not for any of these groups the only problem (if even a desired goal). Nor at any time, even at the earliest when numbers (and, perhaps it might have been felt, needs) were greatest, did the NHS act fast or effectively to meet their needs.[2]

A changing National Health Service

The earliest responses of the health professions to the coming to Britain of immigrants of non-European origins appear to have been distinctly restricted. Most immediate concerns seemed to focus upon issues of what has been termed 'port medicine', seeking to stem the reputed danger of importation of disease to Britain. Concern was particularly expressed about venereal diseases, traditionally blamed on immigrants (Skone 1970: 25), and the scourge of tuberculosis which was just beginning to be brought under control. Even now, references or allusions to this recur from time to time (Handley 1991). Significantly, the danger then was also seen as being a 'moral' one, with constant reference to 'unmarried mothers' (Yudkin 1965; Dodge 1969). That theme also continues, although it is clear that the growth in single-parent families cannot all have been caused by the coming of immigrants from the New Commonwealth, and their subsequent descendants (Marks and Kingman 1991).

There is no doubt that the 1960s, the period during which migration from the 'Third World' was at its most intensive, were a time during which the practitioners of the medical service needed to extend their knowledge base. This would have enabled them to face up to the challenges to existing practices which those with other cultural backgrounds and expectations represented. It is less clear that any substantive changes were made, or that there was then any idea that anything other than a period of transition (while 'immigrants' adapted to 'English' ways) would be required. While the Community Relations Commission and the rest of the young 'race relations industry' were actively publishing and promoting work in the interests of the newcoming population, most of this referred to education, housing and prejudice, and little to health matters. Dodge's early text therefore set a paradigm which has not yet fully been overturned. As he remarks: 'Before one is able adequately to serve the needs of a community, it is necessary to understand the more important differences of belief and custom which distinguish that community . . . These barriers may be based upon differences of language or culture' (Dodge 1969: 15). Similarly, the Community Relations Commission observed in 1970 that: 'There is an urgent need for a central bureau of information and teaching material in health education' (Skone 1970: 29).

Research in the latter part of the 1980s was to demonstrate that this need had in no way diminished (Poulton *et al.* 1987). Indeed, as the association between ethnic minority status and immigrant origin declines, and assumptions may be made about social or cultural integration, it is possible that the need has increased. Cultural sensitivity and knowledge of naming patterns may well not be the sole answer to the problems of those who find themselves in a society structured by racism and inequality, but they are none the less necessary, since ignorance is one of the key instruments of racist oppression. Certainly it remains important that medical workers should be educated to practice in a society characterized by diversity. It is therefore remarkable that the initiative and Government funding to set up just such a central bureau – to be known as Services for Health and Race Exchange (SHARE) King's Fund press release, 4 November 1991 – has had to wait for a further 21 years!

While Dodge and his co-contributors were undoubtedly correct to identify communication issues as of key importance, it is of interest (and concern) to note that there still seems to be a need for such descriptions of naming systems and diet as he sought to provide, sometimes without the sensitivity that he displayed:

> It is easy for the Western European to observe that the culture of the immigrant is different from his own, and as easy to forget that his culture is different from that of the immigrant . . . this is not to imply that the difference is for the worse or that members of the same race or nationality exhibit the same differences . . . (Dodge 1969: 16)

It is not, however, necessarily the case that the training of nurses or other medical staff has overcome these gaps, despite the existence of well-designed and well-circulated training materials, and acknowledgement of these matters in core texts. Nor have the necessary attitudinal changes occurred among the staff themselves, and these continue to form effective barriers to use of services by minority clients:

> The questionnaire responses indicated difficulties over Asian naming systems and over communication with Asian women . . . Non-attendance at the antenatal clinic was attributed mainly to cultural restrictions rather than to the provision of inappropriate services . . . Many interviewees expressed some hostility to Asian users and relatives.
> (Auluck and Iles 1991: 49)

A second theme that can be detected in reading the history of health service provision is one of complaints about the misuse or overuse of the NHS by 'immigrants'. This theme has continued to recur (Wright 1983;

Heatley and Yip 1991) and led to the imposition of charges on 'overseas visitors' in 1981–82, an impost which still rankles and has led to cases of black British citizens (including those born in UK) being asked for passports to prove their entitlement. The apotheosis of this theme was perhaps Enoch Powell's famous 'Rivers of Blood' speech of 20 April 1968, in which he claimed that the native English ' . . . found their wives unable to find hospital beds in childbirth . . .' (cited by Nanda 1989: 273). The irony of this is, perhaps, that then, as on subsequent occasions, the ethnic minorities were making demands and setting trends (in this case for hospital births rather than home confinement) which were shortly be to be recognized as commonplace, and in many cases desirable, among the white population. On other occasions the responses of black and ethnic minority groups to an unmet need, such as 'half-way homes' run by community groups for discharged mental hospital patients, have been followed by government initiatives making a similar virtue out of necessity for the majority (as in the recent move towards 'care in the community').

Since the war, the provision of medical services has changed unimaginably – both technically and in social attitudes towards its practice, as well as in the expectations of the populace for its delivery and capacity. Many diseases which in the 1950s were viewed as fatal are now generally regarded as minor or at least curable. Nevertheless, there have been few developments of particular benefit for ethnic and racial minorities, and barriers to their uptake of services remain. A recent publication for example reminds us that sickle cell disease, a scourge of African-descended populations, was first described in 1910 and the subject of extensive research in the 1940s. Despite the Nobel prizes since awarded to Linus Pauling for his fundamental research and the development of a 'new' science of molecular medicine based upon work exploring this condition, less has been done towards seeking a cure or more effective treatment for this than for many rarer conditions only affecting white patients (Weatherall 1991: 1590). This is not a new observation: the President of the Royal College of Physicians wondered why 'there was no screening programme for thalassaemia, which affects more people than cystic fibrosis' as long ago as 1985 (McNaught 1985a :8). Cystic fibrosis, which affects about one in every 2,500 'white Caucasian' births, was first described at about the same time as sickle cell disease, and while as yet no cure has been found, research into its prevention has developed tremendously in recent years (Vaghmaria 1991). Much the same may be said about phenylketonuria, whose incidence is less than one in 10,000 and yet every child born in Britain is tested for this condition, using a blood sample which might be used to test simultaneously for sickling. Black patients, of whom as many as one in 300 may be at risk of sickle cell disease, are understandably concerned that 'their' disease seems to attract less attention.

Anionwu discusses the politics and provision of services for haemoglo-binopathies in Chapter 5 (this volume).

The debt of the National Health Service

The NHS, indeed, has benefited from major contributions from Britain's black or ethnic minority communities, over and above the financial relationship incurred through the proportion of the cost which they shoulder either in direct or indirect taxation. The role of Enoch Powell's Ministry of Health in recruiting nurses from the Caribbean has been well documented: in 1964, nearly one in five nursing trainees was Commonwealth-born (Skone 1970). To this day the medically qualified personnel on which the NHS depends includes a substantial proportion of 'overseas doctors', largely from the Asian sub-continent. Rather fewer black British have been able to play their part in that work, due in part to the racist exclusion they have met in recruitment to medical schools. However, the contribution goes further back, and includes an intellectual and political role. Increasingly, the work of Mary Seacole has been recognized for its part in creating and legitimating the profession of nursing – even if Florence Nightingale's name is the one which is revered (Lee-Cunin 1989). Similarly, less is heard of other pioneers, such as the Jamaica-born Dr Goffe, sometime GP of Kingston upon Thames, early member of the Fabian Society and father of one of the team who helped develop the Sabin polio vaccine (File and Power 1981: 39), even if Dr Harold Moody (GP in Peckham) and Lord Pitt are well known, as much perhaps for their political prominence as their contributions to medicine. Doctors from India such as Sake Deen Mahomed and his grandson Frederick Akbar Mahomed FRCP, or Dr K.M. Pardhy FRCS, also made early contributions to the practice and development of scientific medicine in Britain (Visram 1986). The current NHS is heavily dependent on Asian doctors and Caribbean origin nurses whose experiences are discussed in detail by Ward (Chapter 9, this volume).

Changes in health services provision

It is, therefore, hard to detect any structural changes in the delivery of health services since the 1960s which would make them more responsive to black and ethnic minority needs, or indeed much awareness that this is required, even in research and policy documents examining the provision of services. Most studies of health services delivery appear to be colour-blind, so that planning takes place in a vacuum informed only by myth and prejudice. The famous study into inequality in health now known as the Black Report (Townsend and Davidson 1982) barely touched on the issue, and while its successor did explore this particular dimension of inequality it does not get very far (Whitehead 1987). The Black Report found, indeed, conflicting evidence that migrants may be healthier and fitter, but that their descendants were more likely to suffer from specific health disabilities and that 'there is evidence of a lack of appreciation among health service staff of the special needs of some immigrant groups and a lack of facilities in the areas where they are forced to concentrate' (Townsend *et al.* 1988: 79).

A survey of district health authorities carried out after the Black Report found that few DHAs had any statistical information about their 'Asian' populations to assist in planning, and that their 'special provision' was largely confined to translated health education materials, dietary provision in hospital, and perhaps 'in-service training' for staff (Donaldson and Odell 1984). That period, however, was noteworthy for the mounting of the Asian Mother and Baby Campaign (AMBC). This grew from another initiative, to counter the perception that rickets was a growing threat to the health of Asian children (McNaught 1987: 16). While this may have been based on shaky grounds, it is clear that there were real problems of communication between health workers and clients. By the identification of the delivery of inappropriate and inaccessible services and the provision of resources coupled with an innovative approach, some of the ideas and mechanisms arising from the AMBC project have had real value (Coad 1986). In particular, the notion of 'link-workers', and language-competent client advocates, has been catalytic, and taken up by a growing number of authorities (Coventry, Southall, and Bristol among them) for work in mental health services as much as in the original maternity areas. They, and the AMBC itself, are frequently 'project based' and likely to be abandoned after two or three years as evaluation studies are being prepared to testify to their value (Bahl 1987), or before their benefits are known and before the material deprivation, which remains a key underlying issue, can be tackled (Rocheron 1988). Underlying causes are rarely attractive to policy-makers, who wish to be seen to be taking action.

As may be noted by consideration of textbooks for health professionals, what analysis and service provision related to ethnic minority need there has been has tended to focus upon the exotic or the specialist. In particular, this has meant genetically transmitted and relatively rare conditions for which little has been done in terms of 'cure', or 'imported' conditions such as leprosy or cholera perhaps related to tropical environments. These are now more likely to be found among globe-trotting business executives or families returning from 'foreign holidays' than among the British black communities. Clearly there are 'ethnically specific diseases', but these can be met in some cases by referral to the appropriate specialist (if the professional first encountering them is alert). Others, while possibly requiring specialized provision or treatment, are not 'common'. The presence of projects and centres to provide appropriate care and support for such cases (such as in the Haringey Sickle-Cell Centre) is perhaps indicative of a degree of sensitivity in the health care provision system, but it does not necessarily indicate that all the health needs of the minority communities are being met. Nor do such initiatives always survive for long. While the first sickle cell project was founded in Brent in 1978 and stimulated others so that by 1985 there were seven, this development can be traced to the activity of a few key individuals. Many have now closed and the sickle cell charities have hit hard times.

However, there are signs of recent trends away from a model whereby minority health issues are seen as confined to such exotic or relatively rare and ethnically specific diseases. There is developing within the NHS a new theme of 'transcultural' or multi-cultural medicine, and of preparation to practise in a multi-racial society. Not all commentators or authors are united in the use of this terminology, and while for some the term is merely an opportunity to demonstrate a variety of quaint oddities, others seem to have made a genuine effort to understand and consider the implications of cultural relativism. This must be seen as healthier than a concentration on problematic cultures and 'special needs'. For it to be adopted more universally, however, both political will and leadership are required (McNaught 1988). Further, perhaps some disturbance to the existing system such as that being brought about in the name of the Patient's Charter will enable this new perspective to be grafted in, without being seen to displace those existing priorities and practices which have grown up to serve powerful established constituencies. There is, therefore, despite many reservations about the details of the reforms, some potential in the current changes in health services, especially in relation to making them more attuned to meeting language and cultural needs and those issues which arise from the development of monitoring and 'quality assurance'.

The British Medical Association, in its attempt to produce a manifesto for the future of the NHS that would complement or pre-empt the proposals of the government, has failed signally to consider any of these issues, and clearly appears to be considering the agenda for a continuing mono-cultural (albeit geographically distinguishable) society (BMA 1991). It does, however, acknowledge that a key issue is the assessment of need, and that this is a 'primitive science'. Since one of the key demands of those fighting for improvements in health services for ethnic minorities has been that their needs should be recognized and built into planning, it may be that the work done to develop means of measuring minority needs will provide the basis of mechanisms to measure needs more generally. As remarked earlier, Whitehead, returning to the territory of the Black Report (Townsend *et al.* 1988), was not convinced that the condition of any of the poorer sections of the British population had been materially improved. The identification of 'ethnic minority' need is only part of a wider rediscovery of the true dimensions of need in society. This will then have to be linked to resource allocation, and consideration of questions of distribution, equity and priority. In all this lies, perhaps, the development of equal opportunities in service delivery, of the coming of 'citizen consumer' status for black and ethnic minority clients.

Special or specific need

We know from the Black Report and from the founding fathers (most were, indeed, male) of epidemiology and sociology that ill health is inequitably distributed. We therefore have to consider equality of opportunity in a need or demand-led and non-normally distributed universe. We might ask if everyone does want an equal chance of a particular operation, or if certain procedures should be equally distributed. This inevitably raises questions about the nature of equal opportunity – should one measure proportionate distribution of resources or outcomes? Given inequality in life circumstances, massive over-representation among the users of certain services might be a proper expectation. And other services may be totally irrelevant to black needs, as some will be irrelevant to the majority of white consumers. Indeed, medically, it remains a necessary fact that there are 'racially' specific special needs, or at least 'alternative' needs. While we argue and agree that 'race' is a social construct and that disease organisms such as HIV pay no attention to ethnic differences, certain biological differentiations do exist – and will not go away. One might argue that with intermarriage between populations the association between a genetic predisposition towards sickle cell and visible blackness may decline. This theme was taken up in the 1991 Reith Lectures, in which Dr Steve Jones (1991: 16) observed: 'There are also black Duffy genes among the American population that sees itself as white. Eighteenth century England had a substantial black population . . . Some of its genes are certainly still around in the streets of Britain.' That process of genetic integration takes many years, and ignores the facts of racial discrimination on the latter basis affecting life chances, and, through income and housing, health. Indeed, such discrimination may be found within the health service, perhaps affecting directly the chances of clients being given appropriate treatment or a diagnosis which will further disadvantage them. This has particularly been reported in the use of certain powers under the Mental Health Acts (Cope 1989; Ineichen 1989). On the other hand, in that field as in other specialisms, there have been some examples of good practice – perhaps provoked by the exposure of examples of bad practice and by the political pressures that have been generated around these! Again, these tend to be local initiatives rather than generally available services, so that a publication of the King's Fund finds it easier to list 'gaps in mental health services' and suggest occasional examples of good practice, than to do the reverse (Christie and Blunden 1991). Much the same was the experience of the compilers of the National Association of Health Authorities publication *Words about Action*; an initiative designed to spread knowledge about good practice which collapsed after only four issues covering mental health, maternity, 'services for older people' and haemoglobinopathies.

Examples can be found of local initiatives addressing issues of concern to specific populations, or targeted towards the communication problems in service delivery of particular groups. These include the Chinese Health Resource Centre in Soho (Li 1992) and the Bengali Health Advisory Service in Tower Hamlets, staffed by bilingual staff, often including volunteers from the relevant communities and professionals working over and above their expected levels of commitment to help those who share their language and culture. Others such as the Coventry Health Information Forum are partnerships between health and community development workers and attract intermittent support from official funds. Rarely are these initiatives fully supported by those who are responsible for mainstream provision. While it may be true that with the passage of time the need for such facilities may decline, that is no reason for ignoring those needs now (McNaught 1985b: 8). However, what all too frequently happens is that these projects are reliant upon the goodwill of a few individuals, or on temporary funding regimes such as the Urban Programme (Department of Health (DoH) 1991a: 21), and fade away in an unplanned fashion before their value has been exhausted. Worse still, their existence may permit a hard-pressed bureaucracy to argue that scarce public resources should not be used to duplicate an existing (voluntary and community-financed) service, or at the least that there is 'no need' to amend mainstream services in the light of such provision.

A black future in the health of the nation?

During the autumn of 1991, many black and ethnic minority readers may have turned to the government's consultative document *The Health of the Nation* (DoH 1991b) with interest. In it they would have noted the observation that 'There are significant variations in health – geographical, ethnic, social and occupational . . . This is a cause for concern and a challenge . . .' (1991b: viii, para. 6). These are sentiments which echo those expressed on many occasions by members of those communities and their friends. They may even have been heartened to observe that the approach has the potential to recognize both that there are racial disadvantages which affect all black and visible minority groups, and that within that there are further specific issues affecting particular groups. On looking into the paper in greater detail to see what specific attention was paid to this issue, however, they will have found little of any specific value apart from the observation that ethnicity is associated with variations in health status; that those born in the Indian sub-continent (not all of whom would be classified as Asian!) have a higher death rate from coronary heart disease, and that 'diabetes shows [similar] marked variations, while some diseases (such as sickle cell disease) affect particular ethnic groups' (1991b: 19, para, 4.14).

It is perhaps a step forward in the sensitivity of official policy to have reached this level of recognition of the specific needs of Britain's black and minority ethnic groups, but unfortunately there appears to be no further initiative exhibited in the paper to tackle these issues, or others which are of at least as great concern to those constituencies. There is no more detailed consideration given to the issue than the pledge that 'specific initiatives to address the health needs of particularly vulnerable groups, whether geographical, ethnic, occupational or others' will be needed (1991b: 20), and the observation that the Department of Environment has funded some 'access' projects under the Urban Programme (1991b: 21). Unfortunately, no examples of these are given, either as a demonstration of good practice or a means of identifying (and perhaps criticizing) what might be provided. Further, the Inner Cities Urban Programme (even if a 'partnership' between agencies) is not a part of the National Health Service, under the direction of the Department of Health, or in any sense 'main programme funding'. It cannot therefore be regarded as being any more than transitional or supplementary provision, in the same way as 'Section 11' funding (Johnson et al. 1989). It is certainly no solution to entrenched disadvantage, racist exclusion or other institutional barriers to equity. That would require action to be included in the 'Key Areas' objectives and targets listed later in the document, and from which mention of race or ethnicity is conspicuously absent.

While it is of interest to observe that, under the heading 'Quality of NHS Service', it is stated that 'the importance of the quality of service in terms of the patients' perception of health care experience should not be underestimated. The quality of service can have a therapeutic value and be of enormous psychological benefit' . . . (1991b: 52, para, 10,3), there is no apparent realization that to many black or ethnic minority patients that 'quality of care' is seriously flawed, either because of cultural insensitivity, or in terms of their experience of racist treatment.

The appendices to the paper continue this apparent 'colour-blind' approach, despite the expectations which had been raised in the introductory passages cited above. Thus Appendices A and B, 'Coronary Heart Disease' and 'Stroke', which are seen as largely preventable, and are known to be raised in certain ethnic minorities, fail to refer to that fact (despite the evidence cited on page 19, para 4.14). Similarly, while Appendix E, 'Eating and Drinking Habits', refers to changing dietary preferences, it could perhaps have acknowledged the increasing popularity among the majority (white) population of foods from ethnic minority cultures – a trend which many recent Health Education Authority booklets seem to ignore, with the result that black readers also may feel that their tastes are marginalized or ignored. The only mention of minority ethnic needs in this part of the document comes in Appendix I, where the higher rates of (non-insulin dependent) diabetes among those of Asian origin are mentioned (1991b: 83). However, there is no suggestion of specific screening or other projects targeted on minority communities, either as examples of good practice (which could be located) or as objectives and targets. Other appendices, such as those on mental health (Appendix J) or environment (Appendix P) are equally colour-blind, even though there are established issues of racial or ethnic concern in those fields. One such is the unsatisfactory nature of 'bed and breakfast accommodation' which is mentioned, but not linked to the unwanted reliance upon this form of housing experienced by Bengali families in the East End of London, for example. The problems of the mental health service have been well documented elsewhere (Ineichen 1989; Ranger 1989; Littlewood and Lipsedge 1990; Crowley 1991; and Sashidharan and Francis in this volume).

The failure of this government initiative to build 'equality of opportunity in service delivery' or ethnic and racial sensitivity into the NHS reforms is to be regretted. It can be done, indeed apparently was done in the design of the Children Act and its associated guidance materials (Johnson 1992). But while these concerns are left to the care of individuals willing to act as 'policy entrepreneurs' or 'product champions' (McNaught 1988: 27), rather than incorporated into central planning and policy formulation, there is little hope that black British citizens will experience a uniformly welcoming and sensitive service, as should be their right.

Conclusion

As the Department of Health (1991c: 12) itself states in a charter distributed to all the nation and which will be available, probably uniquely, in nine minority languages including Turkish, Vietnamese and Gujarati: 'The Charter Standard is that all health services should make provision so that . . . your privacy, dignity and religious and cultural beliefs are respected.'

The centre has spoken, and given a clear lead – even if there has been some delay in the production of those translations. The onus now would appear to be on local health authorities and trusts to demonstrate through their practice, monitoring and reports, that they are doing their best to meet that standard, and the guidelines of the NHS Management Executive. Some of those guidelines have already stipulated the need to meet what are in fact key demands of the minority communities, such as attention to their religious and spiritual lives (HSG1922). It is also possible that they have met with incomprehension, resistance, or simply an inability to release resources to meet them.

It is certain that a prime reason for these expectations being built into the reforms was not a desire to meet the demands of black or minority ethnic British citizens: rather, it is politically fortunate that those demands parallel the desires of the vocal and critical middle classes! It is not that this initiative is designed to create equality of opportunity in the provision of health services, but that it provides an explicit expectation of changes which will enable that, and a requirement that the providers of services can be measured against. In auditing that performance, the role of the 'purchasing authorities', and indeed of the Secretary of State, will be critical. This opportunity to move attention away from the stereotypical and victim-blaming views of minority culture as pathogenic, inherent in campaigns against *surma*, *sikor*, and diets believed to cause rickets, must be grasped.

It remains to be seen whether the political pressure that black and ethnic minorities can exert will be sufficient, or whether the will to monitor the degree to which their interests are met exists. If, as may be suspected, those interests continue to be dependent upon the actions of a few committed and sensitive individuals, then the evidence suggests that progress towards equality of opportunity in service delivery will remain as marginal, impermanent and insubstantial as it has been over the past forty-odd years. If, on the other hand, common cause can be found with those whose interests motivate the management, or if enough reforming managers can be identified (and black or minority ethnic management must be among them), then perhaps the initial vision of Beveridge and his colleagues may be fulfilled in a more radical fashion than was ever envisaged.

Notes

1 This Chapter went to press before the data from the 1991 Census were available.
2 Recently available evidence from the 1991 Census of Population has made it possible for us to have a better understanding of the size and characteristics of the black and minority ethnic population of Britain. Responses to an 'ethnic origin' question showed that 3,015,000 people, 5.5 per cent of the population of Great Britain, declared their identity as one of the minority groups. About half of this number were of South Asian origin, and while there were half a million people described as 'Black-Caribbean', there were also substantial numbers of Chinese descent and in 'Other' categories (Owen 1992). Over half (54.4 per cent) had been born in Britain.
    The black and minority population is still very youthful, only about three in every hundred being aged over 65, compared to 16 per cent of the nation as a whole, and a third were aged under 16. Consequently, household sizes tend to be rather larger, but unexpectedly, there are higher rates of 'persons suffering from a long-term illness or health problem' (Owen 1993).

Conclusions

11

Promoting equitable health and health care: a case for action

W.I.U. Ahmad

Introduction

This chapter looks to the prospects for equitable health and health care in a racially inequitable society. The aim is not to provide a blueprint for action but merely to offer some pointers. That (ill) health is socially produced, mediated by people's social, economic, and racial and gender identities; and more widely by their *de facto* citizenship status, is no longer in doubt. At an official level the World Health Organization (WHO) definition of health as a state of complete mental, physical and social well being, rather than just the absence of disease, extends our understanding of the social conception and reality of 'health', an understanding further elaborated by the Ottawa Convention on Health Promotion and adopted by all the regions of the WHO. The European region agreed the following prerequisites for health: peace, and freedom from the fear of war: equal opportunities for all; satisfaction of basic needs (adequate food and income, basic education, safe water and sanitation, decent housing, secure work, a satisfying role in life); and political will for change at an official level and public support. The strategy for achieving Health for All by the year 2000 had the following underlying principles: equity; health promotion; community participation; multi-sectoral collaboration; primary health care; and international co-operation (Scott-Samuel 1992).

So, above all, two factors are central to the WHO's vision of reducing health inequalities: first that equity is of paramount importance, and second, that health gains can only be achieved through a broad-ranging strategy. I will discuss the implications of both of these for minority ethnic communities.

Equity has been judged to be the most important element for any meaningful strategy for promotion of health and the eradication of health differentials. That disadvantaged groups have poorer health and reduced access to health care is beyond doubt (see Townsend and Davidson 1982; Whitehead 1987). Equally, as disadvantage adversely affects both health status and access to health care, a move towards equity needs to encompass strategies for eradication of inequitable differentials in both health (largely outside the sphere of medicine) and health care.

Whitehead (1992b: 430) summarizes the link between inequality in social life and inequality in health in the European context and shows that inequalities exist in both mortality and morbidity:

> Firstly, there is consistent evidence that disadvantaged groups have poorer survival chances . . . For example, in the United Kingdom a child born to professional parents can expect to live over five years more than a child born to an unskilled manual household. In France, life expectancy of a 35-year old university lecturer exceeds by nine years that of an unskilled labourer of the same age. In Hungary . . . males living in the most depressed neighbourhoods had a life expectancy of about four years shorter than the national average and five and half years shorter than those living in the most fashionable districts.

On morbidity, she cites evidence of disadvantage being related to poor mental health, shorter stature of children, poor dental health, higher rates of chronic illness and disability and the chance of earlier onset of these conditions. It is unhealthy to be born poor or to become poor. The evidence is that the majority of health differentials between populations, defined on the basis of class or race, are avoidable and unjust, and are intrinsically related to the wider life chances of those populations (Ahmad *et al.* 1989; Sheldon and Parker 1992).

The term 'inequity' refers, as in WHO documents, to avoidable differences which are both unnecessary and unjust. A definition of equity in *health* offered by Whitehead (1992b: 433) is 'that ideally everyone should have *fair opportunity* to attain their full health potential and, more pragmatically, that none should be disadvantaged from achieving this potential, if it can be avoided'. Equity in health care must encompass notions of quality, appropriateness and acceptability of service provision to all sections of the population and is summed up by Whitehead (1992b: 434) as 'equal access to available care for equal need; equal utilization for equal need; equal quality of care for all'.

The provision of basic prerequisites for health is therefore essential to achieving equity in health status and health care. Issues of participation, equality of substantive rights of citizenship (Ahmad and Husband 1993) and the provision of basic human needs are essential elements in moving towards racially equitable health and health care. A cursory study of racial inequalities across different indices of social existence – education, housing, employment, law and order – provides ample evidence of racial inequalities in these basic pre-requisites for health (Brown 1984; Bhat *et al.* 1988; Skellington and Morris 1992).

Equally there is substantial evidence of racial inequalities in health care – as discussed in this volume. Clarke and Clayton (1983) and Ahmad *et al.* (1991), in particular, have shown that minority ethnic communities receive poor quality of health care, and that doctors hold negative attitudes towards minority ethnic communities. These findings are consistent with both the general operation of the 'inverse care law' in health care provision (Tudor Hart 1971) and evidence from the USA (Price *et al.* 1988).

It is vital, therefore, that struggles for equity of health and health care are located within the broader context of struggles against racial discrimination and oppression, and for substantive rights of citizenship (Ahmad and Husband 1993). Struggles for racially non-discriminatory immigration policies, better housing, equality of access to the labour market, anti-racist education, equality of legal, social and civil rights and access to meaningful political participation are therefore essential to both building and sustaining a health promoting environment and overcoming the 'inverse care law' in the provision of health care. This provides the structuring theme for this chapter.

National health reforms and the politics of welfare

The recent changes in the National Health Service and social services can only be made sense of against the backdrop of the Thatcherite assault on the welfare state. Wilding (1992: 210) charts the legacies of Thatcherism, the ideas and policies popularized by the Thatcher government, thus:

> The conventional wisdom about the inevitability and the appropriateness of collective action has been challenged. Markets in welfare have been actively promoted. Significant 'cuts' in areas hitherto deemed politically sacrosanct have been made. A new, sharper approach to management of social services has been pressed on the world of welfare. Inequality has been positively promoted as a virtue and a more divided society has resulted. Local government has been systematically shorn of powers, rights and duties so that it is little more than an enabling outpost of a more centralised state. The mixed economy of welfare has been promoted and accepted . . . The rights of citizenship have been

curtailed. Responsibilities have replaced rights as the password. Citizens have become consumers with all the loss of rights which that means. While government may provide less, the forms of regulatory government involvement have expanded and extended its reach. Collectivism may be sick but the regulatory state is in rude health.

The NHS reforms are located, then, in the general package of policies aimed at alleviating the 'crisis of welfare', the causes of which were deemed to be located in the moral failings of society, the inefficiency of state monopolies, and the dependency-creating nature of an over-protective 'nanny state' (Minford 1987).

In relation to the NHS, the assumption was that the combined provider/purchaser role of health authorities in the old system was problematic. A split, creating 'purchasing' health authorities and 'providing' hospital and other trusts, will increase appropriateness, effectiveness and efficiency of service delivery. The district health authorities' major role, under the reforms, would be the identification and prioritization of the health needs of their local population (Harrison 1991). As Ham and Heginbotham (1991) state: 'The successful implementation of the NHS reforms hinges on the development of health authorities as effective purchasers of health care for their residents.' Health authorities consequently have attempted to increase their power in the pseudo-market through joint purchasing arrangements with other health authorities, consortia, mergers and takeovers. This, however, requires time to build up relationships of trust and to win local ownership of professionally determined changes. It also requires a flexibility of approach and putting in place mechanisms for project management, among other considerations. This makes the task of health authorities far from easy. In addition, their 'contracts' with providers are rarely enforceable in reality, and many health authorities have limited or no choice of providers. Questions about both the market power of purchasing authorities and their market choices remain unanswered.

Paton (1991: 23) argues that the reforms are largely about the myths of competition, and suggests that the ironic result of NHS reforms may in fact be higher public spending:

> In the end, we are left with the contracting process and the purchasers' ability to identify need – yet the rhetoric of consumerism lingers on. This may produce two forces for higher spending. First, rationing based on purchasers' priorities translated into contracts with providers may still be politically unacceptable. Yet, second, consumers will demand production-line medicine and trendy procedures, whether they meet expert defined need or not. In aggregate, these will push NHS spending higher.

Harrison (1991), on the basis of early experience of the 'reformed' health service, suggests that the new system is unlikely to function as ostensibly intended. His evaluation of the changes in one authority showed that the guidance from the regional health authority was unclear and unhelpful; the DHA did not know its financial allocation; the authority had no information on referral intentions or the identity of would-be fundholding general practices. He identified difficulties in the assessment of needs at three broad levels:

> a) [The] regional guidance was not considered either helpful or intelligible. b) It proved impracticable to reach agreement on joint provision with the coterminous FHSAs [Family Health Service Authorities]. c) The DHA was already under pressure from major providers to fund certain new models of care. (1991: 631–2)

Harrison shows two types of difficulty faced by DHAs: 'The first of these was immediate . . . *cognitive difficulty* in knowing how to either determine or express needs and priorities as distinct from responding to demands for existing services.' The second difficulty is termed *political difficulty*:

> Explicit priorities and need identification [imply] explicit . . . rationing. This calls into question the political legitimacy of DHAs as appointed rather than elected bodies. As I write at least one health authority in another part of England is facing a potential outcry at its decision not to fund surgery for varicose veins, non-malignant 'lumps and bumps' and the removal of wisdom teeth. (1991: 632)

As for efficiency Harrison, like Paton (1991), does not consider the reforms to carry much potential: cost effectiveness will not necessarily improve as cost is not a major criterion for contracts; increasing bureaucracy needs to be funded; it is not easy or possible to compare costs between rival providers. Harrison (1991: 633) suggests that, at least in private, NHS managers have been briefed by the Department of Health that competition is not expected to any great degree. 'Much of the reason for this is centred upon the recognition – and the fear – that a competitive system would be likely to encourage perverse behaviour on the part of a wide range of actors.' However, costs are an issue when London health authorities face the choice of purchasing services from the prestigious but extremely expensive teaching hospitals in comparison with the much cheaper non-teaching hospitals. At the time of writing, the government is considering closing down a number of the London teaching hospitals while others are being merged.

If the reforms are problematic at a general level, there is even less to encourage black people to hope for meaningful change in the racially inequitable health service. There is reduced public participation in NHS trusts which, along with district health authorities, are to be run as 'businesses'. The indications are and early experience suggests that contracts for services will by and large reflect current practice rather than lead to radical shifts in priorities. Safder Mohammad (1991: ii) argues that:

> the ideological shift that is taking place in the health service does not have people, especially black people, as a focus. Indeed, but for one paragraph in Caring for People, black people are not mentioned. This despite a series of statements by ministers . . . that the needs of the black people have to be taken seriously. The overall impact of reforms is to reinforce the inequalities which currently exist.

A functioning health care market will necessarily involve some service provision by adjacent, or even distant, provider trusts. Under the reforms some 'specialist' services will only be provided at regional level. Health reforms are thus likely to exacerbate the current problems of access and equality for minority ethnic groups. None of these likely developments offers much comfort for the ethnic minorities for whom accessibility and equality may include consideration of language, dietary and other specific needs in addition to the problems of individual and institutional racism.

There are other developments in health and social services provision which concern minority ethnic groups. The NHS and Community Care Act 1990 is part of the package aimed at reforming welfare. The implementation of this Act will require collaboration between local and health authorities and a variety of service providers in the statutory, voluntary and private sectors. The Act assumes the existence of a mythical, active and well-informed consumer able to make rational choices concerning type, quality and source of care. In reality, neither is the 'consumer' enabled to make real choices, nor generally is the initiative adequately funded (Mirza 1991). With regard to the implications of NHS and Community Care Act 1990, the situation in health and social services is characterized by confusion and uncertainty (Wistow *et al*. 1992). There are uncertainties particularly around resource implications, and shifting of and renegotiation of responsibilities between health and social services as well as of inter-professional boundaries between health and social services professionals. The wider implications of the Act are summed up by Walker (1992):

> the Act is the product of ambitions which are socially narrow-minded but ideologically broad. It boils down to four things. First, it shifts responsibility for community care firmly onto local authorities and nebulous 'communities', and detaches central government from direct accountability. Second, it makes a mixed economy of care the objective of the system, and aims to maximise means-tested contributions to the

costs of care. Third, a positive development, it imposes a duty on local authorities to have comprehensive care plans based on consultation and assessment of needs. Fourth, it extends the directive powers of the Secretary of State.

These reforms in NHS or community care make no detailed reference to ethnic minorities. However, by imposing the duty on, respectively, health authorities and local authorities to assess care needs of the population, the reforms offer a window of opportunity for minority ethnic communities which can and should be exploited. I will develop this point later.

Health of the nation

The 38 targets of WHO European region for the strategy *Health for All 2000* were never endorsed by the UK. Independently of this, however, 70 local authorities and health authorities adopted the WHO strategy (Radical Statistics Health Group 1991). There is belated recognition of the need to promote health rather than cure illness in the government strategy for health promotion, *Health of the Nation* (Department of Health 1991b; 1992). The strategy defines 'key areas' for action and sets targets to monitor progress. These targets are restricted by two concerns: first, to change lifestyles and behaviours, and second to maximize the efficiency or output of the NHS. The three guiding principles of the WHO strategy concerning a philosophy of integrated central government approach where all government departments assess health impact of their policies, address and reduce social inequalities, and ensure active community participation, are missing in *Health of the Nation*. The focus is narrowly on the health service with no attempt (and barely an acknowledgement of euphemistically termed 'variations' in health) at structural change in policy on alcohol, tobacco, housing, poverty, transport and environment. As the Radical Statistics Health Group (1991) argues, the strategy is not for health but for the health service, with only six of the document's 151 pages devoted to action outside the NHS.

The disappointing emphasis on the NHS was too much even for sections of the medical profession. Richard Smith (1991), editor of the *British Medical Journal*, wrote: 'The glossy document is disappointingly repetitious and defensive . . . and there is much more on the NHS than on the broader aspects of health.' The accusation that it is more accurately a strategy for the NHS rather than for health appears to be justified by the government's decision to locate the initiative within the Department of Health rather than the arguably more obvious and more influential Department of Environment (Hunter 1991). Smith (1991: 299) comments on the need for cross-departmental collaboration and the pecking order within the ministries:

For the health strategy to have real impact the other groups who may have a part to play in implementing the strategy will also have to take action, especially as health services themselves have only a limited impact on health . . . They will have to be persuaded, which is why real consultation is so important. And most difficult of all to persuade might be other government departments . . . The Department of Health is way down the Cabinet pecking order, and why should the Treasury reduce its income from tobacco, or the Department of Trade and Industry give up its plans to promote the alcohol industry, one of Britain's largest exporters and employers?

A broader strategy, in keeping with the WHO strategy, would have had considerable potential for improving health, particularly of the black population and other socially disadvantaged groups. As it is, the implementation of the narrowly defined goals of *Health of the Nation*, with its limited resource base, is itself a cause for concern. In order to fund health promotion, will the health services shift resources from other areas of policy? If so, which: elderly, minorities, women, fertility, disability or others? As the Radical Statistics Health Group (1991: 302) asked:

Will they be forced to invest in ineffectual health promotion policies in the mistaken belief that these will promote health? What sections of the community will benefit from this shift in resources? Will resources be shifted away from health care of elderly, poor, and disabled people to fund health education campaigns for the younger, healthier, and more affluent people, who are able to respond to campaigns to change behaviour?

At a general level, *Health of the Nation* does mark a shift in government response by putting public health on the agenda and by redefining that agenda from reactive towards preventative medical intervention. However, by defining the strategy in such narrow terms and not making reduction in racial inequalities in health a key area, the strategy gives little hope for improvement in health, particularly health of the black population.

Accountability, democracy and reforms

There is no tradition of meaningful public participation in health policy formulation in Britain. The public watchdogs, in the shape of community health councils, already toothless, have been muzzled under the reforms. The 'leaner' top tier of NHS management, the boards of directors of health authorities and trusts, does not require participation from locally elected representatives, a move which will considerably reduce the influence of local government in health policy (Harrison 1991). Consequently, along with the general fragmentation of the health and social services and the centralization of power with the ministries, the health services are even less accountable at the local level than before. This issue of a lack of local accountability of public services has major consequences for active citizenship and democratic control, and I shall return to this later.

However, in a positive sense, the reforms do charge the health authorities and local authorities with the responsibility to assess, respectively, the health and social care needs of the local population and to purchase services on their behalf. This gives rise to two problems. First, health needs assessment is at best a primitive science (Ong and Humphries 1990; Thunhurst and Macfarlane 1992); the mushrooming literature in this area reflects problems rather than advancement in assessing needs (Bowling 1991). This vital aspect of health and local authority responsibility in the reforms is not well thought out; coupled with the historical unwillingness of authorities to seek active public participation and with inadequate financial resources for the task, this will only encourage health and local authorities to fudge this responsibility. Popular pressure on health authorities to involve communities in needs assessment is therefore of paramount importance. It is important that the relevant authorities are not allowed to emphasize the technical and professional definitions of health needs of their populations at the expense of community participation.

However, the health and local authorities' responsibility to assess local health needs, as defined in *Working for Patients* and the NHS and Community Care Act 1990, does offer an opportunity which needs to be exploited. The black populations can use this mechanism to fight for equality of access and appropriateness and quality of health services. I wish to relate this to debates in equal opportunities more generally.

Two major problems characterize equal opportunity policies on 'race'. First, 'race' is considered in isolation from other policy concerns, which leads to a tendency to create 'special' policies on 'race' issues rather than to consider the implications for ethnic minorities of all policies. Second, British 'race' relations legislation (the 1976 Race Relations Act) is protective rather than enabling: in Britain, an act of racial discrimination needs to have taken place before legal processes can be activated; while in the USA legal action can be taken if certain positive steps are not taken to promote equality. In addition, an employer in the USA who loses a case against an employee for discrimination is deemed to have discriminated against all employees in the same 'class' (women, blacks, gays, and so on).

Lustgarten and Edwards (1992) suggest that in order to make effective progress in terms of equal opportunities we require, first, an administrative approach where the 'ethnic dimension' becomes an essential consideration in all aspects of policy discussion and formulation, and second, a move towards the US laws on discrimination allowing positive action and access to 'class action'. The British government has vigorously resisted any attempts at positive action (consider the demonization followed by the demise of the Inner London Education Authority and the Greater London Council) and although the Fair Employment (Northern Ireland) Act 1989 provides access to class action in Northern Ireland, the provision is not available in other parts of Britain. But effective mechanisms can be instituted to pressure health and local authorities to consider the 'race' implications of all their policies, and not just those specifically targeted at minority ethnic communities.

One means of exploiting the limited opportunity for participation in delivery of health and social services is through setting up locally elected organizations which negotiate on policy and service delivery on behalf of the black communities. It is important that such organizations have community support and a democratic basis. This will aid accountability, help in achieving equitable gender balance, and counter the often heard accusation by health and social service managers that black critics of welfare services are only engaged in self-promotion and therefore need not be taken seriously. It should also help ensure that such forums are not dominated by black professionals. Equally, active participation by black health professionals will help such forums to be proactive and well informed about administrative and policy issues within the health services. Too often black professionals have been abused in advisory roles by their own employing organizations, where the mere act of seeking their 'advice' is used as proof of authority's commitment to 'ethnic sensitivity'. Having such forums will offer an avenue for more effective participation. I do not underestimate the enormity of the task or the strength of a variety of administrative procedures which can be employed to block participation (health and other services have long experience of doing exactly this). However, this is exactly why we need an organized, well-considered and community-led collective approach to effecting anti-racist change in health and social services.

The issues surrounding the lack of public accountability at a local level in health and social services and the blurring of boundaries between the two services in the Community Care Act within a general re-negotiation of the role of health and social services require new questions to be posed. One issue concerns accountability. Within a local democracy, local services should be accountable at a local level. The health service, arguably, has been less accountable than social services, allowing participation largely through locally elected councillors on health authority and family practitioner committee boards and through community health councils. Since the implementation of *Working for Patients* in 1991, there has been no formal link between health services and local government. This raises serious issues about the democratic process and the power of the citizens to effect change through it. NHS trusts are now directly accountable to the central government, thus diminishing what little local democratic influence on health services there was before reforms. A related issue is one of providing a coherent and co-ordinated approach to health and social services. It seems absurd to continue with the traditional divides when the responsibilities for services overlap so much (take child protection, care of elderly, or the long-term ill, for example, all of which require co-ordination of services provided by health and social services as well as the voluntary and private sector). Worse still, the health service itself has become fragmented with the old division between general practitioners and other secondary and community health services now increased by the introduction of the purchaser–provider split, budgetholding general practices and the private sector.

We also need to consider the health impact of local government policies; health-friendly policies on housing, job opportunities, education, clean environment and transport are all important for good health. A logical option appears to be one which attempts to decentralize the health services and combines them with social services, bringing both under the control of local government. Planning can thus be rationalized within a co-ordinated approach and local accountability of public services can be both reintroduced and strengthened (Harrison *et al.* 1991).

This would be to the considerable benefit of ethnic minorities where the standard and availability of services provided by local government can become considerations for the electorate in local elections. Black health forums can act as pressure groups, offer guidance and consultation and monitor services. That the services can operate under local government is not in doubt. It has worked in housing, education and social services, though I do not ignore or underestimate the struggles by minority ethnic groups for equality in these areas.

That it will be strongly resisted by the medical profession, who will see this as an erosion of their professionalism and clinical freedom, is also not in doubt. Here, however, the Conservative government, in pushing through the health reforms against medical opposition, has shown that it is possible to defeat the immensely powerful medical lobby. The biggest hurdle, however, is the central government itself which, through a sustained assault, has been engaged in diminishing local government influence in those services which are under the control of local authorities, through such devices as the introduction of the right to buy council property, the national curriculum in education and the imposition of rate-capping on local authorities which do not toe the central government line. Along with an attack on local democracy, a series of central government interventions (particularly the introduction of the 'poll tax') have resulted in the democratic base being shrunk alarmingly (Wilding 1992). This is an issue of concern to all; it affects minority ethnic communities particularly, as it hampers their struggles for substantive citizenship rights (Ahmad and Husband 1993).

Black community health movement

The black communities have never been passive recipients of state welfare. Black voluntary organizations came into existence to aid their communities in the very early days of large-scale black settlement in Britain (Layton-Henry 1990). Since then a variety of community and religious organizations have been established and become involved in community voluntary work on different fronts. The 'pooling' system which allowed black people to counter housing discrimination by pooling together money to buy residential properties in the 1960s and early 1970s still has many variants. In Bradford, for example, there are numerous networks of Asian women who weekly contribute an agreed sum of money to a 'committee'. The women are then entitled to claim money from this 'kitty', free of interest, for weddings, visits to Pakistan and India, funerals, and so on; the system is controlled exclusively by women, and flexibility and a system of priorities are essential elements of these 'committees'. In other parts of Britain, black communities have organized to protect themselves against deportations, racist immigration laws, racial harassment, and racism in housing allocations (Wardburgh 1990; Hesse et al. 1992).

Black community mobilization is evident in health, with an exciting variety of community health initiatives throughout England, Wales and Scotland (see Jeyasingham 1992). These rightly traverse the artificial divide between 'health' and other services and their success is a testament to black people's willingness to engage with issues facing their communities with courage and imagination. Among others, the Afro-Caribbean Mental Health Association (Francis 1991a; 1991b) and the Leicestershire Black Mental Health Group (Westwood et al. 1989) have done important campaign and research work. However, almost all such projects suffer from the vagaries of short-term funding, often from sources whose commitment to anti-racism is questionable. The list includes the important and successful initiatives such as the London Chinese Health Resource Centre as well as numerous smaller projects (Jeyasingham 1992; Li 1992).

Equally, they have unintended negative effects for the black community. First, they often provide an excuse for mainstream service providers to procrastinate, while creating dependency on a short-term and inadequately resourced 'special service', and consequently maintain the status quo. Second, they often work on the basis of 'ethnicization', of turning communities united in their experience of racism and oppression into discrete cultural groupings who are in competition with each other for state handouts, and are therefore easier to control. This can be highly dangerous for the black communities generally and fits into the wider project of 'new racism'. Third, there is only a fine dividing line between community empowerment, enabling communities to take on the state and its agencies for better services and recognition of unmet needs, and turning the concept on its head into one which emphasizes that the communities create their own needs and should themselves meet these needs. The state agencies, through funding 'special projects', thus often abdicate responsibility for mainstream service provision and through funding for community projects also promote an 'acceptable', supposedly more docile and palatable, black leadership.

The community health movement therefore is in danger of being exploited by the very agencies it wishes to challenge. The movement can perform an important role in meeting unmet and unrecognized needs, defined in terms which are appropriate, in a supportive and enabling environment. However, it is not a substitute for mainstream services; it is important to continue the struggles for recognition of black people's needs, defined in anti-racist ways, and provision of appropriate mainstream services along with adequately resourced community initiatives.

However, one positive consequence of initiatives in community health and in social services is the radicalization of black community activists and a proportion of the black health service workforce. Professional discourses on black pathology and racist constructions of black people's health and social services needs are thus being challenged. Racism in service delivery is being resisted. Consequently, there has been some official recognition of institutional racism and the need to effect anti-racist change in social work (Central Council for Education and Training in Social Work 1991a; 1991b). Regrettably, debates about multi-culturalism and latterly anti-racism which have characterized social work and education in the past two decades are barely beginning to take place in health services. As the chapters by Ahmad, Stubbs, and Sashidharan and Francis (in this volume) show, health research has constructed racialized notions of black health needs and health problems. The health services have responded accordingly. The need for action in health services is clear. A small number of black (and white) health researchers and health professionals are beginning to engage with the racist nature of the health service and health research. However, the majority of health professionals, including black professionals, appear to lack any political vision, seeing the medical profession to be above malice of all kinds and ideologically neutral. Change in thought and action, both in research and practice, needs to be forced by the black communities themselves, but without 'disabling' progressive white support. A more radicalized black health workforce can help in effecting such change. The focus in health research needs to shift away from 'ethnic differences' to racist constructions of black needs, and racism in service provision at individual and institutional levels. The black populations need to become involved in defining their own needs.

Racial inequalities in health are a part, and a consequence of racial inequalities in substantive rights of citizenship. Equally, although the scope for reducing racial inequalities in health lies largely outside the NHS, equity of health care provision too is also of paramount importance. These struggles for equitable health and health care are essentially located in the wider struggles for equity and dignity which have been a part of black people's history.

Acknowledgements

My thanks to Charles Husband and Reg Walker for comments.

Bibliography

Abelin, T. (1987) 'Approaches to health promotion and disease prevention', in Abelin, T., Brzezinski, Z.J. and Carstairs, V.D.L. (eds) *Measurement in Health Promotion and Protection*, WHO Regional Publications, European Series no. 22, Copenhagen: WHO Regional Office for Europe.

Ahmad, B. (1990) *Black Perspectives in Social Work*, London: Venture.

Ahmad, W.I.U. (1989) 'Policies, pills and political will: critique of policies to improve the health status of ethnic minorities', *Lancet*, i: 148–50.

Ahmad, W.I.U. (ed.) (1992a) *The Politics of 'Race' and Health*, Bradford: Race Relations Research Unit, University of Bradford and Bradford and Ilkley Community College.

Ahmad, W.I.U. (1992b) 'The maligned healer: the 'hakim' and western medicine', *New Community*, 18(4): 521–36.

Ahmad, W.I.U. (1992c) 'Is medical sociology an ostrich? Reflections on 'race' and the sociology of health', *Medical Sociology News*, 17(2): 16–21.

Ahmad, W.I.U. and Husband, C. (1993) 'Religious identity, citizenship and welfare: the case of Muslims in Britain', *American Journal of Islamic Social Sciences*, 10(2): 217–33.

Ahmad, W.I.U., Baker, M. and Kernohan, E. (1991) 'General practitioners perceptions of Asian and non-Asian patients', *Family Practice – An International Journal*, 8(1): 52–6.

Ahmad, W.I.U., Kernohan, E.E.M. and Baker, M.R. (1988) 'Alcohol and cigarette consumption among white and Asian general practice patients', *Health Education Journal*, 47: 128–9.

Ahmad, W.I.U., Kernohan, E.E.M. and Baker, M.R. (1989) 'Health of British Asians: a research review', *Community Medicine*, 11: 49–56.

Ahmad–Aziz, A., Froggatt, A., Leung, T., Richardson, I. and Whittaker, T. (1992) *Working with Elders No. 3 – A Training Manual, Anti–Racist Social Work Education Series*, London: CCETSW.

Ahmed, A. and Pearson, M. (1985) *Multiracial Initiatives in Maternity Care*, London: Maternity Alliance.

Alibhai, Y. (1984) 'Forging a new partnership', *Nursing Times*, 80: 19–20.

Allen, I. (1988) *Doctors and their Careers*, London: Policy Studies Institute.

Allen, M.E., Nunley, J.C. and Scott-Warner, M. (1988) 'Recruitment and retention of black students in baccalaureate nursing programs', *Journal of Nursing Education*, 27(3): 107–16.

Allison, A.C. (1957) 'Properties of sickle haemoglobin', *Biochemical Journal*, 5: 212–19.

Alvear, J. and Brooke, O.G. (1978) 'Fetal growth in different racial groups', *Archives of Disease in Childhood*, 53: 27–32.

Amin, K., Fernandes, M. and Gordon, P. (eds) (1988) *Racism and Discrimination in Britain: A Select Bibliography*, London: Runnymede Trust.

Amos, A., Church, M., Forster, F., Robertson, G. and Young, I. (1990) 'A health promotion module for undergraduate medical students', *Medical Education*, 24: 328–35.

Anderson, S. (1976) 'Science, technology and black liberation', in Rose H. and Rose S.(eds) *The Radicalization of Science: Ideology of/in Natural Science*, Basingstoke: Macmillan.

Anees, M.A. (1988) 'Science and control: sex, race and the new biology', in Sardar Z. (ed.) *The Revenge of Athena: Science, Exploitation and the Third World*, London: Mansell.

Angastiniotis, M.A., Kyriakidou, S. and Hadjiminas, M. (1986) 'How thalassaemia was controlled in Cyprus', *World Health Forum*, 7: 291–7.

Anionwu, E.N. (1988) 'Health education and community development for sickle cell disorders in Brent', PhD thesis, University of London, Institute of Education.

Anionwu, E.N. (1989) 'Running a sickle cell centre: community counselling', in Cruickshank, J. K. and Beevers, D.G. (eds) *Ethnic Factors in Health and Disease*, London: Wright Butterworth Scientific.

Anionwu, E.N. (1990) 'Community development approaches to sickle cell anaemia', *Talking Point*, 113: 2, Association of Community Workers (ACW), Grindon Lodge, Beech Grove Road, Newcastle Upon Tyne, NE4 2RS.

Anionwu, E.N., Patel, N., Kanji, G., Renges, H. and Brozovic, M. (1988) 'Counselling for prenatal diagnosis of sickle cell disease and beta thalassaemia major: A four year experience', *Journal of Medical Genetics*, 25: 769–72.

Anonymous (1981) 'X–rays, age and immigration', *Lancet*, i: 1301.

Anwar, M. and Ali, A. (1987) *Overseas Doctors: Experiences and Expectations – A Research Study*, London: Commission for Racial Equality.

Ashton, J. and Seymour, H. (1988) *The New Public Health*, Milton Keynes: Open University Press.

Aslam, M. (1979) 'The practice of Asian medicine in the United Kingdom', PhD thesis, University of Nottingham.

Association of Directors of Social Services (1978) *Multi–racial Britain: The `Social Services' Response*, London: ADDS/CRE.

Atkin, K., Cameron, E., Badger, F. and Evers, H. (1989) 'Asian elders' knowledge and future use of community social and health services', *New Community* 15(3): 439–45.

Audit Commission (1986) *Performance Review in Local Government – A Handbook for Auditors and Local Authorities*, London: HMSO.

Auluck, R. and Iles, P. (1991) 'The referral process: a study of working relationships between antenatal clinic nursing staff and hospital social workers and their impact on Asian women', British Journal of Social Work, 21: 41–61.

Aykroyd, W.R. and Hossain, M.A. (1967) 'Diet and state of nutrition of Pakistani infants in Bradford, Yorkshire', *British Medical Journal*, i: 42–45.

Bagenal, F.S., Easton, D.F., Harris, E., Chilvers, C. and McElwain, T.J. (1990) 'Survival of patients with breast cancer attending Bristol Cancer Help Centre', *Lancet*, ii: 606–10.

Bahl, V. (1987) *Asian Mother and Baby Campaign: A Report by the Director*, London: Department of Health and Social Security.

Baker, M.R., Bandaranayake, R. and Schweiger, M.S. (1984) 'Difference in rate of uptake of immunization among ethnic groups', *British Medical Journal*, 288: 1075–8.

Balarajan, R. (1991) 'Ethnic differences in mortality from ischaemic heart disease and cerebrovascular disease in England and Wales', *British Medical Journal*, 302: 560–4.

Balarajan, R. and Botting, B. (1989) 'Perinatal mortality in England and Wales, variations by mother's country of birth (1982–85)', *Health Trends*, 21: 79–84.

Balarajan, R. and McDowall, M. (1985) 'Mortality from congenital malformations by mother's country of birth', *Journal of Epidemiology and Community Health*, 39: 102–6.

Balarajan, R. and Raleigh, V.S. (1990) 'Variations in perinatal, neonatal and postneonatal and infant mortality by mother's country of birth (1982–85)', in Britton, M, (ed) *Mortality and Geography. A Review in the Mid–1980s, England and Wales*, Series DS no. 9, London: HMSO.

Balarajan, R. and Raleigh, V.S. (1993) 'The ethnic population of England and Wales: the 1991 Census', *Health Trends*, 29: 113–16.

Balarajan, R., Bulusu, L., Adelstein, A.M. and Shukla, V. (1984) 'Patterns of mortality among migrants to England and Wales from the Indian sub–continent', *British Medical Journal*, 289: 1185–7.

Balarajan, R., Raleigh, V.S. and Botting, B. (1989) 'Mortality from congenital malformations in England and Wales: variations by mother's country of birth', *Archives of Disease in Childhood*, 64: 1457–62.

Balarajan, R., Yuen, P. and Raleigh V. (1989) 'Ethnic differences in general practitioner consultations', *British Medical Journal*, 299: 958–60.

Banton, M. (1977) *The Idea of Race*, London: Tavistock.

Barker, J. (1984) *Black and Asian Old People in Britain*, London: Age Concern Research Unit.

Barker, M. (1981) *The New Racism*, London: Junction Books.

Barron, S.L. and Vessey, M.P., (1966a) 'Immigration – a new social factor in obstetrics' *British Medical Journal*, i: 1189–94.

Barron, S.L. and Vessey, M.P. (1966b) 'Birth weight of infants born to immigrant women', *British Journal of Preventive and Social Medicine*, 20: 127–134.

Baxter, C. and Baxter, D. (1988) 'Racial inequalities in health – a challenge to the British NHS', *International Journal of Health Services*, 18(4): 563–571.

Beard P. (1982) 'Contraception in ethnic minority groups in Bedford', *Health Visitor*, 55: 417–21.

Bebbington, A. and Charnley, H. (1990) 'Community care for the elderly – rhetoric and reality', *British Journal of Social Work*, 20: 409–32.

Bebbington, P.E., Hurry, J. and Tennant, C. (1981) 'Psychiatric disorder in selected groups in Camberwell', *Social Psychiatry*, 16: 43–51.

Behrman, R.E. (1987) 'Premature births among black women', *New England Journal of Medicine*, 317: 763–4.

Ben–Tovim, G. and Gabriel, J. (1982) 'The sociology of race – time to change course?', in

Ohri, A., Manning, B. and Curno, P. (eds) *Community Work and Racism*, London: Routledge.

Berger, P. and Luckmann, T. (1979) *The Social Construction of Reality*, Harmondsworth: Penguin.

Bernal, M. (1987) *The Black Athena*, London: Vintage.

Best, G. (1987) *The Future of NHS General Management: Where Next*, King's Fund Project Paper No 75. London: King's Fund.

Beveridge, W. (1942) *Social Insurance and Allied Services*, Cmd. 6404, London: HMSO.

Bhalla, A. and Blakemore, K. (1981) *Elders of the Minority Ethnic Groups*, Birmingham: All Faiths for One Race.

Bhat, A., Carr–Hill, R. and Ohri, S. (1988) *Britain's Black Population* (2nd edn), Aldershot: Gower/Radical Statistics Group.

Bhavnani, K.K. and Coulson, M. (1986) 'Transforming socialist feminism: the challenge of racism', *Feminist Review*, 23: 81–92.

Bhopal, R.S. (1986a) 'The inter–relationship of folk, traditional and western medicine within an Asian community in Britain', *Social Science and Medicine*, 22: 99–105.

Bhopal, R.S. (1986b) 'Asians' knowledge and behaviour on preventive health issues: smoking, alcohol, heart disease, pregnancy, rickets, malaria prophylaxis and surma', *Community Medicine*, 8: 315–21.

Bhopal, R.S. (1988) 'Health care for Asians: conflict in need, demand and provision', in Royal College of Physicians (ed.) *Equity: A Pre–requisite for Health: Proceedings of the 1987 Summer Scientific Conference*, London: Faculty of Community Medicine and World Health Organization.

Bhopal, R.S. (1991) 'Health education and ethnic minorities', *British Medical Journal*, 302: 1338.

Bhopal, R.S. (1992) 'Future research on the health of ethnic minorities: back to basics: a personal view', in Ahmad, W.I.U. (ed.) *The Politics of 'Race' and Health*, Bradford: Race Relations Research Unit, University of Bradford, and Bradford and Ilkley Community College.

Bhopal, R.S. and Donaldson, L.J. (1988) 'Health education for ethnic minorities – current provision and future directions', *Health Education Journal*, 47: 137–140.

Bhopal, R.S. and Samim, A.K. (1988) 'Immunization uptake of Glasgow *Asian* children: paradoxical benefit of communication barriers', *Community Medicine*, 10: 215–20.

Billig, M., Condor, S., Edwards, D., Game, M., Middleton, D. and Radley, R. (1988) *Ideological Dilemmas: Social Psychology of Everyday Thinking*, London: Sage.

Black Health Workers and Patients Group (BHWPG) (1983) 'Psychiatry and the Corporate State', *Race and Class*, 25(2): 49–64 .

Black, J. and Laws, S. (1986) *Living with Sickle Cell Disease. An Inquiry into the Need for Health and Social Service Provision for Sickle Cell Sufferers in Newham.* London: Sickle Cell Society.

Blakemore, K. (1985) 'The state, the voluntary sector and new developments in provision for old of minority racial groups', *Ageing and Society*, 5: 175–90.

Blaxter, M. (1990) *Health and Lifestyles*, London: Routledge.

Blennerhassett, S., Farrant, W. and Jones, J. (1989) 'Support for community health projects in the UK: a role for the NHS', *Health Promotion*, 4(3): 199–206.

Botting, B.J. and Macfarlane A.J. (1990) 'Geographic variations in infant mortality in relation to birthweight, 1983–85', in Britton M. (ed.), *Mortality and Geography. A Review in the Mid–1980s, England and Wales*, Series DS no. 9, London: HMSO.

Bourne, J. (1983) 'Towards an anti–racist feminism', *Race and Class*, 25(1): 1–22.

Bourne, J. and Sivanandan, A. (1981) 'Cheerleaders and ombudsmen: the sociology of race relations in Britain', *Race and Class*, 21(4): 331–52.

Bowl, R. and Barnes, M. (1990) *Approved Social Worker Assessment, Race and Racism: Local Authority Policy and Practice Monitoring the Mental Health Act 1983*, London: Social Services Research Group.

Bowling, A. (1991) *Measuring Health*, Milton Keynes: Open University Press.

Bowling, B. (1990) *Elderly People from Ethnic Minorities: A Report on Four Projects*, London: Age Concern Institute of Gerontology.

Brent Community Health Council (1981) *Black People and the Health Service*, London: Brent CHC.

Breslow, L. (1987) 'Some fields of application for health promotion and disease prevention', in Abelin, T., Brzezinski, Z.J. and Carstairs, V.D.L. (eds) *Measurement in Health Promotion and Protection*, WHO Regional Publications, European Series no. 22, Copenhagen: WHO Regional Office for Europe.

British Medical Association (1986) 'Report of the Board of Science Working Party on Alternative Therapy', *British Medical Journal*, 292: 1407–8.

British Medical Association (1991) *Leading for Health: A BMA Agenda for Health*, London: BMA.

British Medical Journal (1962) 'Tuberculosis in immigrants' (editorial), *British Medical Journal*, 1:1397–8.

British Medical Journal (1988) 'Black nurses', *British Medical Journal*, 297: 39.

Brockington, I.F., Kendell, R.E. and Leff, J.P. (1978) 'Definitions of schizophrenia: concordance and prediction of outcome', *Psychological Medicine*, 10: 665–75.

Brook, P. (1973) *Psychiatrists in Training*, Ashford, Kent: Headley.

Brook, P. (1974) 'Psychiatrists: background, career and career alternative, of a group of recently appointed consultants', *British Journal of Psychiatry*, 125: 1–9.

Brown, C. (1984) *Black and White Britain*, London: Heinemann.

Brown, C. (1990) 'Racial inequality in the British labour market' *Employment Institute Report*, 5(4).

Brown, C. and Lawton, J. (1991) *Training for Equality*, London: Policy Studies Institute.

Brown, I. (1991) 'Singing in tune', *Health Service Journal*: 101: 24.

Bryan, B., Dadzie, S. and Scafe, S. (1985) *The Heart of the Race: Black Women's Lives in Britain*, London: Virago.

Buchan, J. (1989) 'Less equal than others – equal opportunities in the NHS', *Nursing Standard*, 3(8): 43.

Bundey, S., Alam, H., Kaur, A., Mir, S. and Lancashire, R.J. (1989) 'Race, consanguinity and social features in Birmingham babies: a basis for prospective study', *Journal of Epidemiology and Community Health*, 44:130–35.

Bundey, S., Alam, H., Kaur, A., Mir, S. and Lancashire, R. J. (1991) 'Why do UK–born Pakistani babies have high perinatal and neonatal mortality rates?', *Paediatric and Perinatal Epidemiology*, 5: 110–14.

Burke, A. (1986) 'Social work and intervention in West Indian psychiatric disorder', in Coombe, V. and Little, A. (eds) *Race and Social Work*, London: Tavistock.

Burke, A. (1989) 'Psychiatric practices and ethnic minorities', in Cruickshank, J. and

Beevers, D. (eds) *Ethnic Factors in Health and Disease*, London: Butterworth.

Camberwell Community Health Council (1990) *Annual Report*, London: Camberwell CHC.

Campbell Brown, M. and Willmott, M. (1983) 'Perinatal deaths in immigrant Indian women', *British Journal of Obstetrics and Gynaecology*, 4: 2–6.

Carby, H.V. (1982) 'White women listen! Black feminism and the boundaries of sisterhood', in Centre for Contemporary Cultural Studies, *The Empire Strikes Back*, London: Hutchinson.

Carmichael, S. and Hamilton, C. V. (1967) *Black Power: The Politics of Liberation in America*, Harmondsworth: Penguin.

Carney, T. (1989) 'Ethnic population and general practitioner workload', *British Medical Journal*, 299: 930–1.

Carpenter, L. and Brockington, I.F. (1980) 'The study of mental illness in Asians, West Indians and Africans living in Manchester', *British Journal of Psychiatry*, 137: 201–5.

Cashmore, E. (ed.) (1988) *Dictionary of Race and Ethnic Relations*, London: Routledge, 246.

Central Council for Education and Training in Social Work (1991a) *Setting the Context for Change: Anti–racist Social Work Education*, London: CCETSW.

Central Council for Education and Training in Social Work (ed.) (1991b) *One Small Step towards Racial Justice*, London: CCETSW.

Central Statistical Office (1991) *Social Trends* 21, London: HMSO.

Central Statistical Office (1992) *Social Trends* 22. London: HMSO.

Centre for Contemporary Cultural Studies (1982) *The Empire Strikes Back*, London: Hutchinson.

Chen, L.C., Choudhery, A. and Huffman, S.L. (1980) 'Anthropometric assessment of energy–protein malnutrition and subsequent risk of mortality among pre–school aged children', *American Journal of Clinical Nutrition*, 33: 1836–45 .

Chirimuuta, R. and Chirimuuta, R. (1989) *AIDS, Africa and Racism*, London: Free Association Press.

Christie, Y. and Blunden, R. (1991) *Is Race on your Agenda?*, London: King's Fund Centre.

Chrystie, I.L., Palmer, S.J., Kenney, A. and Banatvala, J.E. (1992) 'HIV seroprevalence among women attending antenatal clinics in London', *Lancet*, 339: 364.

Chudley, P. (1989) 'Stuck on the career ladder: racism', *Nursing Times and Nursing Mirror*, 85 (5 July): 36–7.

Clark–Hine, D. (1989) *Black Women in White: Racial Conflict and Cooperation in the Nursing Profession 1890–1950*, Indianapolis: Indiana University Press.

Clarke, M. and Clayton, D. (1983) 'Quality of obstetric care provided for Asian immigrants in Leicestershire', *British Medical Journal*, 60: 866–879.

Clarke, M., Clayton, D.G., Mason, E.S. *et al.*, (1988) 'Asian mothers' risk factors for perinatal death – the same or different? A 10 year review of Leicestershire perinatal deaths', *British Medical Journal*, 297: 384–7.

Coad, H. (1986) 'Linking community and care', *Health Service Journal*, 8 May: 626–7.

Cochrane, R. (1977) 'Mental illness in immigrants to England and Wales: an analysis of mental hospital admissions', *Social Psychiatry*, 12: 25–35.

Cochrane, R. (1984) *The Social Creation of Mental Illness*, London: Longman.

Cochrane, R. and Bal, S.S. (1987) 'Migration and schizophrenia: an examination of five hypotheses', *Social psychiatry*, 22: 181–91.

Cochrane, R. and Bal, S.S. (1989) 'Mental hospital admission rates of immigrants to England: a comparison of 1971 and 1981', *Social Psychiatry and Psychiatric Epidemiology*, 24: 2–11.

Cockerham, W. (1992) *Medical Sociology* (5th edn), Englewood Cliffs, NJ: Prentice Hall.

Cole, A. (1987) 'Racism: limited access', *Nursing Times and Nursing Mirror*, 83 (17 June): 29–30.

Commission for Racial Equality (1983a) *Code of Practice – Race Relations*, London: CRE.

Commission for Racial Equality (1983b) *Ethnic Minority Hospital Staff*, London: CRE.

Commission for Racial Equality (1984) *St Chad's Hospital – Report of a Formal Investigation into the Birmingham A.H.A. (teaching)*, London: CRE.

Commission for Racial Equality (1987) *Ethnic Origins of Nurses Applying for and in Training – A Survey*, London: CRE.

Commission for Racial Equality (1991a) *Annual Report of the Commission for Racial Equality*, London: CRE.

Commission for Racial Equality (1991b) *NHS Contracts and Racial Equality: A Guide*, London: CRE.

Confederation of Indian Organizations (CIO) (1986) *Coronary Heart Disease and Asians in Britain*, London: CIO.

Confederation of Indian Organizations (CIO) (1989) *Information Booklet*, London: CIO.

Constantinides, P. (1986) 'Health care services for populations at risk for genetically determined disease', paper presented at British Association conference, 3 September.

Cooper, J.E., Kendell, R.E., Gurland, B.J., Sharpe, L., Copeland, J.R.M. and Simon, R. (1972) *Psychiatric Diagnosis in New York and London*, Maudsley Monograph no. 20, London: Oxford University Press.

Cooper, J.E., Goodhead, D., Craig, T., Harris, M., Howat, J. and Korer, J. (1987) 'The incidence of schizophrenia in Nottingham', *British Journal of Psychiatry*, 151: 619–29.

Cope, R. (1989) 'The compulsory detention of Afro–Caribbeans under the Mental Health Act', *New Community* 15(3) 343–56.

Cottle, T.J. (1978) *Black Testimony: Voices of Britain's West Indians*, London: Wildwood House.

Coventry Health Information Forum (1991) *It's Our Health: What Do We Want to Know?*, Coventry Health Authority/Coventry City Council.

Cox, B.B. (ed.) (1987). *The Health and Lifestyle Survey: Preliminary Report*, London: Health Promotion Research Trust.

Crawford, L.A. and Olinger, B.H. (1988) 'Recruitment and retention of nursing students from diverse cultural backgrounds', *Journal of Nursing Education*, 27(8): 379–81.

Crawford, R. (1977) 'You are dangerous to your health: the ideology and politics of victim blaming', *International Journal of Health Services*, 7(4): 663–80.

Crowley J. (1991) 'Races apart', *Nursing Times* 87(10): 44–6.

Crowley, P. (1993) 'Elective induction of labour at 41+ weeks of gestation', in Enkin, M.W., Keirse, M.J.N.C., Renfrew, M.J. and Neilson, J.P. (eds) *Pregnancy and Childbirth Module: Cochrane Database of Systematic Reviews*, Oxford: Update Software (published through Cochrane Updates on disk).

Cruickshank, J.K. and Beevers, D.G. (1989) *Ethnic Factors in Health and Disease*, London: Wright.

Cunningham–Burley, S. and McKeganey, N.P. (1990) *Readings in Medical Sociology*, London: Tavistock/Routledge.

Darr, A. and Modell, B. (1988) 'The frequency of consanguineous marriages among British Pakistanis', *Journal of Medical Genetics*, 25: 186–190.

Darr, A.R. (1990) 'The social implications of thalassaemia among Muslims of Pakistani origin in England – family experience and service delivery', PhD thesis, University of London, University College.

Davey–Smith, G., Bartley, M. and Blane, D. (1990) 'The Black Report on socioeconomic inequalities in health 10 years on', *British Medical Journal*, 301: 373–7.

Davis, A. (1981) *Women, Race and Class*, London: The Women's Press.

Dawson, I., Golder, R.Y. and Jonas, E.G. (1982) 'Birthweight by gestational age and its effects on perinatal mortality in white and in Punjabi births; experience at a district general hospital in West London 1967–1975', *British Journal of Obstetrics and Gynaecology*, 89: 896–9.

Dean, G., Walsh, D., Downing, H. and Shelley, E. (1981) 'First admissions of native born and immigrants to psychiatric hospitals in South East England 1976', *British Journal of Psychiatry*, 139: 506–12.

Department of Environment (1979) *National Housing and Dwelling Survey*, London: HMSO.

Department of Health (1989a) *General Practice in the New NHS: A New Contract*, London: HMSO.

Department of Health (1989b) *Caring for People: Community Care in the Next Decade and Beyond*, Cm 849, London: HMSO.

Department of Health (1991a) *Health and Healthy Living – A Guide for Older People*, London: HMSO.

Department of Health (1991b) *The Health of the Nation*, London: DoH.

Department of Health (1991c) *The Patient's Charter: Raising the Standard*, London: DoH/HMSO.

Department of Health (1992) *The Health of the Nation: A Strategy for Health in England*, Cm 1986, London: HMSO.

Department of Health (1993) *Standing Medical Advisory Committee Working Party Report on Sickle Cell Thalassaemia and Other Haemoglobinopathies*, London: HMSO.

Department of Health and Social Security (1985) *Report to the Advisory Committee on Medical Manpower*, March.

Department of Health and Social Security (1989) *Public Health in England: The Report of the Committee of Inquiry into the Future Development of the Public Health Function*, Cm 289, London: HMSO.

Department of Health and Social Security, Office of Population Censuses and Surveys, and Welsh Office (1986) *Hospital Inpatient Enquiry, Maternity Tables, England and Wales, 1977–81*, Series MB4 no. 19, London: HMSO.

Department of Health and Office of Population Censuses and Surveys (1988) *Hospital Inpatient Enquiry, Maternity Tables, England, 1982–85*, Series MB4 no. 28, London: HMSO.

Dodge, J.S. (ed.) (1969) *The Fieldworker in Immigrant Health*, London: Staples Press.

Dohrenwend, B.P. and Dohrenwend, B.S. (1964) *Social Status and Psychological Disorder: A Casual Inquiry*, London: Wiley–Interscience.

Dominelli, L. (1988) *Anti–racist Social Work*, London: Macmillan.

Donaldson, L.J. and Clayton, D.G. (1984) 'Occurrence of cancer in Asians and non–Asians', *Journal of Epidemiology and Community Health*, 38: 203–7.

Donaldson, L.J. and Odell, A. (1984) 'Aspects of the health and social service needs of elderly Asians', mimeo, Dept of Community Health, Leicester University.

Donaldson, L.J. and Odell, A. (1986) 'Health and social status of elderly Asians: a community survey', *British Medical Journal*, 293: 1079–82.

Donovan, J.L. (1984) 'Ethnicity and disease: a research review', *Social Science and Medicine* 19(7): 663–70.

Donovan, J.L. (1986) *We Don't Buy Sickness, It Just Comes: Health, Illness and Health Care in the Lives of Black People in London*, Aldershot: Gower.

Douglas, J. (1991) 'Black women's health matters: Putting black women on the research agenda', in Roberts, H. (ed.) *Women's Health Matters*, London: Routledge.

Downie, R.S., Fyfe, C. and Tannahill, A. (1990) *Health Promotion: Models and Values*, Oxford: Oxford University Press.

Doyal, L. with Pennell, I. (1979) *The Political Economy of Health*, London: Pluto.

Doyal, L., Hunt, G. and Mellor, J. (1981) 'Your life in their hands: migrant workers in the NHS', *Critical Social Policy*. 1(2).

Doyal, L., Gee, F. and Hunt, G. (1982) *Migrant Workers in the National Health Service*, London: Polytechnic of North London.

Durward, L. (ed.) (1990) *Traveller Mothers and Babies: Who Cares for their Health?*, London: Maternity Alliance.

Ebrahim, S., Patel, N., Coats, M., Greig, C., Grilley, J., Bangham, C. and Stacey, S. (1991) 'Prevalence and severity of morbidity among Gujarati elders: a controlled comparison', *Family Practice*, 8: 57–62.

Ecob, R. and Williams, R. (1990) 'Sampling ethnic minorities to assess health and welfare', *Journal of Epidemiology and Community Health*, 45: 93–101.

Ehrenreich, J. (ed) (1978) *The Cultural Crisis of Modern Medicine*, New York and London: Monthly Review Press.

Elliot, K. and Fuller, J. (1990) 'Health education and ethnic minorities', *British Medical Journal*, 302: 802–3.

Emerson, P.A. (1961) 'Tuberculosis in Soho', *British Medical Journal*, 2: 148–52.

Employment Gazette (1991) 'Ethnic origin and the labour market', *Employment Gazette*, February: 59–72.

Faculty of Public Health Medicine (1991) *UK Levels of Health*, London: FPHM.

Fanon, F. (1967) *The Wretched of the Earth*, Harmondsworth: Penguin.

Fanon, F. (1970) *Black Skin, White Masks*, London: Paladin.

Fanon, F. (1978) 'Medicine and colonialism', in Ehrenreich, J. (ed.) *The Cultural Crisis of Modern Medicine*, New York and London: Monthly Review Press.

Farrah, M. (1986) *Black Elders in Leicester: An Action Research Report on the Needs of Black Elderly People of African Descent from the Caribbean*, Leicester Social Services Department.

Farrar, N. and Sircar, I. (1986) 'Social work with Asian families in a psychiatric setting', in Coombe, V. and Little, A. (eds) *Race and Social Work*, London: Tavistock.

Fawdrey, A.L. (1946) *Report on Present State of Knowledge of Erythroblastic Anaemia in Cyprus. Cyprus Medical and Sanitary Report*, Appendix D, 12, Nicosia: Government of Cyprus.

Feder, G. and Hussey, R. (1990) 'Traveller mothers and babies', *British Medical Journal*, 300: 1536–7.

Feinmann, J. (1988) 'The Asian factor', *Nursing Times and Nursing Mirror*, 84 (26 October).

Fenton, S. (1986) *Race, Health and Welfare, Afro–Caribbean and South Asian People in Central Bristol: Health and Social Services*, Bristol: Bristol University, Department of Sociology.

Fenton, S. (1987) *Ageing Minorities: Black People as They Grow Old in Britain*, London: CRE.

Fernando, S. (1991) *Mental Health, Race and Culture*, Basingstoke: Macmillan/MIND.

Field, D. and Woodman, D. (1990) *Medical Sociology in Britain: A Register of Research and Teaching*, London: Medical Sociology Group of British Sociological Association.

Figlio, K. (1980) 'Sinister medicine? A critique of left approaches to medicine', *Radical Science*, 10:14–68.

File, N. and Power, C. (1981) *Black Settlers in Britain 1555 – 1958*, London: Heinemann Educational Books.

Firdous, R. and Bhopal, R.S. (1989) 'Reproductive health of Asian women: a comparative study with hospital and community perspectives', *Public Health*, 103: 307–15.

Ford, G. (1988) 'Science and ideology: the Marxist perspective', in Sardar Z. (ed.) *The Revenge of Athena: Science, Exploitation and the Third World*, London: Mansell.

France–Dawson, M. (1991) 'Sickle cell conditions – the continuing need for comprehensive care services: a study of patients' views', The Daphne Heald Research Unit, Royal College of Nursing, London.

Francis, E. (1991a) 'Mental health, antiracism and social work training', in Central Council for Education and Training in Social Work (ed.) *One Small Step towards Racial Justice*, London: CCETSW.

Francis, E. (1991b) 'Racism and mental health: some concerns for social work', in Central Council for Education and Training in Social Work, *Setting the Context for Change: Anti-racist Social Work Education*, London: CCETSW.

Franklin, I. (1990) *Sickle Cell Disease. A Guide for Patients, Carers and Health Workers*, London: Faber and Faber.

Fraser, F.C. and Biddle, C.J. (1976) 'Estimating the risks for offspring of first cousin marriage', *Annals of Human Genetics*, 28: 522–526.

French, J. and Adams, L. (1986) 'From analysis to synthesis: theories of health education', *Health Education Journal*, 45: 71–4.

Friedson, E. (1970) *Profession of Medicine: A Study of the Sociology of Applied Knowledge*, London: Chicago University Press.

Fryer, P. (1984) *Staying Power: The History of Black People in Britain*, London: Pluto Press.

Fuller, J. (1987) 'Contraceptive services for ethnic minorities', *British Medical Journal*, 295: 1365.

Gabe, J., Calnan, M. and Bury, M. (1991) *The Sociology of the Health Service*, London: Routledge.

General Medical Council Education Committee (1991) *Undergraduate Medical Education*, London: GMC.

Gibbon, P. (1990) 'Equal opportunities and race equality', *Critical Social Policy*, 24: 5–23.

Giggs, J. (1986) 'Ethnic status and mental illness in urban areas', in Rathwell, T. and Philips, D. (eds) *Health, Race and Ethnicity*, London: Croom Helm.

Gilbert, O. (1976) 'Race and disease – the spread of sickle cell anaemia', *Spearhead*, May: 14.

Gillam, S., Jarman, B., White, P. and Law, R. (1989) 'Ethnic differences in consultation rates in urban general practice', *British Medical Journal*, 299: 953–7.

Gillies, D.R.N., Lealman, G.T., Lumb, K.M. and Congdon, P. (1984) 'Analysis of ethnic influence on stillbirths and infant mortality in Bradford (1975–81)', *Journal of Epidemiology and Community Health*, 38: 214–17.

Gilroy, P. (1990) 'The end of Anti–racism', in Ball, W. and Solomos, J. (eds) *Race and Local Politics*, Basingstoke: Macmillan.

Glendenning, F. and Pearson, M. (1988) *The Black and Ethnic Minority Elders in Britain: Health Needs and Access to Services*, Working Papers on the Health of Older People no. 6, Health Education Authority and Keele University.

Goel, K.M., Campbell, S., Logan, R.W., Sweet, E.M., Attenburrow, A. and Arneil, G.C. (1981) 'Reduced prevalence of rickets in Asian children in Glasgow', *Lancet*, 2: 405–6.

Goldberg, D. and Huxley, P. (1980) *Mental Illness in the Community: The Pathway to Psychiatric Care*, London: Tavistock.

Gordon, P. (1983) 'Medicine, racism and immigration control', *Critical Social Policy*, 7:6–21.

Graham, H. (1984) *Women, Health and the Family*, Brighton: Wheatsheaf.

Graham, H. (1991) 'The concept of caring in feminist research: the case of domestic service', *Sociology*, 25(1): 61–78.

Grant, L. (1988) 'Black elderly: the Caribbean perspective', in Mossadaq, M. and Froggatt, A. (ed.) *Black or Asian Elders: Do Our Services Deliver?*, Report of Conference held at Bradford University.

Greater London Council (1984) *A Critical Guide to Health Service Resource Allocation in London*, London: GLC.

Greater London Council (1985) *Ethnic Minorities and the National Health Service in London*, London: GLC.

Grenville–Mathers, R. and Clark, J.B. (1979) 'The development of tuberculosis in Afro–Asian immigrants', *Tuberculosis*, 60: 25–9.

Griffiths, R., White, M. and Stonehouse, M. (1989) 'Ethnic differences in birth statistics from central Birmingham', *British Medical Journal*, 298: 94–5.

Grundy, M.F.B. Hood, J. and Newman, G.B. (1978) 'Birthweight standards in a community of mixed racial origin', *British Journal of Obstetrics and Gynaecology*, 85: 481–6.

Halsey, R.A. (1988) *British Social Trends since 1990: A Guide to the Changing Social Structure of Britain*, (2nd Edn), London: Macmillan.

Ham, C. and Heginbotham, C. (1991) 'Happy ever after', *Health Services Journal*, 14 November.

Hancock, C. and Sutherland, S. (1986) 'When do we discriminate?' in Racial Discrimination: A Guide for Ward Sisters and Charge Nurses', *Health Services Manpower Review*, June: 4–22.

Handley, A. (1991) 'Lives still under threat', *Coventry Evening Telegraph*, 18 September: 17.

Hansard (1986) Written reply, 18 November 1986, *House of Commons Official Report*, col. 78–9.

Hansard (1987a) Written reply, 12 January 1987, *House of Commons Official Report*, col. 133–4.

Hansard (1987b) Written reply, 24 July 1987, *House of Commons Official Report*, col. 713.

Hansard (1992) Written reply, 15 January 1992, *House of Commons Official Report*, col. 590.

Harrington, F. and Finnegan, P. (1989) Factors in the Genesis of Stress and Mental Ill-health Among the Irish in Britain. London: Brent Irish Mental Health Group.

Harrison, G. (1988) Paper presented at the Annual Meeting of the Special Interest Group in Forensic Psychiatry, Royal College of Psychiatrists, Stratford upon Avon.

Harrison, G. (1990) 'Search for the causes of schizophrenia: the role of migrant studies', *Schizophrenia Bulletin*, 16: 663–71.

Harrison, G., Ineichen, B., Smith, J. and Morgan, H.G. (1984) 'Psychiatric hospital admission in Bristol. II: Social and clinical aspects of compulsory admission', *British Journal of Psychiatry*, 145: 605–11.

Harrison, G., Owens, D., Holton, A., Neilson, D. and Boot, D. (1988) 'A prospective study of severe mental disorder in Afro–Caribbean patients', *Psychological Medicine*, 18: 643–57.

Harrison, S. (1991) 'Working the markets – purchaser/provider separation in English health care', *International Journal of Health Services*, 21(4): 625–35.

Harrison, S., Hunter, D., Johnston, I., Nicholson, N., Thornhurst, C. and Wistow, G. (1991) *Health before Health Care* (Social Policy Paper No. 4), Institute for Public Policy Research, 18 Buckingham Gate, London SW1.

Hart, N. (1985) *The Sociology of Health and Medicine*, Ormskirk, Lancashire : Causway.

Harvey, L. (1990) *Critical Social Research*, London: Unwin Hyman.

Haskey, J. (1989) 'Families and households of the ethnic minority and white populations of Great Britain: estimates by ethnic group and country of birth', *Population Trends*, 57: 8–19.

Haskey, J. (1990a) 'The ethnic minority populations of Great Britain: estimates by ethnic group and country of birth', *Population Trends*, 60: 35–8.

Haskey, J. (1990b) 'The ethnic minority populations resident in private households – estimates by county and metropolitan district of England and Wales', *Population Trends*, 63: 22–35.

Hawthorne, K. (1990) 'Asian diabetics attending a British hospital clinic: a pilot study to evaluate their care', *British Journal of General Practice*, 40: 243–7.

Healey, M.A. and Aslam, M. (1990) *The Asian Community: Medicines and Traditions*, Nottingham: Silver Link Publishing.

Heatley, P T. and Yip, R.Y.W. (1991) 'Analysis of general practice consultation rates among Asian patients', *British Journal of General Practice*, 41: 476.

Hemsi, L.K. (1967) 'Psychiatric morbidity of West Indian immigrants', *Social Psychiatry*, 2: 95–100.

Henley, A. (1979) *Asian Patients in Hospital and at Home*, London: Pitman Medical.

Henley, A. (1980) *Asians in Britain: Asian Names and Records*, London: DHSS/Kings Fund.

Henley, A. and Clayton, J. (1982) 'What's in a name?', *Health and Social Service Journal*, 92: 855–7.

Hesse, B., Rai, D.K., Bennett, C. and McGilchrist, P. (1992) *Beneath the Surface: Racial Harassment*, Aldershot: Avebury.

Hitch, P.J. and Clegg, P. (1980) 'Models of referral of overseas immigrant and native born first admissions to psychiatric hospital', *Social Science and Medicine*, 14A: 369–374.

Hodnett, E.D. (1993) 'Support from caregivers during childbirth', in Enkin, M.W. *et al.* (eds) *Pregnancy and Childbirth Module*, Oxford: Update Software.

Hoffenberg, R. (1985) 'The health service and race', Centre for Contemporary Studies Winter Lecture.

Holland, B. and Lewando–Hundt, G. (1986) *Coventry's Ethnic Minority Elderly Survey: Method, Data and Applied Action*, Coventry: Coventry Social Services.

Honeyman, M.M., Bahl, L., Marshall, T. and Wharton, B.A. (1987) 'Consanguinity and fetal growth in Pakistani Moslems', *Archives of Disease in Childhood*, 62: 231–5.

Hooks, B. (1986) 'Sisterhood: political solidarity between women', *Feminist Review*, 23: 124–38.

House of Commons Health Committee (1992) *Maternity services*, 2nd report, session 1991–92, Vol. I, HC 29–I, London: HMSO.

Howlett, B.C., Ahmad, W.I.U. and Murray, R. (1992) 'An exploration of white, Asian and Afro–Caribbean peoples' concepts of health and illness causation', *New Community*, 18(2): 281–92.

HSG (1992) 'Meeting the spiritual needs of patients and staff', *Health Service Guidelines*, London: NHS Management Executive, HSG (92)2.

Hughes, J., McNaught, A. and Pennell, I. (eds) (1984) *Race and Employment in the N.H.S.*, London: King's Fund.

Hulley, T. and Clarke, J. (1991) 'Social problems: social construction and social causation', in Loney, M. with Bocock, R., Clarke, J., Cochrane, A., Graham, P. and Wilson, M. (eds) *The State or the Market: Politics and Welfare in Contemporary Society* (2nd edn), London: Sage.

Hume, J.C. (1977) 'Rival traditions: western medicine and unan–i–tibb in the Punjab, 1849–89', *Bulletin of the History of Medicine*, 51: 214–31.

Hunt, S. (1987) 'Evaluating a community development project', *British Journal of Social Work*, 17(6): 661–8.

Hunter, D. (1991) 'Breaking down barriers', *Health Services Journal*, 3 October: 19.

Husband, C. (ed.) (1982) *'Race' In Britain: Continuity and Change*, London: Hutchinson.

Husband, C. (1991) '"Race", conflictual politics and anti–racist social work: lessons from the past for action in the '90s', in Central Council for Education and Training in Social Work, *Setting the Context for Change*, London: CCETSW.

Husband, C. (1992a) 'Minorities, mobility and communication in Europe', Race Relations Research Unit, University of Bradford, Research and Policy Paper 2.

Husband, C. (1992b) 'A policy against racism', *The Psychologist*, September: 414–17.

Illich, I. (1977) *Medical Nemesis*, New York: Bantam Books.

Ineichen, B. (1989) 'Afro–Caribbeans and the incidence of schizophrenia: a review', *New Community*, 15(3): 335–41.

Ineichen, B., Harrison, G. and Morgan, H.G. (1984) 'Psychiatric hospital admissions in Bristol. I: Geographic and ethnic factors', *British Journal of Psychiatry*, 145: 600–4.

Jackson, S.H.D., Bannon, L.T. and Beevers, D.G. (1981) 'Ethnic differences in respiratory disease', *Postgraduate Medical Journal*, 57: 777–8.

Jain, C. (1985) *Attitudes of Pregnant Asian Women to Antenatal Care*, Birmingham: West Midlands Regional Health Authority.

Jani, B., Mistry, H., Patel, N., Anionwu, E., Pembrey, M. (1992) 'A study of beta thalassaemia in the Gujarati community of north London', *Journal of Paediatric Research*.

Jeyasingham, M. (1992) 'Acting for health: community development and ethnic minorities', in Ahmad, W.I.U., *The Politics of 'Race' and Health*, Bradford: Race Relations Research Unit, University of Bradford, and Bradford and Ilkley Community College.

Joffe, M. and Farrant, W. (1989) 'Medical student projects in practical health promotion', *Community Medicine*, 11 (1): 35–40.

Johnson, A.M., Wadsworth, J., Welling, K. and Bradshaw, S. (1993) 'Sexual Lifestyles and HIV risk', *Nature*, 360: 410–12.

Johnson, M.R.D., Cross, M. and Cardew, S.A. (1983) 'Inner city residents, ethnic minorities and primary health care', *Postgraduate Medical Journal*, 159: 664–7.

Johnson, M.R.D. (1984) 'Ethnic minorities and health', *Journal of the Royal College of Physicians of London*, 18(4): 228–30.

Johnson, M.R.D. (1986) 'Inner city residents, ethnic minorities and primary health care in the West Midlands' in Rathwell, T. and Phillips, D. (eds) *Health, Race and Ethnicity*, London: Croom Helm.

Johnson, M.R.D. (1987) 'Towards racial equality in health and welfare: what progress?', *New Community*, 14(1/2): 128–34.

Johnson, M.R.D. (1992) 'Chartering for black citizens' rights', *New Community*, 18(2): 316–25.

Johnson, M.R.D., Cox, B. and Cross, M. (1989) 'Paying for change? Section 11 and local authority social services', *New Community* 15(3): 371–90.

Jones, C. (1991) 'Birth statistics 1990', *Population Trends 65*, Autumn: 9–15.

Jones, K., Smith, A.D. (1970) *The Economic Impact of Commonwealth Immigration*, Cambridge: Cambridge University Press for National Institute for Economic and Social Research.

Jones, S (1991) 'A message from our ancestors' (edited version of Reith Lecture on BBC Radio 4, 13 November), *The Independent*, 14 November: 16.

Kamin, L.J. (1974) *The Science and Politics of I.Q.*, Harmondsworth: Penguin.

Karenga, M. (1982) *Introduction to Black Studies*, Inglewood, CA: Kawaida Publications.

Karseras, P. and Hopkins, E. (1987) *British Asians' Health in the Community*, Chichester: John Wiley.

Kay, E.J., Shaikh, I. and Bhopal, R.S. (1990) 'Dental knowledge, beliefs, attitudes and behaviour of the Asian Community in Glasgow', *Health Bulletin*, 48: 73–80.

Khlat, M., Halabi, S., Hudr, A. and Der Kaloustain, V.M. (1986) 'Perception of consanguineous marriages and their genetic effects among a sample of couples from Beirut', *American Journal of Medical Genetics*, 25: 299–306.

Killoran, A. (1990) 'An overview of health and lifestyle surveys', in Health Education Authority/Office of Population Censuses and Surveys, *Health and Life-style Surveys: Towards a Common Approach*, London: HEA.

King, P. (1992) 'Modernity: prisoners' dilemma in colour', *New Community*, 18(2): 229–50.

King's Fund (1989) *Health Authority Equal Opportunities Committee*, London: King's Fund.

King's Fund (1990a) *Equal Opportunities Task Force Final Report*, London: King's Fund.

King's Fund Task Force (1990b) *Racial Equality: The Nursing Profession*, position paper, London: King's Fund.

King's Fund (1992) *Health Care U.K. 1991: An Annual Review of Health Care Policy* (edited by A. Harrison), London: King's Fund.

Kirby, J. (1977) 'Sickle cell anaemia', *G.P.*, 18 March: 34.

Kleijnen, J., Knipsehild, P. and Riet, G. (1991) 'Clinical trials of homeopathy', *British Medical Journal*, 302: 316–23.

Kohn, M.L. (1972) 'Class, family and schizophrenia: a reformulation', *Social Forces*, 50: 295–304.

Kramer, M. (1976) 'Issues in the development of statistical and epidemiologic data for mental health services research', *Psychological Medicine*, 6: 185–215.

Kraus, A.S. (1954) 'The use of hospital data in studying the association between a characteristic and disease', *Public Health Reports*, 69: 1211–14.

Kushnick, L. (1988) 'Racism, the National Health Service, and the health of black people', *International Journal of Health Service*, 18(3): 457–70.

Lancet (1974) 'Tuberculosis retreats – slowly', *Lancet*, 1: 1087–8.

Lancet (1990) 'Survival of patients with breast cancer attending Bristol Cancer Help Centre', *Lancet*, 336: 683, 743–4, 1185–8 (correspondence in response to Bagenal *et al.* (1990).

Lancet (1991) 'Consanguinity and health', *Lancet*, 338: 85–6.

Larby, J. (1985) *Black Women and the Maternity Services*, London: Training in Health and Race.

Lawrence, E. (1981) 'White sociology, black struggle', *Multi–racial Education*, 9(3): 13–17.

Lawrence, E. (1982a) 'Just plain common sense: the "roots" of racism', in Centre for Contemporary Cultural Studies, *The Empire Strikes Back*, London: Hutchinson.

Lawrence, E. (1982b) 'In the abundance of water the fool is thirsty: sociology and black pathology', in Centre for Contemporary Cultural Studies, *The Empire Strikes Back*, London: Hutchinson.

Layton–Henry, Z. (1990) 'Immigrant associations', in Layton–Henry, Z. (ed) *op. cit.*

Lee–Cunin, M. (1989) *Daughters of Seacole*, Batley: West Yorkshire Low Pay Unit.

Leff, J. (1988) *Psychiatry Around the Globe*, London: Gaskell.

Leff, J., Fisher, M. and Betelsen, A. (1976) 'A cross–national epidemiological study of mania', *British Journal of Psychiatry*, 129: 428–42.

Lehmann, H. and Huntsman, R.G. (1974) *Man's Haemoglobins*, Amsterdam: North–Holland.

Lewando–Hundt, G. and Grant, L. (1987) 'Studies of black elders – an exercise in window dressing or the groundwork for widening provision', *Social Services Research*, Nos 5 and 6.

Li, Pui–Ling (1992) 'The health needs of the Chinese population', in Ahmad, W.I.U. (ed.) *The Politics of 'Race' and Health*, Bradford: Race Relations Research Unit, University of Bradford, and Bradford and Ilkley Community College.

Lim, S. P. (1979) 'The Chinese elders in Camden' in Glendenning, F. (ed.) *The Elders in Ethnic Minorities*, London: Beth Johnson Foundation.

Lin, M.M. (1991) 'Breast feeding and weaning practices among Pakistani and Chinese communities in Newcastle–upon–Tyne', unpublished MSc dissertation, University of London Institute of Child Health.

Little, J. and Nicoll, A. (1988) 'The epidemiology and service implications of congenital and constitutional anomalies in ethnic minorities in the United Kingdom', *Paediatric and Perinatal Epidemiology*, 2: 161–84.

Littlewood, R. and Lipsedge, M. (1981) 'Acute psychotic reactions in Caribbean–born patients', *Psychological Medicine*, 11: 289–302.

Littlewood, R. and Lipsedge, M. (1982) *Aliens and Alienists: Ethnic Minorities and Psychiatry* (1st edn), Harmondsworth: Penguin.

Littlewood, R. and Lipsedge, M. (1988) 'Psychiatric illness among British Afro–Caribbeans', *British Medical Journal*, 296: 950–1.

Littlewood, R. and Lipsedge, M. (1989) *Aliens and Alienists: Ethnic minorities and Psychiatry* (2nd edn), London: Unwin Hyman.

Littlewood, R. and Lipsedge, M. (1990) 'Institutional racism', *The Psychologist*, July: 319.

Livingstone, F.B. (1985) *Frequencies of Haemoglobin Variants*, New York: Oxford University Press.

Local Government Information Unit (1991) *The Black Community and Community Care*, London: LGIU.

Lock, M. and Gordon, D.R. (1990) *Biomedicine Examined*, Dordrecht: Kluwer Academic Publishing.

London Association of Community Relations Councils (1985) *In a Critical Condition*, London: LACRC.

Lucarelli, G. and Weatherall, D. (1991) 'For debate: bone marrow transplantation for severe thalassaemia', *British Journal of Haematology*, 78: 300–3.

Luck, M. (1991) *A Manual of Market Research for Health Promotion*, Birmingham: West Midlands Regional Health Authority.

Luck, M., Lawrence, B., Pocock, R. and Reilly, K. (1988) *Consumer and Market Research in Health Care*, London: Croom Helm.

Lumb, K.M., Congdon, P.J. and Lealman, G.T. (1981) 'A comparative review of Asian and British–born maternity patients in Bradford, 1974–78', *Journal of Epidemiology and Community Health*, 35: 106–9.

Lustgarten, L. and Edwards, J. (1992) 'Racial equality and the limits of law', in Braham, P., Rattansi, A. and Skellington, R. (eds) *Racism and Anti–racism: Inequalities, Opportunities and Policies*, London: Sage.

Macfarlane, A.J. (1986) 'Anaesthetics – the risks for black women', *Maternity Action*, 26: 6.

Macfarlane, A.J. and Mugford, M. (1984) *Birth Counts: Statistics of Pregnancy and Childbirth* (2 vols.), London: HMSO.

Macfarlane, A.J., and Parsons, L. (in preparation), 'Ethnic differences in maternity care'.

Macluer, J.W. (1980) 'Inbreeding and human fetal death', in Porter, I.H. and Hook, E.B. (eds) *Human Embryonic and Fetal Death*, New York: Academic Press.

Manchester Community Health Group for Ethnic Minorities (1981) 'Sickle cell disease in Manchester: a discussion document for all interested groups and particularly for health professionals', Manchester Community Health Council.

Manning, N. (1987) 'What is a social problem?', in Loney, M. with Bocock, R., Clarke, J., Cochrane, A., Graham, P. and Wilson, M. (eds) *The State or the Market: Politics and Welfare in Contemporary Society* (1st edn), London: Sage.

Mares, P., Henley, A. and Baxter, C. (1985) *Health Care in Multiracial Britain*, Cambridge: NEC/HEC.

Marks, K., Kingman, S. (1991) 'One–parent families double in 20 years', *The Independent*, 18 September: 6.

Marmot, M.G., Adelstein, A.M. and Bulusu, L. (1984) *Immigrant Mortality in England and Wales 1970–78, Studies on Medical and Population Subjects* no. 47, London: HMSO.

Masai, A.T. (1965) 'Potential uses and limitations of hospital data in epidemiologic research', *American Journal of Public Health*, 55: 658–67.

Mason, E.S. (1990) 'The Asian Mother and Baby Campaign (the Leicestershire experience)', *Journal of the Royal Society of Health*, 110: 1–9.

Maynard, A. and Walker, A. (1978) *Doctor Manpower 1975–2000: Alternative Forecasts and Their Implications – A Report for the Royal Commission on the NHS*, York: York University.

McAvoy, B. (1990) 'Contraceptive services for Asian women in the UK: a review', *Family Practice*, 7: 60–64.

McAvoy, B.R. and Donaldson, L.J. (1990) *Health Care for Asians*, Oxford: Oxford University Press.

McAvoy B.R. and Raza, R. (1988) 'Asian women: (i) Contraceptive knowledge, attitudes and usage, (ii) Contraceptive services and cervical cytology', *Health Trends*, 20: 11–17.

McAvoy, B.R. and Raza, R. (1991) 'Can health education increase uptake of cervical smear testing among Asian women?' *British Medical Journal*, 302: 833–6.

McCrudden, C., Smith, D. and Brown, C. (1991) *Racial Justice at Work*, London: Policy Studies Institute.

McEwan, R. and Bhopal, R.S. (1991) *A Review of the Theory, Principles and Practice of Health Promotion about HIV and AIDS for Young People*, Occasional Paper No. 12, London: Health Education Authority.

McFadyen, I.R., Campbell Brown, M., Abraham, R., North, W.R.S. and Haines, A.P. (1984) 'Factors affecting birthweights in Hindus, Moslems and Europeans', *British Journal of Obstetrics and Gynaecology*, 91: 968–972.

McGovern, D. and Cope, R. (1987) 'First psychiatric admission rates of first and second generation Afro–Caribbeans', *Social Psychiatry*, 22: 139–49 .

McKeigue, P.M., Richards, J.D.M. and Richards, P. (1990) 'Effects of discrimination by sex and race on the early careers of British medical graduates during 1981–7, *British Medical Journal*, 301: 961–4.

McKeigue, P.M., Shah, B. and Marmot, M.G. (1991) 'Relation of central obesity and insulin resistance with high diabetic prevalence and cardiovascular risk in South Asians', *Lancet*, 337: 382–6.

McKeown, T. (1976) *The Modern Rise of Population*, London: Edward Arnold.

McNaught, A. (1985a) 'Race on the agenda', *The Health Summary*, 2: 3–8 (report of lecture by Sir Raymond Hoffenberg, President of the Royal College of Physicians, Royal Society of Arts, 29 January).

McNaught, A. (1985b) *Race and Health Care in the United Kingdom*, (Occasional Paper No 2), London: Health Education Council.

McNaught, A. (1987) *Health Action and Ethnic Minorities*, London: National Community Health Resource and Bedford Square Press

McNaught, A. (1988) *Race and Health Policy*, London: Croom Helm.

Meager, N. and Metcalfe, H. (1988) *Equal Opportunity Policies: Tactical Issues in Implementation*, Report no. 156, London: Institute for Management Studies.

Medical Research Council Tuberculosis and Chest Diseases Unit (1985) 'National survey of notifications of tuberculosis in England and Wales in 1983', *British Medical Journal*, 291: 658–61.

Mercer, K. (1986) 'Racism and transcultural psychiatry', in Miller, P. and Rose, N. (eds) *The Power of Psychiatry*, Cambridge: Polity Press.

Merrison, A.W. (1975) *Report of the Committee of Inquiry into the Regulation of the Medical Profession*, London: HMSO.

Miles, R. (1982) *Racism and Migrant Labour*, London: Routledge.

Miles, R. (1989) *Racism*, London: Routledge.

Miller, P. and Rose, N. (1986) *The Power of Psychiatry*, Cambridge: Polity Press.

Minford, P. (1987) 'The role of the social services: a view from the New Right', in Loney, M. with Bocock, R., Clarke, J., Cochrane, A., Graham, P. and Wilson, M. (eds) *The State or the Market: Politics and Welfare in Contemporary Society*, London: Sage.

Mirza, K. (1991) 'Waiting for guidance', in Central Council for Education and Training in Social Work (ed.) *One Small Step towards Racial Justice*, London: CCETSW.

Mitchell, A. and Wilson, A. (1981) *Black People and the Health Service*, London: Brent Community Health Council.

Modell, B. and Berdoukas, V. (1984) *The Clinical Approach to Thalassaemia*, London: Grune and Stratton.

Modell, B., Petrou, M., Ward, R.H.T. Fairweather, D.V.I., Rodeck, C., Varnavides, L.A. and White, J.M. (1984) 'Effect of fetal diagnostic testing on the birth rate of thalassaemia in Britain', *Lancet*, 2: 1383–1386.

Modood, T. (1988) '"Black", racial equality and Asian identity', *New Community*, 14(3).

Mohammad, S. (1991) 'NHS reforms? How will the black population fare?', *Ethnic Minorities Health: A Current Awareness Bulletin*, 1(3): 1–3.

Mohammed, S. (1987) *No Alibi, No Excuse*, London: Greater London Action on Racial Equality (GLARE).

Mohanty, C. (1991) 'Cartographies of struggle' in Mohanty, C., Russo, A. and Torres, L. (eds) *Third World Women and the Politics of Feminism*, Indianapolis: Indiana University Press.

Moodley, P. and Perkins, R.E. (1987) 'Routes to psychiatric inpatient care in an inner London borough', *Social Psychiatry and Psychiatric Epidemiology*, 26: 47–51.

Moore, W. (1991) 'Older Asians lose out in Harrow', *Social Work Today*, 31 October.

Morgan, M., Manning, N. and Calnan, M. (1985) *Sociological Approaches to Health and Medicine*, London: Croom Helm.

Morgan, M., Mays, N. and Holland, W.W. (1991) 'Can hospital use be a measure of need for health care?', *Journal of Epidemiology and Community Health*, 41: 269–74.

Morris, J.N. (1990) 'Inequalities in health: ten years and a little further on', *Lancet*, 336: 491–3.

Mukherjee, S., Shukla, S., Woodle, J., Rosen, A.M. and Olarte, S. (1983) 'Misdiagnosis of schizophrenia in bipolar patients – A multiethnic comparison', *American Journal of Psychiatry*, 140: 1571–2.

Murphy, H.B.M. (1982) *Comparative Psychiatry: The International and Intercultural Distribution of Mental Illness*, New York: Springer-Verlag.

Nanda, P. (1989) 'White attitudes, rhetoric and reality' in Bhat, A., Carr-Hill R. and Ohri, S. (eds) *Britain's Black Population: A New Perspective*, Aldershot: Gower.

National Association of Health Authorities (1988) *Action Not Words: A Strategy to Improve Health Services for Black and Minority Ethnic Groups*, Birmingham: NAHAT.

National Association of Health Authorities (1990) *Words about Action Bulletin 1: Mental Health*, Birmingham: NAHA.

National Association of Health Authorities and Trusts (1990a) *Words about Action Bulletin 2: Maternity services*, Birmingham: NAHAT.

National Association of Health Authorities and Trusts (1990b) *Words about Action Bulletin 3: Services for Older People*, Birmingham: NAHAT.

National Association of Health Authorities and Trusts (1991) *Words about Action Bulletin 4: Services for Haemoglobinopathies*, Birmingham: NAHAT.

Navarro, V. (1976) *Medicine under Capitalism*, London: Croom Helm.

Newsweek (1992) Report on biological basis of gender, *Newsweek*. 17 February.

NHS Management Executive (1991) *Priorities and planning guidance for the NHS for 1992/93*, Executive Letter EL(91)103, London: Department of Health.

NHSME DHA Project (1992) *Local Voices: The Views of Local People in Purchasing Health*, London: NHS Management Executive (Department of Health).

Noack, H. (1987) 'Concepts of health and health promotion', in Abelin, T., Brzezinski, Z.J. and Carstairs, V.D.L. (eds) *Measurement in Health Promotion and Protection*, WHO Regional Publications, European Series No 22, Copenhagen: WHO Regional Office for Europe.

Norman, A. (1985) *Triple Jeopardy: Growing Old in a Second Homeland*, London: Centre for Policy on Ageing.

O'Shea, M. (n.d.) 'Introduction' in Brent Irish Mental Health Group, The Irish *Experience of Mental Ill–health in London*, Brent Irish Mental Health Group.

Oakley, A. (1980) *Women Confined: Towards a Sociology of Childbirth*, Oxford: Martin Robertson.

Office of Population Censuses and Surveys, (1982) 'Sources of statistics on ethnic minorities' (editorial), *Population Trends*, 28: 1–8.

Office of Population Censuses and Surveys (1986) *General Household Survey*, London: HMSO.

Office of Population Censuses and Surveys (1990) *General Household Survey*, London: HMSO.

Office of Population Censuses and Surveys (1991) unpublished data from the EC Labour Force Survey.

Office of Population Censuses and Surveys (1992a) *Birth Statistics, England and Wales 1990. Series FM1 no. 19*, London: HMSO.

Office of Population Censuses and Surveys (1992b) *General Household Survey: Preliminary Results for 1991, OPCS Monitor SS 92/1*, London: OPCS.

Office of Population Censuses and Surveys (1992c) *Mortality Statistics, Perinatal and Infant: Social and Biological Factors, England and Wales, 1990, Series DH3 no. 24*, London: HMSO.

Old, J.M., Petrou, M., Ward, R.H.T., Karazoglu, F., Modell, B. and Weatherall, D.J. (1982) 'First trimester fetal diagnosis for the haemoglobinopathies: three cases', *Lancet* ii: 1413–16.

Old, J.M., Fitches, A., Heath, C., Thein, S.L., Weatherall, D.J., Warren, R., McKenzie, C., Rodeck, C.H., Petrou, M. and Modell, B. (1986) 'First trimester fetal diagnosis for haemoglobinopathies: report on 200 cases', *Lancet*, ii: 763–8.

Ong, B.N. and Humphries, G. (1990) 'Partners in need', *Health Services Journal*, 5 July: 102–3.

Owen, D. (1992) *Ethnic Minorities in Great Britain: Settlement Patterns*, 1991 Census Statistical Paper 1, National Ethnic Minority Data Archive, University of Warwick.

Owen, D. (1993) *Ethnic Minorities in Great Britain: Housing and Family characteristics*, 1991 Census Statistical Paper 4, National Ethnic Minority Data Archive, University of Warwick.

Pam, A. (1990) 'A critique of the scientific status of biological psychiatry', *Acta Psychiatrica Scandinavica*, 82, Suppl. 362.

Pandya, S.K. (1988) 'Yearning for baby boys', *British Medical Journal*, 296: 1312.

Parmar, P. (1981) 'Young Asian women: a critique of the pathological approach', *Multiracial Education*, 9(3): 19–29.

Parmar, P. (1982) 'Gender, race and class: Asian women in resistance', in Centre for Contemporary Cultural Studies, *The Empire Strikes Back*, London: Hutchinson.

Parsons, L. and Day, S. (1992) 'Improving obstetric outcomes in ethnic minorities', *Journal of Public Health Medicine*, 14: 183–92.

Parsons, T. (1951) *The Social System*, Glencoe, IL: The Free Press.

Patel, N. (1990) *A 'Race' against Time? Social Services Provision to Black Elders*, London: Runnymede Trust.

Paton, C. (1991) 'Myths of competition', *Health Services Journal*, 30 May: 22–3.

Paul, J.A. (1978) 'Medicine and imperialism', in Ehrenreich, J. (ed.) *The Cultural Crisis of Modern Medicine*, New York and London: Monthly Review Press.

Peach, G.C.K., Robinson, V., Maxted J., Chance, J. (1988) 'Immigration and ethnicity' in Halsey, R.A. *British Social Trends since 1900: A Guide to the Changing Social Structure of Britain* (2nd edn), London: Macmillan, 561–615.

Peach, H. (1984a) 'A critique of survey methods used to measure the occurrence of osteomalacia and rickets in the United Kingdom', *Community Medicine*, 6: 20–28.

Peach, H. (1984b) 'A review of aetiological and intervention studies on rickets and osteomalacia in the UK', *Community Medicine*, 6: 119–26.

Pearson, M. (1983) 'Ethnic minority health studies: friend or foe?' paper presented to Medical Conference, Leeds (reprinted as 'The politics of ethnic minority health studies', in Rathwell, T. and Phillips, D. (eds) *Health, Race and Ethnicity*, London: Croom Helm).

Pearson, M. (1986) 'Racist notions of ethnicity and culture in health education', in Rodmell, S. and Watt, A. (eds) *The Politics of Health Education*, London: Tavistock.

Pearson, M. (1987) 'Racism – the great divide', *Nursing Times and Nursing Mirror*, June 17.

Pearson, M. (1989) 'Sociology of race and health', in Cruickshank, K. and Beevers, D.G. (eds) *Ethnic Factors in Health and Disease*, London: Wright.

Pearson, M. (1991) 'Ethnic differences in infant health', *Archives of Disease in Childhood*, 66: 88–90.

Peteirse, J.N. (1991) 'Fictions of Europe', *Race and Class*, 32: 3–10.

Petrou, M., Modell, B., Darr, A., Old, J., Kin, E.I. and Weatherall, D. (1990) 'Antenatal diagnosis: how to deliver a comprehensive service in the United Kingdom', *Annals of the New York Academy of Sciences*, 612: 251–63.

Pharoah, C. (1991) 'Health and social care provision for older people', *SHARE*, no. 1, (November).

Pharoah, C. and Redmond, E. (1991) 'Care for ethnic elders', *The Health Service Journal*, 16 May.

Phoenix, A. (1990) 'Black women and the maternity services', in Garcia, J., Kilpatrick R. and Richards, M. (eds) *The Politics of Maternity Care*, Oxford: Clarendon Press.

Pilger, J. (1992) 'Counting the costs: the humiliation of sick and dying goes on', *New Statesman*, 3rd January: 10–11.

Pledger, H.G. and Watson, H.M.S. (1986) 'Health promotion and disease prevention: two definitions and another framework to use in developing district plans', *Community Medicine*, 8(4): 337–9.

Popay, J. and White, M. (1993) *A Review of Survey Research and Related Training and Advice Needs in the NHS in England*, Salford: Public Health Research and Resource Centre.

Posner, T. (1991) 'What's in a smear? Cervical screening, medical signs and metaphors', *Science as Culture*, 2(11): 167–87.

Poulton, J., Rylance, G. and Johnson, M.R.D., (1987) 'Medical teaching of the cultural aspects of ethnic minorities', *Medical Education*, 20: 492–7.

Powell, E. (1969) *Freedom and Reality*, London: Paperfront.

Prasad, R.K. (1991) *ODA Survey of the General Practitioners on Their Views on GP Contracts – a Year after Its Implementation*, Manchester: Overseas Doctors Association (UK).

Prashar, U., Anionwu, E. and Brozovic, M. (1985) *Sickle Cell Anaemia – Who Cares?*, London: Runnymede Trust.

Price, J.H., Desmond, S.M., Synder, F.F. and Kimmel, S.R. (1988) 'Perceptions of family practice residents regarding health care and poor patients', *Journal of Family Practice*, 27: 615–21.

Proctor, S.R. and Smith, I.J. (1992) 'A reconsideration of the factors affecting birth outcome in Pakistani Muslim families in Britain' *Midwifery*, 8: 76–81.

Qureshi, B. (1989) *Transcultural Medicine*, Dordrecht: Kluwer Academic Publishers.

Qureshi, B. (1992) 'How to avoid pitfalls in ethnic medical history, examination and diagnosis', *Journal of Royal Society of Medicine*, 85: 65–66.

Rack, P. (1980) *Race, Culture and Mental Disorder*, London: Tavistock.

Radical Statistics Health Group, (1987) *Facing the Figures: What Really Is Happening to the National Health Service*, London: Radical Statistics Health Group.

Radical Statistics Health Group (1991) 'Missing: a strategy for health of the nation', *British Medical Journal*, 303: 299–302.

Ranger, C. (1989) 'Race, culture and "cannabis psychosis": the role of social factors in the construction of a disease category', *New Community*, 15(3) 357–69.

Rao, P.S.S. and Inbaraj, S.G. (1977) 'Inbreeding effects on reproduction in Tamil Nadu of India', *Annals of Human Genetics*, 41: 87–98.

Rashid, A. (1990) 'Asian doctors and nurses in the NHS' in McAvoy, B.R. and Donaldson, L.J. (eds) *Health Care for Asians*, Oxford: Oxford University Press.

Rathwell, T. and Philips, D. (eds) (1986) *Health, Race and Ethnicity*, London: Croom Helm.

Research Unit in Health and Behavioural Change (RUHBC) (1989) *Changing the Public Health*, Chichester: John Wiley.

Rhodes, P. (1992) 'The emergence of a new policy: racial matching in fostering and adoption', *New Community*, 18(2):191–208.

Richards, E. and Henryk–Gutt, R. (1982) 'Diagnosis of psychiatric illness in immigrant patients', *British Journal of Clinical and Social Psychiatry*, 1: 78–81.

Robinson, M.J., Palmer, S.R., Avery, A., James, C.E., Benyon, J.L. and Taylor, R.W. (1982) 'Ethnic differences in perinatal mortality – a challenge', *Journal of Epidemiology and Community Health*, 36: 22–6.

Rocheron, Y. (1988) 'The Asian Mother and Baby Campaign: the construction of ethnic minorities health needs', *Critical Social Policy*, 22: 4–23.

Rocheron, Y. and Dickinson, R. (1990) 'The Asian Mother and Baby Campaign: a way forward in health promotion for Asian women', *Health Education Journal*, 49: 128–133.

Rocheron, Y., Dickinson, R., and Khan, S. (1989) *Evaluation of the Asian Mother and Baby Campaign*, Leicester: Centre for Mass Communication Research.

Rocheron, Y., Khan, S. and Dickinson, R. (1989) 'Links across a divide', *Health Service Journal*, 99: 951–52.

Rooney, B. (1987) *Racism and Resistance to Change: A Study of the Black Social Workers Project – Liverpool SSD*, Liverpool: Merseyside Area Profile Group.

Rose, H. and Rose, S. (eds) (1976) *The Radicalisation of Science: Ideology of/in Natural Science*, Basingstoke: Macmillan.

Rose, S., Kamin, L. and Lewontin, R.C. (1984) *Not in Our Genes: Biology, Ideology and Human Nature*, Harmondsworth: Penguin.

Royal College of Physicians (1989) *Prenatal Diagnosis and Genetic Screening: Community and Service Implications*, London: RCP.

Runnymede Trust (1980) *Britain's Black Population*, London: Runnymede Trust and Radical Statistics.

Runnymede Trust (1982) *Britain's Black Population*, Aldershot: Gower.

Runnymede Trust (1986) *The New Right: Image and Reality*, London: Runnymede Trust.

Runnymede Trust (1991) *Race Issues Opinion Surveys 1991: Preliminary Findings*, London: Runnymede Trust.

Rwegellera, G.G.C. (1977) 'Psychiatric morbidity among West Africans and West Indians living in London', *British Journal of Psychiatry*, 137: 428–32.

Rwegellera, G.G.C. (1980) 'Differential use of psychiatric services by West Indians, West Africans and English in London', *British Journal of Psychiatry*, 137: 428–432.

Sackett, D.L. B., Haynes, R. and Tugwell, P. (1985) *Clinical Epidemiology. A Base Science for Clinical Medicine*, Boston: Little, Brown and Company.

Saedi–Wong, S. and Al–Frayh, A.R. (1989) 'Effects of consanguineous matings on anthropometric measurements of Saudi newborn infants', *Family Practice*, 6: 217–20.

Said, E.W. (1978) *Orientalism*, Harmondsworth: Penguin.

Sardar, Z. and Wynn Davies, M. (1990) *Distorted Imaginations: Lessons from the Rushdie Affair*, London: Grey Seal.

Sashidharan, S.P. (1986) 'The politics and ideology of transcultural psychiatry', in Cox, J.L. (ed) *Transcultural Psychiatry*, London: Croom Helm.

Saunders, N. and Paterson, C. (1991) 'Can we abandon Naegele's rule?', *Lancet*, 337: 600–1.

Sayal, A. (1990) 'Black women and mental health', *The Psychologist* 3: 24–7.

Scott–Samuel, A. (1992) 'Still got a long way to go: an international perspective', in Public Health Alliance and Radical Statistics Health Group, *The Health of the Nation: Challenges for a New Government*, Birmingham: PHA and Radical Statistics Health Group.

Scrivens, E. and Hillier, S. (1982) 'Ethnicity, health and health care', in Patrick, D.L. and Scambler, G. (eds) *Sociology as Applied to Medicine*, London: Baillière Tindall.

Scully, D. and Bart, P. (1978) 'A funny thing happened to me on the way to the orifice: women in gynaecology textbooks', in Ehrenreich, J. (ed.) *The Cultural Crisis of Modern Medicine*, New York and London: Monthly Review Press.

Secretary of State for Health (1989) *Caring for People*, London: HMSO.

Secretary of State for Health (1990a) *The NHS and Community Care Act (1990)*, London: HMSO.

Secretary of State for Health (1990b) *Working for Patients*, London: HMSO.

Serjeant, G.R. (1985) *Sickle Cell Disease*, Oxford: Oxford University Press.

Shahjahan, M. (1991) 'Infant and toddler feeding patterns and related issues in the Bangladeshi community', Unpublished MSc dissertation, University of London, Institute of Child Health.

Shaw, C. (1988a) 'Components of growth in the ethnic minority population', *Population Trends*, 52: 26–30.

Shaw, C. (1988b) 'Latest estimates of ethnic minority population', *Population Trends*, 51.

Sheldon, T. and Parker, H. (1992) 'Use of 'ethnicity' and race in health research: a cautionary note', in Ahmad, W.I.U. (ed.) *The Politics of 'Race' and Health*, Bradford:

Race Relations Research Unit, University of Bradford, and Bradford and Ilkley Community College.

Sickle Cell Society (1981) *Sickle Cell Disease: The Need For Improved Services*, Leicester: Sickle Cell Society.

Siegel, J.S. (1974) 'Estimates of coverage of the population by sex, race and age in the 1970 census', *Demography*, 11: 1–23.

Sillitoe, K. (1987) *Developing Questions on Ethnicity and Related Topics for the Census*, Occasional Paper no 36, London: OPCS.

Sivanandan, A. (1982) 'Introduction' in *Roots of Racism*, London: Institute of Race Relations.

Sivanandan, A. (1983) *A Different Hunger*, London: Pluto.

Sivanandan, A. (1990) *Communities of Resistance: Writings on Black Struggles for Socialism*, London: Verso.

Skellington, R. and Morris, P. (1992) *Race in Britain Today*, London: Sage.

Skone, J.F. (1970) *Public Health Aspects of Immigration*, London: Community Relations Commission.

Smith, D. and Gay, P. (1985) *Police and People in London*, London: Policy Studies Institute.

Smith, D.J. (1977) *Racial Disadvantage in Britain: The PEP Report*, Harmondsworth: Penguin.

Smith, D.J. (1980) *Overseas Doctors in the National Health Service*, London: Policy Studies Institute.

Smith, D.J. (1981) *Unemployment and Racial Minorities*, London: Policy Studies Institute.

Smith, N.J. and McCulloch, J.W. (1977) 'Immigrants' knowledge and experience of social work services', *Mental Health and Society*, 4: 190–7.

Smith, R. (1987) 'Prejudice against doctors and students from ethnic minorities', *British Medical Journal*, 294: 328–9.

Smith, R. (1991) 'First steps towards a strategy for health' (introduction to the series of articles under the heading 'The Health of the Nation: Responses'), *British Medical Journal*, 303: 297–9.

Smithies, B. and Fiddick, P. (eds) (1969) *Enoch Powell on Immigration*, London: Sphere.

Smythe, M.G and Sashidharan, S.P. (1990) 'The unreliability of Census data in the estimation of ethnic minority populations', *Psychiatric Bulletin*, Supplement 4: 15.

Spectator (1986) 'How to stop the plague', *The Spectator*, 8 November: 5.

Spencer, D.A., Venkataraman, M. and Weller, P.H. (1993) 'Delayed diagnosis of cystic fibrosis in children from ethnic minorities', *Lancet*, 342: 238.

Springett, V.H. (1964) 'Tuberculosis in immigrants', *Lancet*, i: 1094.

Stacey, M. (1990) 'Women with breast cancer attending the Bristol Cancer Help Centre: a note about the findings of the research', *Medical Sociology News*, 16(1): 8–10.

Stainton–Rogers, W. (1991) *Exploring Health and Illness: An Exploration of Diversity*, Hemel Hempstead: Harvester Wheatsheaf.

Stevenson, A.C. and Davison, B.C.C. (1976) *Genetic Counselling*, London: William Heinemann.

Stimson, G and Webb, B. (1975) *Going to See The Doctor: The Consultation Process in General Practice*, London: Routledge.

Stonham, K. and Sims, P. (1986) 'Asian women having babies in Luton, 1983: a controlled study', *Health and Hygiene*, 7: 10–12.

Strong, P (1979) *The Ceremonial Order of the Clinic*, London: Routledge and Kegan Paul.

Stubbs, P. (1985) 'The employment of black social workers: from "ethnic sensitivity" to anti–racism?', *Critical Social Policy*, 12: 6–27.

Stubbs, P. (1987) 'Professionalism and the adoption of black children', *British Journal of Social Work*, 17(5).

Swayne, J.M.D. (1989) 'Survey of the use of homoeopathic medicine in the UK health system', *Journal of Royal College of General Practitioners*, 39: 503–6.

Tannahill, A. (1985) 'What is health promotion?', *Health Education Journal*, 44: 167–8.

Tannahill, A. (1988) 'Health promotion and public health: a model in action', *Community Medicine*, 10: 48–51.

Tannahill, A. and Robertson, G. (1986) 'Health education in medical education: collaboration not competition', *Medical Teacher*, 8: 165–70.

Terry, P.B., Condie, R.G. and Settatree, R.S. (1980) 'Analysis of ethnic differences in perinatal statistics', *British Medical Journal*, 281: 1307–9.

Thiedermann, S. (1989) 'Managing the foreign born nurse', *Nursing Management*, 20: 13.

Thomas, M. and Williams, J.M. (1972) *Overseas Nurses in Britain: A PEP Survey for the UK Council for Overseas Student Affairs*, London: Political and Economic Planning.

Thunhurst, C. and Macfarlane, A. (1992) 'Monitoring the health of urban populations: what statistics do we need', *Journal of Royal Statistical Society A*, 155(5).

Torkington, P. (1983) *The Racial Politics of Health: A Liverpool Profile*, Liverpool: Merseyside Area Profile Group.

Torkington, P. (1987) 'Racism, sorry, wrong colour', *Nursing Times and Nursing Mirror*, 83 (17 June): 27–8.

Torkington, P. (1991) *Black Health: A Political Issue*, London and Liverpool: Catholic Association for Racial Justice/Liverpool Institute of Higher Education.

Torrey, E.F. (1980) *Schizophrenia and Civilization*, London: Jason Aronson.

Townsend, P. (1990) 'Individual or social responsibility for premature death? Current controversies in the British debate about health', *International Journal of Health Services*, 20(3): 373–92.

Townsend, P. and Davidson, N. (1982) *Inequalities in Health: The Black Report*, Harmondsworth: Penguin.

Townsend, P., Davidson, N. and Whitehead, M. (1988) *The Black Report/The Health Divide*, London: Penguin.

Training in Health and Race (1984) 'Review paper – January 1984', London: Training in Health and Race.

Tuckett, D. (1976) *An Introduction to Medical Sociology*, London: Tavistock.

Tudor Hart, J. (1971) 'The inverse care law', *The Lancet*, i: 405–12.

Turner, B.S. (1987) *Medical Power and Social Knowledge*, London: Sage.

UK Health for All Network–Community Participation Group (UKHFAN–CPG) (1991) *Community Participation for Health for All*, Liverpool: UKHFAN.

U.K. Thalassaemia Society (1991) 'News Review', September: 6–7, UK Thalassaemia Society, 107 Nightingale Lane, London N8 7QY.

Vaghmaria, A. (1991) 'Caring for cystic fibrosis patients', *Medical Monitor*, 25 October: 57–9.

Vermylen, C.H., Cornu, G., Philippe, M., Ninane, J., Borja, A., Latinne, D., Ferrant, A., Michaux, J.L. and Sokal, G. (1991) 'Bone marrow transplantation in sickle cell anaemia', *Archives of Disease in Childhood*, 66: 1195–8.

Victor, C.R. (1991) 'Continuity or change: inequalities in health in later life', *Ageing and Society*, 2(1).

Visram, R. (1986) *Ayahs, Lascars and Princes: Indians in Britain 1700–1947*, London: Pluto Press.

Walker, R. (1992) 'Elder outsiders: elders of ethnic minorities and the ideology of care on the community', unpublished MSc dissertation, University of Bradford.

Wardburgh, J. (1990) 'Asian women and housing: the potential for community action', unpublished PhD thesis, University of Stirling.

Warner, R. (1985) *Recovery from Schizophrenia: Psychiatry and Political Economy*, London: Routledge and Kegan Paul.

Watt, A. and Rodmell, S. (1987) 'Community involvement in health promotion: progress or panacea?', *Health Promotion*, 2(4): 359–68.

Weare, K. (1986) 'What do medical teachers understand by health promotion?' *Health Education Journal*, 45: 235–8.

Weatherall, D. (1991) 'Bookshelf: the sickle cell disease patient', *Lancet* 337: 1590.

Weatherall, D.J. and Clegg, J.B. (1981) *The Thalassaemia Syndromes*, Oxford: Blackwell Scientific.

Webb, P. (1981) 'Report of an ethnic health project', *Health Education Journal*, 40: 69–74.

Webb, P.A. (1982) 'Ethnic health project 1979–80', *Journal of Royal Society of Health*, 102(1): 29–34.

Webb, S.J. (1991) *Primary Care for All? A Report on Black and Minority Ethnic Primary Health Care Needs*, Bradford Family Health Services Authority.

Wennburg, J. (1986) 'Which rate is right?', *New England Journal of Medicine*, 314: 310–11.

Werner, D. (1977) *Where There Is No Doctor*, Palo Alto, CA: Hesperian Foundation.

Westwood, S. and Bachu, P. (1988) 'Images and Realities', *New Society*, 6 May.

Westwood, S., Couloute, J., Desai, S., Mathew, P. and Piper, A. (1989) *Sadness in My Heart: Racism and Mental Health*, Leicester: Leicester Black Mental Health Group, University of Leicester.

Whelan, J. (1988) 'Conscience or catalyst? Putting equal opportunities into practice in the NHS', *Radical Community Medicine*, 34 (Summer): 31–4.

While, A.E. and Godfrey, M. (1984) 'Health visitor knowledge of Asian cultures', *Health Visitor*, 57: 297–8.

Whitehead, M. (1987) *The Health Divide: Inequalities in Health in the 1980's*, London: Health Education Council.

Whitehead, M. (1992a) *The Health Divide*, (revised edn), Harmondsworth: Penguin.

Whitehead, M. (1992b) 'The concepts and principles of equity and health', *International Journal of Health Services*, 22(3): 429–45.

WHO Regional Office for Europe (1985) *Targets for Health for All by the Year 2000 in the European Region*, Copenhagen: WHO Regional Office for Europe.

WHO Regional Office for Europe (1992) *Targets for Heath for All: The Health Policy for Europe*, Copenhagen: WHO.

WHO Working Group on the Concepts and Principles of Health Promotion (1984) *Health Promotion: A Discussion Document on the Concepts and Principles*, Copenhagen: WHO Regional Office for Europe.

WHO/Health and Welfare Canada/Canadian Public Health Association (1986) *Ottawa Charter for Health Promotion*, Ottawa: WHO/HWC/CPHA.

Widgery, D. (1988) *The National Health: A Radical Perspective*, London: Hogarth.

Wilcox, A.J. and Russell, I.T. (1983) 'Perinatal mortality: standardizing for birthweight is biased', *American Journal of Epidemiology*, 118: 857–64.

Wilding, P. (1992) 'The British welfare state: Thatcherism's enduring legacies', *Policy and Politics*, 20(3): 201–12.

Williams, F. (1989) *Social Policy: A Critical Introduction*, Cambridge: Polity.

Williams, J. (1985) 'Redefining Institutional Racism', *Ethnic and Racial Studies*, 8(3).

Williams, R. (1992) 'The health of the Irish in Britain', in Ahmad, W.I.U. (ed) *The Politics of 'Race' and Health*, Bradford: Race Relations Research Unit, University of Bradford, and Bradford and Ilkley Community College.

Williams, R., Bhopal, R.S. and Hunt, K. (1993) 'The health of a Punjabi ethnic minority in Glasgow: a comparison with the general population, *Journal of Epidemiology and Public Health Medicine* 47(2): 96–102.

Wing, J.K. and Fryers, T. (1976) *Psychiatric Services in Camberwell and Salford. Statistics from the Camberwell and Salford Psychiatric Registers 1964–1974*, London: MRC Social Psychiatry Unit.

Wing J.K., Cooper, J.E. and Sartorius, N. (1974) *The Measurement and Clarification of Psychiatric Symptoms*, Cambridge: Cambridge University Press.

Winkler, F. (1986) *The Multi-ethnic Women's Health Project*, London: City and Hackney Community Health Council.

Wistow, G., Knapp, M., Hardy, B. and Allen, C. (1992) 'From providing to enabling: local authorities and the mixed economy of social care', *Public Administration*, 70: 25–42.

World Health Organization (1987) *Mental Health Services in Pilot Study Area*, Copenhagen: WHO Regional Offices for Europe.

World Health Organization (1988) *The Haemoglobinopathies in Europe. A Combined Report on Two WHO Meetings*, Copenhagen: World Health Organization, Regional Maternal and Child Care.

Wright, C. (1983) 'Language and communications problems in an Asian community', *Journal of the Royal College of General Practitioners*, 33: 101–4.

Yankener, A. (1982) 'Refugees, immigrants and the public health', *American Journal of Public Health*, 72: 12.

Young, I.D. and Clarke, M. (1987) 'Lethal malformations and perinatal mortality: a 10 year review with comparison of ethnic differences', *British Medical Journal*, 295: 89–91.

Young, M. (1971) *Knowledge and Control*, Basingstoke: Collier–Macmillan.

Young, R. (1977) 'Science is social relations', *Radical Science Journal*, 5.

Yudkin, S. (1965) '*Health and welfare of the immigrant child*', paper delivered to *Immigrants and their Babies conference*, National Committee for Commonwealth Immigrants and the National Council for the Unmarried Mother and her Child; London, 12 March. Reprinted by London Community Relations Commission.

Zaidi, S.A. (1988) *The Political Economy of Health in Pakistan*, Lahore: Vanguard.

Zola, I.K. (1972) 'In the name of health and illness', *Social Science and Medicine*, 9: 83–7.

Zola, I.K. (1977) 'Healthism and disabling medicalization', in Illich, I., Zola, I.K. and McKnight, J., Caplan, J. and Shaiken, H. *Disabling Professions*, New York: Maryon Boyars.

Index